This Day In Game Show History

365 Commemorations and Celebrations

Volume 2: April-June

Adam Nedeff

This Day In Game Show History:
365 Commemorations and Celebrations
Volume 2: April through June

Published in the USA by
BearManor Media
P.O. Box 1129
Duncan, OK 73534-1129
www.BearManorMedia.com

ISBN: 1-59393-570-6

Design and layout by Allan T. Duffin

Printed in the United States of America

Dedications

For my grandparents, Chauncey and Sue Estep, who were ceaselessly amazed at how quickly their little grandson was able to solve *Wheel of Fortune* puzzles, even as a preschooler; my parents, Roger and Linda Nedeff, who supported their son's hobby and endless pursuit of it, even when none of us knew if it would ever lead to anything, and my high school English teachers, James Vaughn, Stephanie Frank, and John T. Smith, for nurturing whatever aptitude I might have shown for doing this.

Table of Contents

April 1

1963 – *You Don't Say!* Premieres

The third time was the charm for Tom Kennedy on the national stage. His first two game shows, *Big Game* and *Dr. I.Q.*, were there and gone in a matter of months, but he finally got a hit show all his own when Ralph Andrews Productions tapped him to host *You Don't Say!*

You Don't Say! wasn't actually all Tom's to begin with. It had started in a trial run on Los Angeles station KTLA Channel 5 in December 1962, hosted by Jack Barry. The game was an immediate hit, and NBC picked it up for a national run. The problem was that in 1963, the industry was still licking its wounds from the quiz show scandals, and the network didn't want Jack Barry involved with the show. The KTLA run finished out its commitment with a series of guest hosts auditioning, and Tom Kennedy got the nod to come along when *You Don't Say!* bowed in front of a national audience.

You Don't Say! was the word game that made its players work just a little bit harder. The object of the game wasn't just to discern an unknown word, but to figure out something else that the word sounded like. Two celebrity-contestant teams competed against each other. One member of each team would see the name of a famous person, fictional character or place and give a clue describing something that sounded like part of the name. The clue had to be structured so the last word would be whatever the clue-giver was describing—and that's the word that you don't say!

Tom Kennedy drops by for a rehearsal at *You Don't Say!*, joining contestants getting accustomed to playing the game. (Jody Lund Collection)

Confused? You don't say! The game does require an example or two if you've never seen it played. Suppose the player were trying to convey the name "Tom Kennedy." A good series of clues could be:

·"2,000 pounds equals one…"

·"When its master is on vacation, a dog might stay in a…"

·Somebody might decline coffee, preferring to drink…"

It was the partner's task to guess the words "ton," "kennel" and "tea" and figure out that "Ton Kennel Tea" sounded like "Tom Kennedy." The first team to guess three names won the game and a chance to earn a maximum of $300 by guessing a name from a similar series of clues on The Bonus Board. Contestants lucky enough to shut out their opponents and win the maximum $300—which the show called a Blitz—received a car as an added bonus.

Supplying clues in a way that led only indirectly to the answer confused some of the celebrity guests who appeared in the beginning. In a 1987 interview, Tom described the trouble the show had with one particular star:

"I really don't want to use his name. He was one our best screen actors. Played many roles and always gave an outstanding performance. Anyway, he shows up to tape the show...If you remember the object of the game was to give a sentence, leaving off the last word. That word should sound like part of the name being played. This particular subject name was John Wayne. Our celebrity player proceeded to whistle the theme from *The High and The Mighty*.

"I of course tried not to embarrass him, but I had to stop the game and stop the tape from rolling. I told him he wasn't allowed to give clues like that. He looked at me, with a very serious expression on his face and said, 'But he was in that movie.' I again explained the concept of the game to him and we then again started the taping. It wasn't thirty seconds into the taping and he again blurted out an answer that was completely against the rules. I again stopped the tape.

"I felt so sorry for him. Here he was this giant of an actor but he simply didn't understand the game. He finally just looked offstage at our producer and said he just didn't get it and he felt it would be better to just call it a night. We of course agreed, and he left and we simply replaced him with another celebrity. But that was funny—this great actor whistling the theme from *The High and The Mighty* and then saying, 'But he was in that movie.'"

A wide shot of the set. Notice the cheat sheet at the edge of the stage, reminding players of the rules. (Jody Lund Collection)

The program circumvented future problems with confused clue-givers by putting a cheat sheet on an easel at the edge of the stage, out of view of the audience. As the series grew in popularity, producers managed to find plenty of eager stars who understood how to play the game and played it quite well. Lee Marvin, Tippi

Hedren, Beverly Garland, Mel Torme, Peter Lawford, Michael Landon, Rowan & Martin and Charles Bronson became familiar faces on the stage of *You Don't Say!* over the next six and a half years. Audiences liked the game too, enough to merit a home game as well as a prime time edition, which hit the air in 1964.

Not everybody was a fan, though. The people at Mark Goodson-Bill Todman Productions, specifically, were outraged by what they saw. It was a word game with the announcer whispering the correct answer to the audience, a game that teamed up celebrities with contestants who alternated rounds of giving and guessing clues—sound familiar? Goodson-Todman felt the game was similar enough to *Password* that the company took the case to court.

While not successful in getting *You Don't Say!* pulled from the airwaves, Goodson-Todman won some smaller concessions. The court ordered the show's set to be slightly redesigned to differ more from the *Password* set. Tom Kennedy could no longer stand between the two teams, because that's where Allen Ludden stood on *Password*, so Tom's podium was moved to the side of the stage. Goodson-Todman eventually learned to live peacefully with the alleged imitator, and eventually the dynasty's hosts, including Bill Cullen, Gene Rayburn, and even Allen Ludden himself, had turns at playing the game. It was good publicity, after all.

As the years went by, *You Don't Say!* kept itself fresh and fun with a number of theme shows. Every year, the show celebrated Christmas with a week of games in which children competed. Tom's brother Jack Narz always dropped by once a year to act as guest host while Tom acted as a partner to the contestants; Tom would admit years later that he enjoyed these weeks but was always perfectly happy when they ended, not totally comfortable with the pressure of trying to earn money for contestants. *You Don't Say!*

also took the act on the road, with the show airing for a week from Cyprus Gardens in Florida.

Michael Landon and Mary Tyler Moore are game for *You Don't Say!* (Jody Lund Collection)

The longer the show stayed on the air, the more popular it became. Beginning in 1964, it consistently ranked among the top three rated game shows on television and, during the 1967-68 season, it was number one. Tom Kennedy began expanding his horizons with guest appearances on television shows and theatrical roles, and he even recorded a single because the demand was there for him.

In 1969, NBC cancelled the show in an attempt to revamp its daytime line-up. The ratings were there, but the network simply got restless with the sameness of their schedule and cleaned out a number of hit shows. It was an ill-advised move. The replacements all bombed, while Ralph Andrews made a few bucks by selling reruns of *You Don't Say!* episodes in syndication.

In 1974, *You Don't Say!* returned to television with another run on KTLA. In this revamped version, two contestants competed against each other with the aid of a four-star panel. Contestants would listen to clues from the panelists one at a time and alternate guessing the answer for a chance at $200, $150, $100 or $50. Reaching $500 won the game and a chance to try for $10,000. In this round, the contestant gave up to a total of six clues to the celebrities in an attempt to convey a total of four names. Correct answers paid $500, $1,000, $2,000 and $5,000; if a contestant used only one clue to convey all four names, the payday was $10,000.

Tom Kennedy and Clark Race on *You Don't Say!* Nobody outside of southern California ever saw this incarnation of the series. (Fred Wostbrock Collection)

In the beginning, Tom was actually a panelist for this version instead of a host. Los Angeles disc jockey Clark Race, previously the host of *The Parent Game* for Chuck Barris, was the host of this incarnation. By the time ABC picked it up for a national run, Tom had been promoted back to his old post as host. The new version set sail for ABC on July 7, 1975.

Audiences didn't gravitate to this version the way they had to the original, and the show was pulled rather hastily. In one of the last episodes taped, Tom promoted Christmas week with children competing, but the show disappeared from ABC on November 26, 1975. Although it was short-lived, it had its moments. In one classic bonus round, the contestant had to convey "Saigon" to Peter Haskell. Trying to give a clue for "sigh" to lead to it, the contestant gave Haskell the clue, "When I won the game a few minutes ago, I made a sound and I let out some air." Tom and the panel were reduced to tears of laughter as the contestant realized what she had just said.

You Don't Say! returned for one last go in syndication during the 1978-79 season with new host Jim Peck and the same four-celebrity format. The show fizzled and faded away, and audiences haven't seen it since. A great game show fading away? You don't say...

Tom has as much fun as the viewers during *You Don't Say!* (Author's Collection)

BONUS ROUND

The contestants on *You Don't Say!* had to guess words, and then guess the famous name that the words sort of sounded like. Here, you'll get three clues to common words, and you have to put those words together to figure out a name of a game show host.

1.) A puny potato is a tater ___(1)___.
A Playboy centerfold poses fully ___(2)___.
When it's finished, you're ___(3)___.
2.) Your grades in school are sometimes called your ___(1)___.
If you can't sing or whistle, you might ___(2)___.
The funeral parlor's car is the ___(3)___.
3.) You exercise at a ___(1)___.
If you have the eight of hearts and the eight of spades, you have a ___(2)___.
It's not she, it's ___(3)___.
4.) A ball player swings a ___(1)___.
A speech writer plans what he will ___(2)___.
If you go for onesies, you pick up a single ___(3)___.
5.) A knock to the head is a ___(1)___.
It's not me, it's ___(2)___.
The hair hanging over your forehead is called your ___(3)___.
6.) A baby rooster is a ___(1)___.
A great big grizzly is a ___(2)___.
A snake sound is a ___(3)___.
7.) A unit of measurement slightly longer than a yard is a ___(1)___.
It's wasn't yesterday or today, it's ___(2)___.
Your family is your kith and ___(3)___.

8.) The organ in your chest is your ___(1)___.
Plumbers fix faucets that ___(2)___.
A mother's newborn kittens are her ___(3)___.

April 2

1962 – *Window Shopping* Premieres

In a world without *Top Secret* (see March 4), *Window Shopping* would probably go down in history as the shortest-lived game show ever to release a lovely copy of the home game to the American consuming public. The show was off the air by June 29, making the boxed adaptation of the thirteen-week wonder a cherished find for collectors.

The game pitted three contestants against each other. They were shown a series of photographs and accumulated points by remembering details about the photos. Contestants were gradually eliminated as the game progressed. The last player standing was shown a window filled with fabulous merchandise and won prizes by describing each one in detail from memory. Describing a randomly pre-selected prize earned the contestant all of the prizes in the window.

The host of the show was Bob Kennedy, a singer who had been all over the place as a series host (*Wingo*), a pilot host (*Choose Up Sides*), a guest host (*The Price is Right*, *Feather Your Nest*, *Beat the Clock*, *Treasure Hunt*), and an announcer (*Name That Tune*, *Password*). In the year 1962, he was quite transparently hired for this show as a bid for publicity. Co-producer Danny Dayton told the press, "If the public wants to think it's JFK's brother—good luck to 'em."

Kennedy opened the series by smiling into the camera and quipping, "No relation." To his chagrin, it wouldn't be the cleverest thing anybody said in the three-month run of *Window Shopping*. That honor belonged to the winner of an ermine wrap, who proudly told Kennedy, "It's great to be on a show that gives a wrap about its contestants."

Unfortunately for the show, the audience didn't give one about *Window Shopping*.

BONUS ROUND

It's time to see if you can recall what you're seeing in photos the way the contestants did. Study each of the following photos for fifteen seconds, and then turn the page to answer some questions about what you're seeing.

Play the Percentages (Author's Collection)

Cross-Wits (Author's Collection)

Wheel of Fortune (Author's Collection)

Password (Author's Collection)

Bullseye (Mike Klauss Collection)

1. On *Play the Percentages*, what number was in the bottom circle of the percent sign?
2. There were four men in that photo from *Cross-Wits*. How many of them were wearing ties?
3. How much did Luella win on *Wheel of Fortune*?
4. What time was showing on Carol Channing's clock necklace?
5. Jim Lange or the contestant—which one was wearing a dark jacket?
6. Which hand was Geoff Edwards holding his cards in for *Play the Percentages*?
7. How many men were standing on the set of *Cross-Wits*?
8. How many microphones were visible in that shot of *Password*?
9. How many arms did Jim Lange have in the air?

For the correct answers, flip back and look at the photos again.

April 3

1956 – Ray Combs' Birth

Ray gives a big thumbs-up. He was ready to go places in 1988.
(Author's Collection)

Ray Combs was a prisoner of his own success—a man who got to do exactly what he wanted in life, then struggled to find something to follow it up. He rose to stardom virtually overnight and faded just as quickly.

Ray was born in Hamilton, Ohio, and raised in the Mormon faith. His first public speaking experience was delivering a sermon when he was five but, as he grew older, he came to realize he had a knack for comedy. He attended classes at Miami University of Ohio, where a speech teacher told Ray he had to do something with his gift for making people laugh.

He dropped out of college to spend two years doing missionary work before marrying his childhood sweetheart, Debra, and getting a job as a furniture salesman, where Ray's gift for making people laugh served him well. Barely twenty-two years old, he was the youngest salesman in the company but wound up making $70,000 a year selling couches. He wanted more, though, and sought a career in comedy. He dreamed of being a talk show host like his idol, Johnny Carson.

Ray and Debra were living in Indianapolis when Ray began working on a nightclub act and went from booking to booking. Seeking advice, he wrote a letter to another rising star from Indianapolis, David Letterman. Letterman wrote back and told Ray in no uncertain terms that he needed to move to Hollywood.

Not ready to risk the move, Ray spent the next few months flying back and forth to Los Angeles for low-paying stand-up bookings. His big break came when he got a job doing audience warm-ups for situation comedy tapings. Ray made the audiences laugh so hard as a warm-up man that in writer Mike Metzger's words, it was a "takeover" by Combs at every taping.

He warmed up the audiences for *Diff'rent Strokes*, *The Facts of Life* and *The Golden Girls*, and soon began raking in $200,000 a year as a warm-up man. Sitcom producers came to appreciate his talents so much that if Ray was unavailable for a taping, they rescheduled the taping.

Ray's idol, Johnny Carson, dropped by the studio one night when the sitcom *Amen* was about to start taping because he needed to talk to the show's star, Sherman Hemsley. As they chatted in Sherman's dressing room, Johnny was caught off-guard by the loud and near-constant sounds of laughter. Hemsley told him about the incredible warm-up guy they had working for the show.

On October 23, 1986, Ray Combs did an amazing set of jokes on *The Tonight Show Starring Johnny Carson*. The audience gave him a standing ovation, and Johnny did something he almost never did. He waved "come here" at Ray and invited him, on the spot, to sit down for a spontaneous interview. The last time Johnny had beckoned an unknown comic was eight years previously, when he'd invited a new guy named David Letterman to talk with him after an impressive set.

NBC Entertainment President Brandon Tartikoff and Johnny Carson both recognized that they had a Next Big Thing on their hands and began looking for projects for Ray. He assisted with some of the pranks on *TV's Bloopers and Practical Jokes* and played one-shot roles on several NBC sitcoms. When the time came for Ray to settle into a regular series, though, it turned out to be for CBS.

NBC and Mark Goodson had initially auditioned Ray in 1987 to host *Classic Concentration*, but Alex Trebek got the nod instead. The following year, Goodson was set to re-launch *Family Feud* and, since he had such a poor relationship with original host Richard Dawson, Goodson sought a new host. Countless auditions with potential hosts were held, but Combs got the job.

Let the feud begin! Ray Combs ably stepped into the established hit. (Author's Collection)

On Independence Day, 1988, Ray Combs took over *Family Feud*, with a nightly syndicated version premiering two months later.

Combs deflected any pressure about the new assignment. "I don't hesitate to follow Richard at all," he said. "People say those are big shoes to fill. I don't have to wear his shoes. I've got my own."

Not only was the show a hit, but it proved to be a more peaceful affair backstage than it had been under the temperamental Richard Dawson. Ray was humble in the wake of his success. Ray reviled in his achievements and happily shared the rewards. He frequently returned to Ohio and Indiana to host fundraisers for numerous causes. He was generous with his money. Years later, two of his brothers told E! the story of a time when Ray stopped shaving and wore tattered clothes to disguise himself and went to a homeless shelter to see how he'd be treated. When the volunteers at the shelter greeted him warmly and fed him, Ray whipped out his checkbook and handed over $30,000.

The year 1989 was possibly the first time anything went truly wrong for Ray. He opened a large nightclub in Cincinnati, Caddy Combs Comedy Club, but clashed with his business partner, Charles Schneider, about how to operate the club. Things came to a head when Schneider's attorneys warned Ray not to come to the building one night when he was in town. Ignoring the warning, Combs headed to the stage to perform his act and was arrested for trespassing as soon as he was finished.

It was the first time he had ever been arrested and he called the experience "the grossest injustice of human rights I have ever seen." Ray shut down Caddy Combs shortly after the incident and eventually opened another club in Cincinnati, The Ray Combs Cincinnati Comedy Connection. That was in 1991. The following year, things began slowly drifting downhill for Ray.

His dream had always been to be a comedian/talk show host like Johnny Carson, but after four years as host of *Family Feud*, well, he was still the host of *Family Feud*. The CBS version expanded to one hour in 1992 in a move to spike ratings. In one interview, Ray boasted that an hour and a half of *Feud* per day made it the most-seen game show on television. In a telling moment, though, he then shook his head and said, "That's a lot of *Feud*."

Ray was becoming restless and frustrated with the day-in, day-out sameness of a TV game show. He sought a sympathetic ear in friend Mike Metzger, but Metzger had worked for Chuck Barris for years and, while sympathetic, he told Ray, "That's the nature of the beast."

Combs began talking to *Family Feud* producers about possible changes that could be made to the show. According to producer Howard Felsher, his changes seemed geared toward turning it into *The Ray Combs Show*, and his ideas were rejected. Meanwhile, his marriage to Debra was falling apart. They separated and Ray moved into a Burbank apartment. His nightclub began faltering, and Ray asked friends to perform there as favors for very low pay to keep the club afloat.

With game shows on a sharp decline in the early '90s, CBS cancelled the daytime *Family Feud*, and the nighttime version sagged in the ratings. Mark Goodson had died, and there was now turmoil behind the scenes as his company tried to run the ship without their captain. Goodson's son, Jonathan, hired a consultant to analyze how to raise the slowly deflating ratings, and the consultant suggested bringing back Richard Dawson.

Despite protests from longtime staffers, in 1994 Richard Dawson was rehired, and Ray Combs was fired after six years on *Family Feud*. The closing minutes of his final episode were brutally awkward. While he didn't explicitly mention that it was his last show, Ray reacted to a family that fared very poorly in the bonus round by passive-aggressively joking, "I thought I was the biggest loser here today."

At the end of the show, Ray gave a curt goodbye to the camera and walked straight offstage with the cameras still running and the credits rolling. *Family Feud* viewers last saw Ray Combs silently rushing offstage while the contestant family looked at him curiously, then looked into the camera, puzzled about what to do with no host joining them onstage. Backstage, Ray rushed to his car and drove straight out of the studio lot without saying goodbye. He was furious.

That summer, shortly after taping his final *Feud*, Ray was in a serious car accident. Doctors were amazed that he survived, but for several months he was paralyzed. Through rehabilitation, he gradually regained the use of his body and he was back to his old self, at least physically. Many of friends noticed, however, that his personality had changed. He was darker, moodier and melancholy.

Sadly, his attempts at goodwill and sharing his fortune began backfiring. His nightclub shut down. With all of his generosity, he had amassed $500,000 in debt. He took on another game show job, hosting *Family Challenge*, a *Double Dare* ripoff for The Family Channel. Ray didn't think much of the show and neither did friends who saw it. When the bank foreclosed on one of his homes, he became disjointed and it came to a head at the next *Family Challenge*. Ray struggled with a job that he had done countless times, forgetting what the score was, forgetting how to explain the game and seeming completely out of sorts.

In 1996, the decline became more alarming and rapid. He called his wife to threaten suicide. He was taken to a hospital, released the next morning and, on his way home, jumped out of the car and ran down the freeway until another driver stopped him. He showed up at a friend's house and began banging his head against the walls, trying to injure himself. Later that night, he went to his wife's house and, finding it empty, ransacked it. Police arrived and took him to a hospital in nearby Glendale.

The hospital placed him in a psychology unit for seventy-two hours of observation. Nurses would come to his room every fifteen minutes to check on him. At four o'clock a.m. on June 2, 1996, one nurse made the rounds, came into his room and found that he had hanged himself. Taking his life proved a tragic end for a man who had given so much to audiences.

(Author's Collection)

April 4

1983 – *The New Battlestars* Premieres

Only a year after the end of *High Rollers*, Alex Trebek went back to work for Merrill Heatter, as host of *Battlestars*.
(Fred Wostbrock Collection)

At the height of the success of *The Hollywood Squares*, producers Merrill Heatter and Bob Quigley sold off the rights to the show and continued operating it for their new bosses. *Hollywood Squares* ended in 1981 and Merrill Heatter, wanting to continue the success of a show to which he no longer owned the rights, did the next best thing: he plagiarized himself. On October 26, 1981, he launched *Battlestars* on NBC, although discerning people who recognized what they were seeing would, with a wink, refer to it as *Hollywood Triangles*. Alex Trebek was tapped to host.

With a spacey motif that included silver "battle stations" and a command post, *Battlestars* featured two contestants and a six-star panel playing a game that was just different enough from its legendary predecessor. Trading out Tic-Tac-Toe for another childhood game, Dots, the two contestants faced the six stars, seated in a grid of six triangles connected to each other by ten dots. In turn, the contestants would press a button to randomly select one dot, and Alex would ask a question. Looking at a battle station monitor displaying two answers, the star would choose one as correct. The contestant would agree or disagree, and a correct response captured that dot and kept the turn for the contestant.

When all three dots surrounding a triangle had been captured, the contestant that gave the last correct answer won that triangle. Three triangles won the game and the chance at the big bonus round.

In the bonus round, the contestant faced a photo of a famous person covered by numbered squares and drew randomly from a stack of cards to remove three of the squares. Correctly guessing the identity of the star won $5,000. Failure to do so gave the contestant an opportunity to draw up to three more cards to see more of the picture for $3,000, $2,000 or $1,000. From the second chance onward, the celebrity panelists could offer help.

The game withered in the face of the stiff competition of *The Price is Right* on CBS and went off the air after six months, but got a reprieve a year later to replace *Just Men!* on the line-up. The game was tinkered with a bit. This time, contestants could choose the dots they wanted rather than depending on random chance, and a new bonus round, The Main Event, gave the contestant a chance to tackle three questions, with the help of the celebrities, for a chance at the Battlestar Bonanza—cash and prizes totaling more than $10,000. With competition from *Family Feud*, this version didn't fare much better than the first. *The New Battlestars*—which, on the final day, Alex referred to as "The Old Battlestars"—ended on July 1, 1983.

Although the game didn't have the "zingers" from stars that made *The Hollywood Squares* legendary, producers found enough quick-witted panelists that the show had its moments:

ALEX: The first income tax levied in America was to pay for something famous. What?
JOAN RIVERS: A set of dishes for Martha Washington.

ALEX: After mating with a male, she turns on the creature and devours it. What is she?
JOAN RIVERS: Shelley Winters.

ALEX: Who said, "Oh, that view is tremendous"?
FRED WILLARD: It's funny, I was talking to Dolly Parton's hairdresser the other day...

ALEX: What is Ayatollah Khomeini's first name?
TIM REID: Mud.

ALEX: Sir Thomas Crapper invented the flush toilet in 1878. What did Queen Victoria do when she found out?
RICHARD SIMMONS: She was very relieved.
NELL CARTER: You've heard of the throne, right?

ALEX: What did the Romans do when the peacock laid an egg?
TOM POSTON: Same as NBC, they put it on the air.

ALEX: *Cosmopolitan* calls it "the dreaded question," and they warn that even a good date may ask it. What's the question?
TOM POSTON: "Has a doctor seen that?"

ALEX: There is something of the President's that tradition holds no one else may sit on. What is it?
RIP TAYLOR: Nancy.

ALEX: Congress is considering naming something in Los Angeles after Bob Hope. What?
TOM POSTON: The Bank of America.

ALEX: Queen Elizabeth always eats it alone. What?
RIP TAYLOR: Chili.
TOM POSTON: I got wind of that, too.

ALEX: The amount of energy needed to make love is about the same as the amount of energy needed to climb how many flights of steps?
TOM WOPAT: Depends on how you go about it. I'm a seven-flight man, myself.

BONUS ROUND!

On "Battlestars," Alex Trebek hosted as contestants faced a grid of squares concealing the face of a famous person. They randomly selected cards to remove squares from the board and could win thousands of dollars by identifying the famous face from what little they could see.

Here, take a look at these eight game show hosts. Can you tell who they are from what we're showing you?

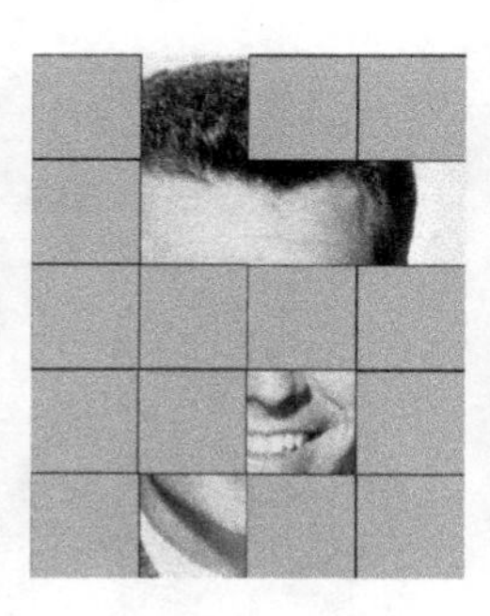
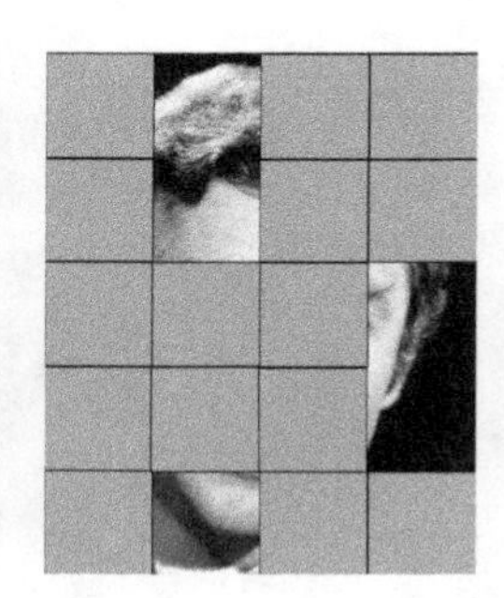

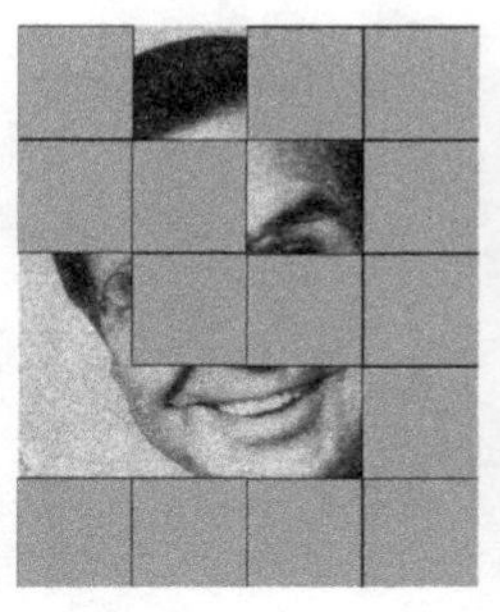

April 5

1985 – *Trivia Trap* Ends

Casual cool Bob Eubanks on *Trivia Trap*. (Author's Collection)

On April 5, 1985, a forty-year era of creativity and innovation came to a close, although at the time nobody realized it had quite that much significance. *Trivia Trap* was a game show from Mark Goodson Productions that premiered October 8, 1984, and vanished after only twenty-six weeks. From 1985 through Mark Goodson's death in 1992, the production company's output would see revivals of *Card Sharks*, *Blockbusters*, *Concentration*, *Family Feud*, *Now You See It*, *To Tell the Truth* and *Match Game*. *Trivia Trap* was the last original game to come from the most productive game show factory in the genre's history.

In the early 1980s, the board game Trivial Pursuit was taking the country by storm, and Goodson loved playing it. He asked his staff to whip up a new game show that involved Trivial Pursuit-style questions. The game was hosted by Bob Eubanks. On each episode, two teams competed: the juniors, dressed in blue sweaters and all under the age of thirty against the senior, decked in red, all thirty and older.

In the first round, the teams alternated playing trivia questions with four possible choices for the correct answer. The counterintuitive twist to *Trivia Trap* was that the teams had to select the three *wrong* answers to win money. Selecting one wrong answer paid $50, selecting two paid a total of $100 and naming all three earned $300. Picking the correct answer, called the Trap, ended the team's turn. A total of four questions were played in this manner.

Following that, the teams played the Trivia Race, during which Bob asked rapid-fire trivia questions to the teams, starting with the team in the lead. As long as one teammate knew the correct answer, the team retained control. If all three teammates were stumped, control of the round passed to their opponents. Each correct answer paid $100, then $200 after the tenth question, with $1,000 winning the game and a shot at $10,000.

In the bonus round, the Trivia Ladder, the teammates competed individually. Each of them played a question for $1,000. Everybody who gave a correct answer played a final question for $10,000.

The first round, which required the teams to eliminate wrong answers rather than chose the correct answer, was the source of a great deal of debate in the production offices. Even host Bob Eubanks had issues with it, because he felt the twist of selecting the wrong answers actually hurt the game. In situations in which all three teammates knew the correct answer, picking wrong answers one at a time dragged out the game and eliminated the suspense, but Mark Goodson stonewalled and refused to change the game after Bob and numerous staffers pointed that out. When Goodson took the show to American Film Institute and had them do focus groups, the focus groups made exactly the same complaint.

Goodson caved in and overhauled the show, starting each game with the teams taking turns answering a total of six true/false questions at twenty-five dollars per correct guess. They then played questions with one teammate picking an answer and the other teammates choosing whether to agree or disagree. If a correct answer was picked and everybody agreed, it paid $200. If a correct answer was picked and one teammate disagreed, it paid $100. If nobody agreed, it paid fifty dollars. The Trivia Race and the Trivia Ladder were left intact.

Audiences were as indifferent to the new format as they were to the first format, and ponder this: there was no more "trap" in the first round, so the show's title was meaningless. *Trivia Trap* was canceled. Goodson attempted to produce new, original formats in the ensuing years, but none sold, and *Trivia Trap* proved an inauspicious end to a legendary career. Despite the clashing over formats, Bob Eubanks closed the series by looking into the camera and saying some kind words to his boss:

"It took me almost twenty years to be able to work for your company, and I want you to know that I feel you're a man of class and everybody around you carries that same kind of class. Thank you, Mark Goodson."

April 6

1997 – *Animal Planet Zooventure* Premieres

The host was J.D. Roth, the veteran host of the kids' game show *Fun House*. The producer was Robert Noah, the veteran producer of fourteen games. The unique setting was the San Diego Zoo. The mission: present a kids' game show that could educate viewers about wildlife.

The title was *Animal Planet Zooventure*. It was one of few shows of any kind to air on two networks at once. New episodes could be seen each week on the Discovery and Animal Planet cable channels. Like most kids' game shows, it was a combination of trivia questions and wild, prop-filled stunts. Stunts are messy, but many on *Zooventure* had good intentions. They involved stuffed animals, and the kids were often told to recreate some kind of animal behavior, such as a "tiger mom" clenching stuffed tigers between her teeth to carry them, or "otters" sliding and slithering across the stage to retrieve food.

The final round was a picture puzzle, with puzzle pieces obscuring a photo of an animal. Players drew numbered balls to reveal the pieces one at a time until one of them identified the creature.

The game was structured as a small tournament, with two complete games played in each episode. The winners faced off in a final, sixty-second round of trivia. The holder of the high score at the end was declared "Zookeeper of the Day" and received a behind-the-scenes tour of the zoo.

Throughout the show, staffers from the San Diego Zoo would drop by with animals, rattling off fun facts about everything from meerkats to moles. The wild, lively game of wildlife connected with viewers well enough to stay on the air for three years.

April 7

2001 - David Graf Dies

David Graf is best-remembered to movie fans as Sergeant Tackleberry in the *Police Academy* films of the 1980s, but in the 1970s, he was little more than a struggling actor trying to keep his head above water in New York City. In December 1979, Graf appeared as a contestant on *The $20,000 Pyramid* and, with Patty Duke's help, he cleared the Winner's Circle on his first attempt and walked away with $10,000. Six years later, with Graf's profile on the rise thanks to the *Police Academy* films, he appeared on the show as a celebrity partner. The opposing celebrity was Patty Duke, and host Dick Clark opened the show by surprising Patty with the video tape of the big win.

David Graf is by no means alone. Many big stars who struggled at the beginning of their show business careers turned to game shows for a quick infusion of funds. Among them:

KIRSTIE ALLEY – Before *Cheers*, she was a champion on *Match Game* in 1979. The following year, she was a champion on *Password Plus*.

SANDRA BERNHARD – Using the alias "Malvina Rae," she was a contestant on *The $1.98 Beauty Pageant*.

BRIAN BILLICK – The one-time head coach of the Baltimore Ravens was a contestant on "Match Game PM" in 1977.

DR. JOYCE BROTHERS – Her road to stardom began with a big win on *The $64,000 Question* (see June 7).

LAURA CHAMBERS – The Game Show Network hostess was a contestant on *Tic Tac Dough* and *Sale of the Century*.

LYNN DEERFIELD – She appeared as a contestant on the original '60s incarnation of *The Match Game*. After she became a cast member on *The Guiding Light*, she appeared as a panelist on *Match Game '76*.

DONNY DEUTSCH – The CNBC correspondent was a contestant on *Match Game* in 1980.

PHYLLIS DILLER – The comedienne launched her career with a show-stealing appearance with Groucho Marx on *You Bet Your Life*.

DANNY ELFMAN – The noted film and TV composer, along with his band, Oingo Boingo, appeared on *The Gong Show*.

CHIP ESTEN – Before he became a regular performer on *Whose Line is it Anyway?*, he played *Scrabble* toward the end of that show's run in 1990.

FARRAH FAWCETT – She was a bachelorette on *The Dating Game*.

TERESA GANZEL – Johnny Carson's "Tea Time Lady" was once a contestant on *The $1.98 Beauty Pageant.*

STACY GUALANDI – The *Inside Edition* correspondent was a contestant on the final episode of the 1990-91 incarnation of *Match Game.*

CUBA GOODING, JR. – "Show me the honey!" he could have shouted when he was a contestant on *The Dating Game* in 1986.

MEL HARRIS – The future *thirtysomething* co-star was a contestant on *The $20,000 Pyramid.*

PHIL HARTMAN – He was a bachelor on *The Dating Game* in 1979.

CONNIE HINES – Before *Mister Ed*, she was a big winner on the controversial quizzer *Dotto* in 1958. The show was abruptly cancelled shortly after.

MYKE HORTON – *American Gladiators* fans know him best as Gemini, but before that he was a contestant on *Press Your Luck.*

ANNE-MARIE JOHNSON – The future co-star on *In the Heat of the Night* and *In Living Color* was a champion on *Card Sharks* and *Child's Play.*

DON JOHNSON – He went looking for love on *The Dating Game.*

JENNY JONES – The controversial daytime talk show host of the 1990s was a big winner on *Match Game* and *Press Your Luck.*

MITZI KAPTURE – The future co-star of *Silk Stalkings* played *The $25,000 Pyramid* in 1984 and won $1,100 and a Caribbean cruise.

BRIANNE LEARY – She won more than $10,000 as a contestant on *Match Game '76.* Two years later, she was starring on *CHiPS* and returned to *Match Game '78* as a panelist.

JACK LEMMON – After he became a star, he appeared on *I've Got a Secret* with the secret that, in 1948, he had won a gas range on a radio quiz show hosted by panelist Bill Cullen.

KELLIE MARTIN – A few years before *Life Goes On*, the actress appeared on a special Young People's Week of *Card Sharks*.

STEVE MARTIN – He was a contestant on *The Dating Game* years before he fell for Roxanne.

JOHN MCCAIN – The future Senator was a champion on Art Fleming's version of *Jeopardy!*

KATHY NAJIMY – The actress and voice artist appeared on *Family Feud* and *The $25,000 Pyramid*.

GIOVANNI RIBISI – As a child, he and his twin were contestants on NBC's Saturday morning game *I'm Telling*.

MICHAEL RICHARDS – Would you want to go on a dream date with Kramer? He was a bachelor on *The Dating Game* in 1968.

JOHN RITTER – Well before *Three's Company*, he was on *The Dating Game*.

JUDD ROSE – The CNN correspondent was a contestant on the final episode of *Split Second* in 1975.

RHONDA SHEAR – The sexpot cable hostess was a contestant on *The $1.98 Beauty Pageant*.

O.J. SIMPSON – He appeared as a contestant on the original version of *The Hollywood Squares*. Years later, producer Art Alisi recalled that O.J. became upset when he learned he had to wait ninety days to collect the $400 he'd won.

McLEAN STEVENSON – A decade before *M*A*S*H*, he was a contestant on *Password*. He recalled years later that he lost but received a lovely set of American Tourister luggage as a consolation prize. He later appeared on *The Dating Game*.

LINDSAY WAGNER – She was a bachelorette on *The Dating Game*. One of the bachelors she had to choose from was McLean Stevenson.

VANNA WHITE – Two years before she began turning letters, she was called to "come on down" on *The Price is Right*. She remained in Contestants' Row for the entire hour.

MARE WINNINGHAM – The Academy Award-nominated actress appeared, using an alias, as a contestant on *The Gong Show*.

ROBERT WUHL – TV's *Arli$$* was a big winner on *The $20,000 Pyramid*. A clip of the episode was used in a story on *Arli$$*, establishing that the title character had started his sports agency with the money he won as a contestant

April 8

1956 – *The $64,000 Challenge* Premieres

Ten months into the reign of *The $64,000 Question*, it became apparent that there was a problem. From the moment it premiered, the show exploded. It quickly rose to become the number-one show on television; it was raking in a fortune for CBS, and the show's sponsor, Revlon, couldn't keep its products on shelves because viewers were snapping them up left and right.

The show was so popular that it turned its contestants into stars. They made public appearances, granted newspaper interviews, and did just about anything else befitting celebrities, since that's what they had become in the wake of their appearances on the show. But the game was structured to limit each contestant's maximum stay to five weeks.

And there was the problem. The show created celebrities but couldn't take advantage of it. The $64,000 *Challenge* was the solution to that problem. As of April 8, 1956, the next stop for big winners on *The $64,000 Question* was a stint on the first game show spin-off.

Challenge welcomed every contestant who had won at least $16,000 on *Question* to face an expert in the same subject as the one that garnered the first win. The expert and contestant were placed in separate isolation booths, both immodestly designed to look like castles, and were asked identical questions. As long as both contestants gave the correct answer, both remained. They continued competing against each other with the money growing the same way that it did on *Question*, doubling until reaching $64,000. If one player missed a question and the other player was correct, the player who goofed was eliminated. The winning contestant was guaranteed to leave with no less than the value of that particular question and continued playing solo until either erring, deciding to quit or reaching the magic number of $64,000.

To keep the well of big winners from running dry every week, the show also included celebrities competing in special competitions over a series of weeks. Edward G. Robinson and Vincent Price dueled for several weeks in the category of Art, before ending the game in a tie at $32,000. Xavier Cugat and young Patty Duke took part in other games.

The original host of the show was Sonny Fox, who later became far better known for his role as host of the children's show *Wonderama*. Fox was struck by an omen on the premiere broadcast. He stood in the wings waiting for his introduction when announcer Bill Rogers bellowed, "Here is your host, Bill Fox!" Sonny stood backstage, confused for a moment until a stagehand told him that was his name and he needed to walk onstage. He was later told that a man named "Sonny" couldn't believably be in charge of a $64,000 prize.

Fox was ill at ease on *Challenge*, stuttering during his introductions and misidentifying the isolation booths as "the control room." He was fired in September and replaced by Ralph Story, who had been one of the finalists in consideration to host *Question* a year earlier before being passed over in favor of Hal March. Ralph Story remained with the series until the end of the run on September 7, 1958, with ratings crumbling in the wake of the ugly rumors gathering steam about what went on behind the scenes. *Question* itself was gone two months later.

One of the matches presented on the show pitted a $16,000 *Question* winner named Stoney Jackson against a woman named Doll Goostree. Their category was Great Love Stories. Years later, Jackson told the story of how a staff member had casually asked him, "Who, other than Christopher Marlowe, wrote a song about Hero and Leander?" She immediately answered her own question, telling Jackson that it was Thomas Hood.

The following week, Ralph Story asked the contestants that same question. Jackson answered "Thomas Hood," while Goostree answered "Shakespeare." A bit suspicious, Jackson called Goostree the following day and asked why she had given that answer. The same staff member had told Goostree to study Shakespeare, because the question was going to be about him. Feeling sorry for his opponent, Jackson mailed her $400.

The show's greatest champion was a $64,000 winner from *Question* named Teddy Nadler. He was a file clerk from St. Louis with only an eighth grade education. Nadler was such a smash with viewers that *Challenge* kept bringing him back again and again until he finally retired altogether with $256,000, a record for game show winnings that would stand until 1980. Nadler had no "comfort zone" to speak of, as far as viewers knew. The recurring gimmick of his appearances was that he always returned with a new field of expertise. He won the grand prize in categories spanning fields of classical music, history, mythology, and baseball.

Nadler was never implicated in the quiz show scandals. He was never subpoenaed by Congress to testify during their investigations, and one obituary maintained that even though the rest of the show may have been rigged, his wins were totally legitimate. The only time his credibility was ever questioned was in 1960, when *Time* reported that he had applied for a job as a census taker but didn't get hired because he failed a preliminary test; Teddy Nadler couldn't read a map.

April 9

1953 – *TV Guide* Debuts

From the dawn of television, there were countless regional magazines devoted to the local listings for that week, but when *TV Guide* arrived in 1953 it quickly became the most influential and popular publication. A good review could singlehandedly save a low-rated show from cancellation, while a scorching review of a show or its star could signal impending downfall (see July 12).

TV Guide has always given a fair share of coverage to game shows and never hesitated to devote a cover story to the genre. If you can find a collector, maybe you can get your hands on these *TV Guide* covers.

July 24, 1953 – Groucho Marx of *You Bet Your Life*
November 6, 1953 – Warren Hull of *Strike It Rich*
January 22, 1954 – Cast of *I've Got a Secret*

March 19, 1954 – Groucho Marx of *You Bet Your Life*

July 9, 1954 – Arlene Francis of *What's My Line?*

August 21, 1954 – Jayne Meadows of *I've Got a Secret* and husband Steve Allen of *What's My Line?*

August 28, 1954 – Roxanne of *Beat the Clock*

January 15, 1955 – Cast of *I've Got a Secret*

August 13, 1955 – Roxanne and Bud Collyer of *Beat the Clock*

August 20, 1955 – Hal March of *The $64,000 Question*

August 27, 1955 – Groucho Marx of *You Bet Your Life*

March 3, 1956 – Hal March and Lynn Dollar of *The $64,000 Question*

March 31, 1956 – John Daly and Arlene Francis of *What's My Line?*

April 7, 1956 – Cast of *I've Got a Secret*

September 22, 1956 – Hal March of *The $64,000 Question*

February 23, 1957 – Charles Van Doren of *Twenty One*

May 4, 1957 – Hal March and Robert Strom of *The $64,000 Question*

June 22, 1957 – Jack Bailey of *Queen for a Day*

July 6, 1957 – Cast of *What's My Line?*

July 27, 1957 – Garry Moore of *I've Got a Secret*

April 19, 1958 – Polly Bergen of *To Tell the Truth*

July 5, 1958 – Bill Cullen of *The Price is Right*

August 30, 1958 – Cast of *To Tell the Truth*

August 22, 1959 – Cast of *I've Got a Secret*

May 14, 1960 – Ernie Kovacs and Edie Adams of *Take a Good Look*

July 23, 1960 – John Daly of *What's My Line?*

September 3, 1960 – Arlene Francis of *What's My Line?*

June 23, 1962 – Arlene Francis of *What's My Line?*

July 28, 1962 – Bill Cullen and contestant Barbara Benner of *The Price is Right*

August 18, 1962 – Cast of *I've Got a Secret*

July 27, 1963 - "The Odd Science of Picking Game Show Contestants"

August 10, 1963 – Cast of *I've Got a Secret*

January 21, 1984 – Jack Barry, Pat Sajak, Bob Barker, Wink Martindale, Bill Cullen and Monty Hall

March 4, 1989 – Vanna White of *Wheel of Fortune*

December 9, 1989 – Vanna White of *Wheel of Fortune*

July 3, 1993 - Vanna White of *Wheel of Fortune*

November 6, 1999 – Regis Philbin of *Who Wants to be a Millionaire?*

January 15, 2000 – Regis Philbin and contestants from *Who Wants to be a Millionaire?*

January 27, 2001 – Regis Philbin and Alex Trebek: *The 50 Greatest Game Shows of All Time*

April 10

1955 - Dr. Jonas Salk Successfully Tests the First Polio Vaccine

A full-body shot of Bill Cullen from 1963. Notice his unusual stance; Bill's legs grew unevenly and he had to lean when he stood. (Author's Collection)

At first glance, sure, this milestone seems a little out of place, but the vaccine is worth noting for bringing an end to a long epidemic that had struck, among millions of other victims, the "Dean of Emcees," Bill Cullen, who devoted himself to dodging excuses and living a fulfilling life despite the ailment.

Cullen once wrote, "I would rather not have people who see me limp along show any pity, distress, or compassion...a little limp doesn't stop me from enjoying work, and living, and playing, too."

Bill was afflicted by polio at the age of eighteen months. It caused his legs to grow irregularly. He wore a brace until he was ten and, when he grew up, it caused one leg to be slightly longer than the other, hence his seemingly strange posture in some publicity photos. He went through therapy for a time to try to rehabilitate the leg, but gave up when doctors told him the muscles were too badly damaged.

He was determined to live an active life. He relentlessly pursued sports, playing sandlot baseball as a kid in Pittsburgh; he once said he couldn't run very fast, but compensated by hitting the ball farther than most of the other kids. When he got older, he took boxing lessons and competed briefly in auto racing.

When it came to settling on a career, though, Bill went with broadcasting. Speaking tongue-in-cheek years later, he credited polio with helping him make the decision about his future. He had been a class clown throughout school and decided to pursue radio, he said, because he could be a ham while sitting down.

Bill thrived just fine in radio but initially resisted the new medium of television, fearful that his limp would make him unattractive to viewers. He significantly underestimated the reputation he had built for himself as a master of ceremonies by this point. Producers who had already worked with him in radio were eager to have him at the helm for their new television games.

For all of Bill's concerns about his limp making him unattractive, the producers and directors he worked with in television struck upon a simple solution: don't show the leg. Although Bill maintained in a newspaper article that he never actually requested this and it was merely something that all of the directors had chosen to do, game shows featuring Bill as a host or a guest were typically staged differently from other game shows.

Bill sat on a counter for *The Price is Right* and sat on a tall chair for most of his other games. (Author's Collection)

Whereas emcees on other game shows bounded across the stage for their entrance and stood behind a podium or next to the prizes and players during the games, Bill usually opened his shows by taking two or three steps, if he took any at all, and had a seat, usually on a tall chair. If a point arose in the game where Bill absolutely had to walk, the camera would cut to anything else—the audience, the game board, maybe a commercial message—until Bill was done walking. When Bill was a guest player on a game show, the usual entrance where the guests smiled, waved, greeted each other and walked across stage was eschewed in favor of having Bill already seated or standing where the game would be played.

Not interested in sympathy, Bill rarely discussed his ailment, although he was very open and talkative about it on the rare occasions when it was brought up. His low-key approach of not discussing polio, combined with the fact that he was never seen walking, precluded many people from being aware that there was anything wrong. He once wrote that whenever fans met him on the street, their first question almost always was, "What's the matter with your leg?"

Bill gave them the honest answer, but assured his fans that as much as he appreciated their sympathy, polio hadn't bothered him at all. He spoke glowingly of his parents and the medical professionals who cared for him during his childhood and credited his wife Ann with a happy home life during adulthood. Besides that, he had become an established television star despite a significant physical handicap. Because of the love and success that surrounded him throughout his life, Bill simply never got around to feeling sad about his impairment.

In an interview conducted years after Bill's death, his wife Ann recalled that there was really only one type of special consideration that Bill ever asked for. When they were planning a vacation, he would ask the hotel for a room on one of the lower floors. He tried to avoid stairs when he could.

His discreet approach to living with polio caused a particularly embarrassing moment for Mel Brooks, who shared the anecdote in a 2009 *GQ* interview. Mel appeared as a contestant on a special all-star week of Bill's game, *Eye Guess*, in the fall of 1966. After the taping, Bill stepped out from behind his podium and walked across the stage. Struck by the strange way Bill was moving, Mel presumed that the cheerful, hammy Bill was doing a "funny walk" to get a laugh from the audience. Wanting to get into the spirit, the comedian stood up and followed Bill around the stage, limping and flailing his arms about, while Julia Meade, the other celebrity guest that day, desperately tried to get Mel's attention and tell him that the limp was Bill's natural walk.

After the show, Bill walked up to Mel, all smiles, shook his hand and told him, "You know, you're the only comic who's ever had the nerve to make fun of my crippled walk. Everyone's so careful; it makes me feel even worse."

April 11

1967 - *Snap Judgment* Premieres

Snap Judgment, hosted by Ed McMahon, went through a strange journey during its two-year run on NBC. It started out as a knockoff of a more popular show from the same producers. Eventually, it simply transformed into the show that it had borrowed from.

Premiering as a replacement for *Reach for the Stars*, a failed three-month effort produced by Merv Griffin, *Snap Judgment* serves as another example of Mark Goodson-Bill Todman Productions' habit of ripping off their own shows as a means of staying ahead of the competition. *Password* had been a major hit for the company, and Goodson-Todman churned out *The Match*

Game and *Get the Message* to take advantage of it. *Snap Judgment* was going to be another spin on *Password*.

The difference between *Password* and *Snap Judgment* was simple and subtle. Just as on *Password*, there would be two celebrity-contestant pairings competing against each other, and the teammates would alternate giving and receiving clues to guess words. The spin provided by *Snap Judgment* was that before the show, the four players were separately shown lists of all the words that would be used, and they had to write down five clues for each word. Once onstage, lists in hand, they were committed to using only the clues they had written down.

Despite some impressive star power in celebrity bookings—Johnny Carson spent a week on the show, as did Bob Hope—ratings for the game were mediocre at best and even the staff at Goodson-Todman was apparently unimpressed with the finished product. *What's My Line?* producer Gil Fates called *Snap Judgment* "anemic" in his memoirs.

On December 23, 1968, *Snap Judgment* solved the problems of its lame game by just becoming *Password*. Although cancelled by that point after *The Newlywed Game* burst onto the scene (see July 11), *Password* had still been an incredibly strong game for the company. It was an unusual choice, but it certainly was a sensible one.

The plan was a bust; thirteen weeks later, *Snap Judgment* was off the air, replaced by *It Takes Two* on the NBC schedule. Goodson-Todman wound up having considerably more success selling reruns of *Password* into syndication before re-launching that show in 1971.

April 12

1976 - *Break the Bank* Premieres

We have a winner! The lips defeat the mustache on
Break the Bank. (Author's Collection)

Hey, remember that game show where two contestants competed against each other with the help of nine celebrities who were asked questions and might give a joke answer and then give a bluff answer, and the contestants were trying to get three of the same symbol on the game board? No, not that one, the other one. The game was *Break the Bank*. The title had already been used for radio and TV quizzes in the 1940s and 1950s, but this incarnation bore no resemblance. The show was produced by Jack Barry and Dan Enright; Jack had already rebuilt his reputation with the three-year run of *The Joker's Wild* on CBS, but *Break the Bank* was a milestone for Dan Enright. It was his first American production credit since the quiz show scandals.

The new series was clearly inspired by *The Hollywood Squares*, which was closing in on ten years on NBC at the time. Maybe Barry and Enright were hoping viewers were ready to move on or maybe they figured the playground was big enough for two similar games, but either way the new game set sail on ABC with host Tom Kennedy, who had firmly established the network as a home after four years with *Split Second* and *You Don't Say!*

Break the Bank pitted a man and a woman against each other. The nine stars did not sit in a game board as on *Squares*. Rather, they surrounded it. The game board consisted of twenty boxes, all hiding different rewards. Three connected boxes hid $100; three connected boxes hid $200; three connected boxes hid $300; one box hid a wild card; five boxes hid money bags, and five boxes were blank.

A contestant would select a box, and the star sitting next to it and the star sitting above it would hear a question. One star gave the correct answer; the other gave a bluff. To capture the box, the contestant had to decide whom to believe. A correct decision kept the contestant's turn, who then continued to choose another

Tom Kennedy couldn't stay away from ABC. *Break the Bank* was his third consecutive series for the network. (Author's Collection)

box. An incorrect decision turned the game over to the opponent. Uncovering one of the blank squares also cost a turn. The winner was the first player to capture three identical money amounts.

And then there were those five money bags. A contestant who uncovered one could keep the money without having to deal with a question but, in that event, would lose the turn. Any contestant who managed to claim three money bags "broke the bank," which started at $5,000 and grew by $250 or $500 for each game it went unclaimed.

When it launched, *Break the Bank* proved to be somewhat symbolic of the changing nature of television. ABC approved of the pilot that Barry and Enright screened but warned that the series would get picked up only if it was "punched up"—code for adding off-color elements.

Jack Barry explained in an interview, "[T]he networks believe that very risqué material is what makes it on television."

It was difficult to argue with that. The most popular game shows on television included *The Hollywood Squares*, which was famous for daring jokes from the celebrities about sex, racism and molestation; *Match Game '76*, where Gene Rayburn and the panel giggled their way through thirty minutes of double-entendres, and *Tattletales*, often requiring celebrities to give honest answers to intimate questions about their personal lives. Meanwhile, talk shows and soap operas were breaking barriers by the day with previously prohibited subject matter.

Barry & Enright probably could have argued with the ABC executives, pointing out that there were still plenty of game shows, like *The Price is Right* and *The $20,000 Pyramid*, that were thriving entirely on the strength of the engaging game, but they quietly accepted the command in the name of getting the show on the air. As the new show bowed on ABC, Jack Barry got to work selling a weekly prime time version of the show in first-run syndication for the fall, hastily assuring station managers at a convention that the prime time counterpart would be toned down and suitable for airing at 7:30 p.m., "the family hour."

In an unfortunate twist, the daytime version would be gone by the time the prime time version premiered. ABC canceled the show after just thirteen weeks. It was a surprising decision by the network; in a market flooded with game shows, *Break the Bank* was the number three game on daytime TV. But soap operas were king, and when the networks began expanding soap opera time slots from thirty minutes to forty-five minutes, and from forty-five

Creator Jack Barry acted as host for the nighttime edition of *Break the Bank*. (Fred Wostbrock Collection)

minutes to one hour, game shows got squeezed out. One of the victims was *Break the Bank*.

The nighttime version of *Break the Bank* premiered in September 1976 with creator Jack Barry acting as host, since Tom Kennedy was already committed to a third season of *Name That Tune*. This version added a bonus round giving contestants a chance to uncover money hidden behind each celebrity's nameplate for a chance at up to $5,000. It faded after only one season.

TOM: You have a soft pretzel and you want to make it hard. What do you do with it?
JAN MURRAY: I'd kiss it.

TOM: You've just been given something with spots, fishers, bubbles, and a yellow tinge. What have you been given?
LIZ TORRES: A very rare Puerto Rican disease.

TOM: It's twelve feet long and four inches in diameter, and it's found below the diaphragm. What is it?
JAN MURRAY: A world's record.

TOM: What were the grounds for divorce for Richard Burton and Elizabeth Taylor?
LIZ TORRES: Neither of them wanted Eddie Fisher.

TOM: It's a muscular organ and mine is the size of my clenched fist. What is it?
JAN MURRAY: What are you asking me for? It's your fist.

TOM: At what age are you considered too old for sex?
ABE VIGODA: Last Wednesday.

TOM: It's your fiftieth anniversary. What gift are you expecting?
ABE VIGODA: A transfusion.

TOM: The biggest concern among senior citizens is money. What's the second biggest concern?
ABE VIGODA: The rising cost of prunes.

TOM: How long does the average engagement last?
JAN MURRAY: Nine months.

TOM: If you're playing the French horn, where do you put your fist?
JAN MURRAY: If you want a high note, in the trumpet player.

TOM: What entertainer was famous for saying, "You ain't seen nothin' yet"?
JAN MURRAY: Linda Lovelace.

TOM: How often should you turn your mattress over?
ABE VIGODA: Depends on who you're sleeping with.

TOM: You can tell the sex of an eggplant because the female has a bigger one than the male. What?
LIZ TORRES: Stretch marks.

TOM: When you get the blues, the most likely cause is a lack of something. What?
JAN MURRAY: Lack of what you were up all night trying to get.

TOM: A lion often does something so much at one time that he won't do it again for a week. What?
ABE VIGODA: A week? I sometimes don't do it for a month.

TOM: What is the major form of gambling in the United States?
JOEY BISHOP: Marriage.
BILL DANA: Politics.

TOM: Where do you get mohair from?
JOEY BISHOP: If you're bald, you go to a wigmaker, and that's where you get mo' hair from.

TOM: Where does the cork come from?
FOSTER BROOKS: The bottle.

TOM: When you follow a group of fish, you're following a school. When you follow a group of birds, you're following a flock. When you follow a group of elephants, what are you following?
FOSTER BROOKS: A man with a shovel.

TOM: What causes a squeaky bed?
JAN MURRAY: Three people with asthma.

TOM: Eddie Fisher says that when you're worried, you should count something. What?
JAN MURRAY: Alimony payments.

TOM: Pigeons are known for their uncanny ability to find something. What?
LONNIE SHORE: Statues of generals.

JACK: What exactly is a sponge?
JOEY BISHOP: Someone who doesn't pick up a check.

JACK: Each night, a wild chimpanzee picks a different tree and does something in it for about five minutes. What is he doing?
PAT MORITA: I don't know, but I'm not standing underneath that tree.

JACK: A doctor's cure for it is putting a fist in a patient's stomach. What is it?
JOEY BISHOP: Overdue bills.

JACK: George Washington never shook hands as President. What did he do instead?
JAYE P. MORGAN: He was a pincher.

JACK: You've just been canonized. What does that mean?
JOEY BISHOP: You've been sat upon by William Conrad.

JACK: What city is known as the chocolate capital of the world?
CLIFTON DAVIS: Harlem.

April 13

1954 - *Pantomime Quiz* Ends...For Now

Pantomime Quiz first appeared on the DuMont network on October 20, 1953, and lasted just the season. What was particularly remarkable about this second run of *Pantomime Quiz* was that, in nine years on national television, it was the longest that the show had stayed in one place.

Pantomime Quiz was created and hosted by Mike Stokey, born September 14, 1918, in Shreveport, Louisiana. He attended Los Angeles City College, and, during his spare time, enjoyed playing charades with other students. He rounded up some of them and put the game on experimental station W6XAO. Since they didn't really have a name for the game and the show didn't have a huge audience anyway—Stokey said years later that it attracted a total of twenty viewers—the experimental broadcasts were plainly titled

The Game. After working briefly as a staff announcer for NBC, Mike decided to revive *The Game.*

In 1947 the show began its new life with a new title on Los Angeles TV station KTLA, where *Pantomime Quiz* enjoyed a two-year run and even pocketed one of the first Emmys, in the nebulous category of Most Popular Television Program. In 1950, CBS picked up the game as a summer replacement series; it aired from July 3 to September 25 that year, sealing the show's fate as the go-to series for filling space. CBS was so pleased with it that the show got another summer run in 1951, airing July 2 through August 20. Early the following year, NBC needed to plug some holes created by cancellations and picked up *Pantomime Quiz* from January 2 to March 26. That summer, it bounced back to CBS for its annual run there from July 4 to September 26.

Stay with this, now....The returned to CBS the following summer, 1953, then bounced to DuMont for the only full season it would ever know. In 1954, it was back to CBS from July 9 to August 27. In 1955, ABC was the network dealing with midseason vacancies and aired the show from January 22 to March 6. Then it was back to its little summer home at CBS for a July 8-September 30 run.

In 1956 and 1957, the show repeated only its annual summer run on CBS, but ABC snapped it up the following year and aired it from April 8 to September 2. The following May, ABC tried it as a daytime show, but it was gone in five months. A simultaneous run in prime time lasted through the summer. Did you get all that?

So what exactly was this show called *Pantomime Quiz*? Charades, that's all. Each week, two teams of three celebrities apiece competed against each other in a series of rounds with particularly challenging material. Most charades players are accustomed to acting out movie titles or famous sayings. *Pantomime Quiz* made the stars work harder. They had to act out quotations, short poems, puns and complete sentences. A typical night's puzzles might include:

·"Of all the felt I ever felt, I never felt felt like that felt felt."

·"Put an egg in your shoe and beat it."

·"Double, double, toil and trouble, fire burn and cauldron bubble."

·"Little pig, busy street, motor car, sausage meat."

·"Though I tried to be aloof, when you pushed me off the roof, I feel our romance is dead."

·"Oh where oh where has my little dog gone, oh where oh where can he be? With his ears cut short and his tail cut long, oh where, oh where can he be?"

·"Hail, hail, the gang's all here, what the heck do we care, what the heck do we care. Hail, hail, the gang's all here, what the heck do we care now?"

·"He crossed his chicken with a racing form and now he's laying odds."

·"The Case of the Female Centipede, or 20,000 Legs Under the She."

·"With spectacles on nose and pouch on side, his youthful hos, well saved, a world too wide for his shrunk shank."

·"When the outlaw ripped his britches, the sheriff found his hideout."

One teammate would try to act out the message, one word at a time, to the other teammates within the two-minute time limit. After each team played, the team that used less time won one point for each second saved over the opposing team's time. All of the material used on the show was submitted by home viewers, who won prizes for having a submission used and for baffling the stars if they used the full two minutes.

As the show stayed on the air, it gradually developed its own supply of signals and movements to convey clues. Touching fingers to the forearms would convey how many syllables were in a word. Placing a hand around the neck indicated that the solution would be a gag saying or pun. Crossing index fingers to resemble a "T" meant the word was "the" or "to." Touching the nose signaled that the partner just said the correct word. Sometimes the clues were too good. Stokey had to step in one night and forcibly restrain Laya Raki when her clue for "nude" became too graphic.

The show's set was elegant, built to look like the living room of a penthouse apartment with plush seating for the stars and a large window framing a faux-skyline of the city's night lights. The impressive galaxy of celebrities, always clad in formal wear, who joined Mike Stokey included Kirk Douglas, Paul Newman, Jack Webb, Lucille Ball, Marilyn Monroe, Robert Stack, Angela Lansbury and Dick Van Dyke.

During the 1960s, the show was retitled *Stump the Stars* and had several runs slightly longer than a summer. It returned to CBS on September 17, 1962, and lasted an entire year. In 1964, it went into syndication for one season, followed by a second syndicated run in 1969-70. In January 1979, the show returned under yet another title, *Celebrity Charades*, with new host Jay Johnson, best known to TV viewers as the ventriloquist on *Soap*. AMC tried a brief run in 2005 co-hosted by Chad Lowe and Hilary Swank, with the teams playing for charity, but the experiment ended after five broadcasts.

April 14

1956 - Practical Videotape is Introduced

For people behind the scenes and the regular folks sitting at home tuning in, the introduction of videotape made life a little easier and a little more pleasant. Ampex, a Redwood City, California-based firm, demonstrated a videotape recording system in public, and it proved to be a breakthrough for a variety of reasons.

Prior to the development of videotape, airing a television show on a delay was only possible through one means, kinescope. Kinescope was a process in which a film was made by putting a camera in front of a television receiver. There were problems with the kinescope process. Film was expensive, the picture quality suffered, and it required extra time to be developed in a lab after it was shot. Often it could take up to three hours, which meant a kinescope of a program that aired live on the east coast and then aired three hours later in the Pacific Time Zone often went on the air straight from development, often still hot from the dryer. Videotape was cheaper, quality degradation was minimalized, and no extra development was needed.

Television adapted to videotape very quickly, mainly because it worked and the industry was desperate for an alternative for kinescopes. A game show was on the ground floor of the development. The January 22, 1957 episode of *Truth or Consequences* was the first television show ever aired via videotape across every time zone in the United States.

By the 1970s, videotape cassettes and recorders were commercially available for home audiences. Some merely looked at it as a means of catching a show you wouldn't be home for, but it ended up being much more. With minimal foresight, many television broadcasts, like sports events, soap operas, and yes, even game shows, were erased by networks and producers because there was no expectation that the tapes would be of any value. Series that were entirely or almost entirely wiped out by this practice survive today because of viewers at home who recorded episodes and hung onto them for decades. Among these treasures are episodes of *The $10,000 Pyramid*, *Three on a Match*, *High Rollers*, *Concentration*, and other classic game shows.

April 15

1960 - *Play Your Hunch* is Ready for Prime time

Merv Griffin's breakout game was one that he didn't create.
(Author's Collection)

Mark Goodson-Bill Todman Productions always looked for a way to put a new spin on an established premise. In 1956, they had struck gold with *To Tell the Truth*, where a celebrity panel heard a story and tried to determine which of the three contestants was telling the truth. Amazingly, the great minds at work for Goodson-Todman were able to conjure up a second format based on trying to pick something out of a group of three.

The name of the game was *Play Your Hunch*, and at the helm would be a rookie in the world of game shows: a singer, disc jockey and sometimes-actor named Merv Griffin. Both the game and host clicked with viewers immediately. Premiering on CBS on June 30, 1958, the show jumped to ABC beginning with the January 5, 1959, telecast. By December, it was on NBC, where it finally settled down and remained for the next four years. NBC aired prime time versions in 1960 and 1962 to fill holes as needed on the schedule.

Two married couples competed and were presented with a series of "problems" involving three people or objects labeled as X, Y and Z. The couples had to decide which of the three possible solutions was correct. For example:

· Which of three dogs is the father of the other two?

· Which of three musicians in a brass band isn't actually playing his instrument?

· Which of three oddly shaped pitchers can hold all the water in a nearby bucket?

· Which of three people engaging in pantomime is actually pantomiming the thing they do for a living?

·Which of three pictures of lips depicts the lips of Marilyn Monroe?

· Which of three brush strokes was the first stroke an artist applied at the beginning of her picture?

· Which of three children with violins actually knows how to play it?

· Which of three covered wheelbarrows contains a pile of bricks? (Merv moved each one back and forth before the contestants decided.)

· Which man dressed as a cop is actually a cop? This one was acted out as a skit in which announcer Johnny Olson got pulled over for speeding three times, and the contestants observed the maybe-cops' demeanors as they filled out the ticket.

Merv Griffin and Tad Tadlock present the choices on *Play Your Hunch*. (Ernie G. Anderson Collection)

The first couple to solve three problems won the game and $150. For the bonus round, the couple drew straws. For every long straw they drew from a choice of seven, they won $100. If they drew five long straws without drawing either of the short straws, they won $500 and a car.

It was the right game at the right time. Audiences were feeling burned by question-and-answer shows after the scandals erupted and gravitated toward a guessing game based on keen observation. Merv explained in a 1960 interview that he thought human nature alone attracted people to the show.

"People love to play hunches, even if they turn out to be wrong. Ever watch a kid at a carnival wheel, a girl with a gift she can't open yet or a fellow in a card game? They're all playing hunches for the fun of it."

Merv modestly avoided giving credit to himself for the show's success, although the show's staff was all too eager to acknowledge his casual, freewheeling style as host as a key part of the show's popularity. One morning when Johnny Olson introduced Merv, he strode onstage wearing his shirt and tie, but no jacket. It was an unusual look for a game show host. Merv leveled with the audience about what was wrong.

"Yep, I did it again. I locked the dressing room with the key inside, so I can't wear my jacket today."

Another morning, Merv was in the middle of introducing the contestants when he realized he'd forgotten to put on his cufflinks. He turned his mistake into a bit of entertainment. The audience watched and waited while Merv cajoled producer Ira Skutch to run backstage and find the cufflinks.

Although he would never admit it himself, the case could be made that Merv was an indispensable part of the program. After he left on September 28, 1962, to launch his talk show, new host Gene Rayburn took over and the ratings plummeted. Robert Q. Lewis replaced Rayburn in November, and the show was off the air ten months later, disappearing on September 27, 1963.

Robert Q. Lewis in the final months of *Play Your Hunch*. (Fred Wostbrock Collection)

April 16

2001 – *The Weakest Link* Premieres

Every competitor tried to launch their own big money prime time game show in the wake of ABC's success with *Who Wants to be a Millionaire?* The biggest success among the competitors was *The Weakest Link*, a game show that was antithetical to *Millionaire* in so many ways. *Millionaire* had Regis Philbin openly declaring that he wanted the contestants to win as they furrowed their brows, sometimes for minutes at a time, on questions. *The Weakest Link* featured a hostile emcee who belittled contestants for failing to answer a tough question as a clock ticked away, and each round concluded with players plotting against each other.

Randy West, the warm-up man who greeted the studio audience before every taping, remembers, "When I got the job, they sent me a tape of some episodes of the British version. I didn't think I'd need that, but they said, 'No, you'd better watch this, because it's a different animal than what you're used to.' And it *was*."

Each week, host Anne Robinson, star of the original British version, stood on the dim stage, dressed in a long black trench coat, stared icily at the camera and the contestants, and snapped off everything she said with the tone of a woman who was disgusted by everybody around her.

The eight contestants would alternate answering questions against the clock, building up the money with every correct answer. They could hang onto that money by saying "Bank" before a question was read, or the players might choose to keep building it up, at the risk of wiping out all of the money with a wrong answer. At the end of each round, Anne would recap the players' progress, often with demeaning terms like "sad" and "embarrassing," and often interrogating the players one by one.

"You should request a refund from your university."

"You're quite honestly the most stupid person I have ever met. Are you intelligent enough to be on the show?"

"Who is suffering from vacancy of mind?"

"Whose doughnut has run out of jam?"

"Who's gone from dim to downright stupid?'"

The contestants voted on who they considered to be "the weakest link" of the team. The one who collected the most votes was tersely told by Anne, "You are the weakest link. *Goodbye*."

The audience was alarmed by the mean streak of the show, but they were equally intrigued, and NBC finally had a hit game show in prime time. They followed it up with a daily syndicated version, originally to be hosted by *Survivor* champion Richard Hatch, but the job ultimately went to George Gray.

Despite the vicious outward appearances of the hosts, Randy West had unreserved kindness for them, and fond memories of seeing their true colors when the cameras were off. "During taping breaks, Anne would give me an introduction and she would call me her 'co-host,' which was such a sweet gesture.

"The other thing I recall about Anne was that 9/11 happened while that show was in production, and she was commuting by plane from England to Los Angeles to tape the NBC version, and the network offered to postpone tapings after 9/11 because they figured she'd be nervous about flying in the aftermath of that. And she told the network, 'No, don't do that, I'll be there.' She didn't miss one taping. She was a real trooper."

As for George Gray, Randy recalls, "I loved George Gray; he had done a lot of warm-ups himself, so we were kindred spirits, we knew a lot of similar routines, and we'd team up and do jokes together, and he'd come out with me to talk to the audience to take breaks."

Both versions were gone from the U.S. by 2003, but a globetrotting game show fan wouldn't have to miss it for very long. By the end of the decade, more than forty countries had launched their own versions of *The Weakest Link*.

April 17

2007 – Kitty Carlisle Dies

Kitty Carlisle kept good company in six decades of *To Tell the Truth.* Here she's joined by host Bud Collyer and fellow regular Tom Poston. (Author's Collection)

She had a distinguished performing career that included film, theater, and opera, but to television viewers, all that took a backseat to her years as the grand dame of *To Tell the Truth*. Kitty Carlisle went down in game show history as the only celebrity to appear as a guest on the same game show in six different decades.

She was born in 1911, and raised by a mother who had extraordinary expectations for her. She took Kitty to capital cities throughout Europe and gave her voice lessons and drama training, expecting Kitty to marry into royalty eventually. No king or prince ever made their way to Kitty, but the expectations were still high. Kitty rejected proposals from playwright Norman Krasna, George Gershwin, and financier Bernard Baruch before settling down with playwright Moss Hart.

Kitty began performing on Broadway in 1932 and eventually worked her way up to opera and eventually to a Hollywood film contract. By her own admission, her film career was a "bust," but she thrived in theater for years to come. As television began to take over the world, Kitty appeared on the small screen, rarely in acting roles and more often as herself. She appeared as a panelist for *What's My Line?* and *I've Got a Secret* on several occasions.

Kitty was a regular panelist from the beginning of *To Tell the Truth* in 1956; the show was based in New York and when Kitty and husband Moss Hart moved to the west coast, she left the show. When Hart suddenly died in 1962, she turned back to her old job to bring some sense of normalcy back to her life. She began commuting from California to New York to sit on the nighttime panel each week.

Bruno Zirato, producer of the prime time version of *To Tell the Truth*, told a reporter, "She has a remarkable general knowledge—I've never known her to be at a loss for a question. She knows about the craziest things—and she fires the questions with great rapidity...she's got a lot of pizzazz...It's most unusual to find someone with real elegance and who obviously enjoys being alive."

The elegance and pizzazz made Kitty stand out in any crowd or panel. Panelists always had a nice suit or dress, but Kitty showed up dressed to kill, wearing lavish evening gowns, jewels, furs, and anything else befitting a member of high society. Her highfalutin wardrobe and her knack for persistent glamour earned her some friendly tweaking of the nose from her co-stars; Peggy Cass called her "Madame Butterfly"; Garry Moore once joked that Kitty was absent from the panel because she was on tour with roller derby. And Kitty had no problem laughing at herself or being the victim for the sake of laughs; she and the rest of the panel once got tricked into eating "meatballs" that were actually dog food, but Kitty laughed it off and went right on with the game, interrogating three players claiming to be the makers of the meatballs.

Kitty described to a reporter one of her favorite moments. Three contestants all claimed to be experts about gorillas. Kitty asked one of them, "How do gorillas breed?" and one of the contestants answered, "Through the nose."

No matter how much she may have laughed, she took the game seriously. Kitty kept coming back over the years because she played masterfully and Mark Goodson-Bill Todman Productions knew a great player when they saw one. She was there when the original series wrapped up in 1968. When the series returned in 1969, she came back for another nine-year run. For the 1980-81 version, she wasn't a regular panelist, but she did make frequent appearances. In 1990, She spent another season on the panel when *To Tell the Truth* was revived by NBC. And in 2000, she took one final turn sitting in as a guest panelist when the show returned in first-run syndication.

Game show announcer Randy West was one of the "imposters" for an episode in 1990 and saw first-hand how much Kitty Carlisle cared about *To Tell the Truth*.

He remembers, "I was told that Kitty Carlisle played the game for blood. She really, really wanted to win. The staffers told me that fooling her was going to be my toughest challenge...one trick she used was to stare at the contestants. An imposter is being dishonest, and is likely to look away from a stare. So I was warned to not look away when Kitty Carlisle stares at me.

"So we play the game and she asks us all the questions, and the round ends, and it's the part where the host says, 'Is it number one...or is it number two...or is it number three?' And the camera pans across us. Kitty knows that she's not on camera for that part. Well, not only does she stare at us, she pulls out opera glasses, friggin' binoculars on a stick, and stares at us through those! If she could have brought the Hubble telescope to that taping, she would have. And I just stared back and smiled, and we stumped the panel. And at the end of the show, she said, 'I was sure it was you!'"

(Fred Wostbrock Collection)

April 18

1983 - *Contraption* Premieres

Despite extravagant prizes and big money, game shows can be deceptively inexpensive to produce, which is possibly why fledgling cable networks feature them so frequently. TNN had *Fandango* from the beginning, Comedy Central, when it was called Ha!, featured *Clash* and even the Playboy Channel had a few game shows in its early years.

The Disney Channel was no different. The day it launched, a game called *Contraption* was on the lineup, and it remained a part of the network for six years. Hosted by Ralph Harris, the game pitted three kids against three other kids. Coach Robin led the red team, and Coach Kevin guided the blue team. The players' passports instructed them to go to one of four stations—Books; Animals; Heroes and Villains; or Magic.

At each station, the kids would watch a film clip from a Disney movie and then take turns answering a series of questions about what they just saw. Every correct answer earned a "contraptile." Afterwards, they would compete in a small race along a track, using assorted wacky modes of transportation like pedal-powered cars or giant tires. The winner received an additional contraptile; the final station was worth five contraptiles per correct answer.

The big winners of the day won a batch of Disney-related prizes, as did the losers. Everybody got passes to Disneyland, lunch boxes, sleeping bags, records, books and an electronic game. As a bonus, the winners received a computer, the TI-99/4A, which came with a staggering 16K of RAM. The page you're reading now took twice as much memory to type and save as the entire computer contained.

April 19

1969 - *Storybook Squares* Ends

Peter Marshall and Kaye Ballard, a.k.a. Cleopatra.
(Author's Collection)

In his memoirs, host Peter Marshall recalled the show as the most fun he'd ever had doing television. Producer Art Alisi remembered going to NBC after the series had ended and personally asking the network to please make sure that the tapes of the twenty-six episodes were never erased. (At the time, it was normal practice to erase game show episodes.) Yet *Storybook Squares* has been largely forgotten by fans.

In the fall of 1968, responding to mounting complaints about violence depicted in children's programming, NBC axed two cartoons from its Saturday morning line-up. Merrill Heatter & Bob Quigley, who already had some experience adapting a grown-up property into a kids' venture with their *Video Village Jr.* spin-off, stepped in to fill the programming gap with a cute twist on *The Hollywood Squares*.

Called *Storybook Squares*, the game would pit two children against each other on a lavish set that resembled a fairy tale castle. The Guardian of the Gate, announcer Kenny Williams, introduced Peter Marshall, who then introduced the celebrities. But *Storybook Squares* didn't have an ordinary panel. The stars on *Storybook Squares* wore a variety of costumes. It was the perfect way to draw in both kids and parents. The kids would get a kick out of seeing Peter Pan, Little Bo Peep and Captain Hook, while any parents tuning in would get a kick out of seeing celebrities in their disguises.

Lonesome George Gobel was so lonesome he was blue—Little Boy Blue, that is. Leslie Uggams was Snow White; in this pre-PC era, she carried a watermelon instead of an apple. Ted Cassidy played Tarzan to Charo's Jane. Nanette Fabray was the Old Lady in the Shoe. Paul Winchell and Jerry Mahoney played assorted pairs, like Romeo & Juliet and Sherlock Holmes & Watson.

The characters weren't limited to fairy tales. Great names from history joined the fun. Arte Johnson was Thomas Edison, Wally Cox was Paul Revere, Soupy Sales portrayed Henry VIII, Pat Harrington, Jr. was Leonardo DaVinci and Kaye Ballard was Cleopatra. Anybody who already had an established reputation as a fictional character recreated that character. William Shatner was Captain Kirk, Carolyn Jones was Morticia and Arte Johnson usually played one of his *Laugh-In* characters. Michael Landon was Little Joe Cartwright, and Cliff Arquette stayed right in character as Charlie Weaver. Sometimes the Muppets were there, too and Roy Rogers and Dale Evans simply appeared as themselves.

The historical aspect, along with safety tips, helped to convince parents that *Storybook Squares* had more substance than the cartoons it had replaced. The kids played for prizes like portable TVs and sailboats. Win or lose, they had fun.

So did Peter Marshall, who happily ignored W.C. Fields' advice about not working with children. He told a newspaper reporter, "I was a little nervous about working with children as contestants in the beginning. But now I treat them as little adults and it works out fine. In fact, they're better at the game than adults. When they're asked to verify or deny an answer...they take their first instinct. And it's usually right."

The ornate sets and costumes turned the show into a surprisingly expensive venture. Peter Marshall observed one other problem: the introductions at the beginning of the show took too long, sacrificing a lot of game-playing. He wanted to expand the show to one hour to accommodate both the elaborate introductions and the game-playing. NBC balked and canceled the show.

Everyone had so much fun with it, though, that the format was salvaged as an idea for *Hollywood Squares* sweeps weeks in the coming years. *Storybook Squares* popped up a few more times with

From La-la-Land to Storybook Land, Peter Marshall greets the cast of characters on *Storybook Squares*. (Author's Collection)

a fresh supply of stars as the '70s rolled along. Doc Severinsen played Gabriel, Bill Hayes & Susan Seaforth-Hayes were Adam & Eve, Rip Taylor became Rip Van Winkle and Karen Valentine was Mary, Mary, Quite Contrary. For the *Storybook Squares* week-long specials, the game was usually a multigenerational family affair instead of being restricted to kids. Three games would be squeezed into each half-hour, with kids playing game one, their parents playing game two and their grandparents stepping in for game three.

By the 1970s, Paul Lynde was entrenched as the Center Square. Although he disliked having to wear costumes—Peter Marshall noted that he could be quite vain about his looks—the staff of *Squares* had a blast finding ways to showcase Paul. Even in a more conservative time and on a game aimed at kids, they winked and nudged quite a bit by deliberately miscasting Paul, dressing him as Frankenstein's Monster, Hercules or Paul Bunyan. But Paul was never more perfectly or accurately cast as he was on the day he dawned a crown, black gown and purple face paint to play the role of the Wicked Queen. When called on by a contestant, he gazed into a mirror, which shattered on cue as he sang the song, "I Feel Pretty," with the show's audio man making it a point to add an echo effect when Paul uttered the word "gay."

Storybook Squares was so much fun that they glitzed it up and made it a game suited for grown-ups for a few specials on the adults' version. In the late 1970s, *The Hollywood Squares* featured a series of specials called "parties" with yet another new set in Broadway black and silver, Peter Marshall donned a tuxedo, the contestants dressed a little more extravagantly than your typical game show contestants and the stars dressed up as characters but, with no children present, they got a little wilder. Paul Lynde dressed as Narcissus, the mythological character who fell in love with himself, and explained that he was walking funny because "I hurt my back when I bent over, trying to kiss myself." With that, the premise had graduated from a kids' show to teenage humor.

April 20

1968 – J.D. Roth's Birthday

He started as a contestant on a talent show. He became the host of a few game shows. And he wound up a producer/mogul of reality television. J.D. Roth has had his hands in just about every form of competition on television that doesn't involve cleats, and he's been a success at every one of them.

J.D. Roth started out as a contestant on *Star Search* in 1985, competing in the acting category. That provided the springboard he needed to become an actor, appearing throughout the '80s on *The Equalizer*, *Charles in Charge* and *The Twilight Zone*. In 1988, at the age of twenty, he became the youngest person ever to host a national TV game show when he emceed *Fun House* (see September 5). J.D. immediately established a distinctive hosting style with a smile and high energy not seen in an emcee since the heyday of Bert Parks. The show was a hit, and J.D. was at the helm for three years on Fox and in syndication. Roth even took the show on the road, performing as host of *Fun House* in more than seventy cities.

In 1992, JD took his first step into the realm of producing when he sold NBC on an original creation called *Double Up*. He hosted this game, too. It was a spin on *The Dating Game* in which a boy grilled three guys trying to find the perfect date for his sister, and then a girl would interrogate three potential mates for her brother.

Two years later, Roth hosted another kids' game, *Masters of the Maze*, for The Family Channel (see August 29). JD left the show after one season and moved on to more acting and voice work, but he returned to game shows in 1997 with *Animal Planet Zooventure* (see April 6).

In 2000, he hosted his first game for adults, *Sex Wars*, in which three men and three women competed to identify the most popular answers to survey questions posed to the opposite sex. The show expired after only one season, and Roth moved onto behind-the-camera production. It proved an extraordinarily successful venture for him. His company, 3 Ball Productions, was behind some of the decade's top reality shows, including *Beauty and the Geek*, *The Pickup Artist* and its biggest success, NBC's *The Biggest Loser*.

Perhaps one of the things guiding Roth's success in reality TV is passion. As a producer, he expects the same kind of enthusiasm he projected as a host. He even has a term for stars who fail to project that enthusiasm: "robo-hosts," whom he describes: "They have an earpiece in their ear, and we tell them what to say. Finding guys who actually know how to do it is hard. Needle in a haystack."

As for the ones who are good at their job, all he asks is that they hang on and keep doing it. "If they have to wheel you out in your wheelchair twenty-five years from now, you stay with it."

April 21

1975 - *Blankety Blanks* Premieres

People who missed the run of *Blankety Blanks* have only themselves to blame for blinking at an inopportune time. The show was in and out of ABC's daytime line-up in just ten weeks. Host Bill Cullen would argue later in a magazine interview that the show "didn't get a fair shake," and it's possible he was onto something. ABC did serious housecleaning in the summer of 1975, ending four game shows in only three weeks. *Blankety Blanks* was one of the heads that rolled.

The game was produced by Bob Stewart, whose *The $10,000 Pyramid* had delivered extraordinarily good results to the network the previous year. *Blanks* pitted two celebrity-contestant teams against each other in a game of wordplay and puns. The players would be shown a category and a clue to the correct answer.

For example, "Movie...*Kill*." They faced a screen that hid three sentences, divided into six fragments. On their turn, a player picked one fragment to reveal and could guess the puzzle after that. As each fragment was revealed, the puzzle got easier.

"That crazy lady...is no lady."
"The audience didn't...shower for days."
"It ends with a...Hitchcock twist."

The answer is *Psycho*, but knowing the answer wasn't helpful unless fate worked in your favor. Turns did not just alternate back and forth; they were determined by a card that was dropped into a scanner. Bill sat next to a rotating drum containing one hundred identical-looking cards, randomly pulled one and dropped it into an electronic scanner built into his podium. The scoreboards in front of the players would reveal whose turn it was and how much money the correct answer would be worth—anywhere from $100 to $1,000. Once players solved the puzzle, they still didn't quite win the money, which sat "in escrow" until their team solved a "Blankety Blank," which was a cute pun. For example:

1. "If you could send all your pains to Mars, what would it be called? ______ __ ___ _____"
2. "The Mafia Chief who bosses a big fish market is called ___ _________."

1. Planet of the Aches
2. The Codfather

Failing to solve the Blankety Blank kept the money in escrow, and money from correct puzzle solutions kept accumulating until the player solved a Blankety Blank to claim it all. Solving a Blankety Blank also cast one strike against the opposing team. Three strikes, and the team was out.

There was a chance to rack up quite a bit of dough, and the game had an extremely laid-back atmosphere to it. Knowing they were granted three strikes before having to leave had a way of putting the contestants at ease, as did host Bill Cullen and his attention to the game play. Bill told a reporter, "I don't emphasize the prizes or the amount of money. I just try to have fun and not use the old clichés."

Whatever failed about the show apparently couldn't be blamed on Bill. *Variety* referred to his performance on *Blankety Blanks* as "affable glossiness." Another critic said that "he works hard at making his job as host appear effortless." After June 27, *Blankety Blanks* was gone, replaced on the ABC line-up by *Brady Bunch* reruns. Bill's career carried on, though; with one cancellation, he still had *The $25,000 Pyramid* and *To Tell the Truth* keeping him on the airwaves every week. Clearly, adoring critics were right about him.

April 22

1920 – Hal March's Birthday

Hal March's career in game shows was a shooting star. His actual time as a master of ceremonies adds up to about four years, but for three of those years no host's star shone brighter, none was a bigger star, none attracted as much attention. From 1955-58, Hal March was the quizmaster of note, hosting the biggest game—in more ways than one—that the genre and the medium had ever seen to that point.

Hal was born in San Francisco, where he would spend his high school years acting in class productions. He liked it so much that after graduating, he headed to Hollywood. He had a nightclub act and performed in burlesque shows until World War II broke out. Kept away from active combat due to flat feet, he was asked by his commander to organize a Christmas show. Hal wrote, produced and performed two shows for the troops before earning his discharge in 1943.

Once Hal returned to San Francisco, his career in show business had no boundaries. He continued with theater, acted in films, performed on radio and moved into television once TV started to take over the world. In 1955, he took a job hosting a quiz show. He initially wanted nothing to do with quiz shows. He took the job figuring that it would last only through the summer, and then he'd work on the sitcom he was starring in for NBC.

The show was *The $64,000 Question*, and Hal March's career plans were drastically altered when the show began averaging more than 47 million viewers per week, while his NBC sitcom fizzled in three months. *The $64,000 Question* was a monster. March appeared on the cover of TV Guide four times. He replaced the vacationing Garry Moore for the summer on *I've Got a Secret.* He was recognized everywhere. Fans would regularly shout, "See you on Tuesday night!" when they saw him in public. He was making great money by the standards of the time—$3,500 a week, or about $28,000 a week in today's money—and, given the popularity of the show, that was actually quite a bargain for the folks signing the checks.

Hal delivered a stand-out performance as emcee, largely because he wasn't sure how to do it. He was an actor by trade, not a quizmaster, and couldn't fake his way through a high-energy, explosive performance. As a result, he naturally delivered a low-key, soft-spoken performance on the big money game. He quite unintentionally added tension and drama to the proceedings by keeping things so subdued, delivering a strong performance without really performing at all.

This didn't sit well with producer Louis Cowan, who once chided him for not squeezing out more suspense from an exciting moment in the game. Hal argued, "It was better to play it straight. What could be more dramatic than a guy who's earning $50 a week trying for $50,000?"

Sometimes, he appeared ill at ease. During one stay in Las Vegas, a fan asked him, "Are you as nervous as you usually are on Tuesday nights?" He got cards mixed up, fumbled rules, damaged props and forgot to pause for commercials. Being prone to error didn't bother Hal at all. He thought it was a big help.

"I was the perfect quizmaster, because I didn't know what I was doing," he said in 1962. "I fluffed and made mistakes, but it all helped to make the whole thing seem more natural."

In 1958, the bottom dropped out. As rumors began swirling and circulating about chicanery behind the scenes, the ratings began to dip. CBS gave the show a three-month break in the summer of 1958 and, when it returned in the fall, the magic was gone. *The $64,000 Question* lasted only two more months, disappearing in November 1958.

As government investigations turned up more and more evidence, March avoided any implication of being in on the deception. Hal was oblivious to any rigging going on behind his back. His career survived, although Hal made it a point to get away from game shows for a while. Toward the end, *The $64,000 Question* was wearing on him anyway and he resisted doing more game shows. Revlon had offered him a second game, *The Most Beautiful Girl in the World*, in 1956 at the height of the popularity of *Question*, but March refused, saying that he had too many things he wanted to do in the entertainment field and hosting two game shows would pigeonhole him.

He went back to theater, starring in *Two for the Seesaw* and *Come Blow Your Horn*. He nearly made a return to game shows in 1961 when NBC launched a prime time version of *Concentration* and asked him to host. The sponsor balked, insisting on daytime host Hugh Downs, so March returned to the comfort of theater, touring with *Come Blow Your Horn* for several months. He briefly hosted a 1963 game show for ABC in prime time titled *Laughs for Sale*, but that show ended quickly after being hastily launched to replace *100 Grand*, an attempt at bringing back big money quiz shows that was cancelled after two episodes. Audiences just weren't yet ready to forgive.

Hal moved his family to Los Angeles so he could pursue television work. He never starred in a regular series, but he worked quite steadily in guest appearances on numerous shows during the 1960s, including *The Monkees* and *The Lucy Show*. He also resumed his film career and briefly dabbled in television directing. He still kept one foot in the theater, starring in *Of Thee I Sing* during 1968.

That same year, March managed to kick his a two-pack-a-day habit for a time, but resumed smoking the following summer. In the fall of 1969, he started work on a new game show, *It's Your Bet*, but was soon diagnosed with lung cancer. Two months after *It's Your Bet* premiered, Hal entered the hospital and had the cancerous lung removed. After being discharged, he contracted pneumonia and had to check right back into the hospital. With only one lung, however, his body was too weak to fight off the illness. March's stricken body gave out on January 19, 1970.

April 23

1979 - *Whew!* premieres

Jay Wolpert is the mind behind the characters of the immensely popular *Pirates of the Caribbean* film series. Although films have been his most notable success, his greatest passion has always been game shows.

In 1969, Wolpert appeared as a contestant on *Jeopardy!* and played it as well as it could be played. He was a five-day undefeated champion and returned to conquer that year's Tournament of Champions. He made his way to Canada to produce games for Dan Enright before briefly returning to the U.S. for a stint at Chuck Barris Productions.

Jay came into his own when he jumped to Mark Goodson-Bill Todman Productions and produced *The Price is Right*, establishing many of the production conventions that his successors continued.

He established the way certain game segments were set up, determined how to rotate them within the show and introduced sketch comedy as a means of presenting the fabulous Showcases.

In 1976, Jay developed a quiz show, *Double Dare* (see April 29), for the company. He later departed from Goodson-Todman to strike out on his own. In a joint venture with veteran producer Burt Sugarman, he launched his first independent game show project in 1979, when *Whew!* arrived on the CBS daytime schedule.

Like fans of every genre, game show fans have cult favorites. With a run that fizzled in just over a year after unspectacular ratings, *Whew!* is an example of a game show cult hit. It's still talked about, mostly with fondness, by game show lovers. There are fan websites, episodes in the so-called "trade circuit" and clips on YouTube. When host Tom Kennedy appeared at conventions more than two decades after cancellation, fans posed for photos with him in signature mannerisms, wiping their brows the same way Tom did every time he said the title of the game.

Merv Griffin once said that it if a game show takes more than one sentence to explain, it has already failed, and this could explain how *Whew!* met its demise. The show aired at 10:30 a.m. on CBS. One day when Richard Dawson took the stage on ABC's *Family Feud* at 11:30 a.m., he opened the show by looking at his watch and joking, "Tom Kennedy is wrapping up explaining the rules on *Whew!* right about now."

The game was played by two contestants, one designated the Blocker and the other the Charger. They faced a twenty-eight-space game board that bore a passing resemblance to the *Jeopardy!* game board. The board was divided into six levels, each one containing "bloopers"—sentences that contained mistakes. For example: "Kato was the faithful sidekick of The Green Giant."

The Charger had sixty seconds to solve one blooper on each

level and would win the round by solving six bloopers with time to spare. Standing in the way of the win was the Blocker. The Blocker secretly placed six blocks on the game board, not more than one on the top level or more than three on any of the other levels. If the Charger uncovered one of those blocks, play stopped while five seconds ticked away. If the clock hit zero, the Blocker won the round. The contestants traded blocking and charging duties for each round, with two out of three rounds winning the game.

For the bonus round, the contestant dealt with villains. Other game shows had used villains, *Tic Tac Dough* had the Dragon and *The Joker's Wild* had the Devil. *Whew!* had ten, an array called the Gauntlet of Villains. Contestants were allotted sixty seconds plus one second per $100 that they had already won to clear the Gauntlet by solving another series of bloopers. If the villain gave the correct answer before the contestant, the contestant had to stay there and keep trying. A contestant who gave the correct answer first could advance to the next villain. If the contestant could defeat Alphonse the Gangster, Bruno the Headsman, Mister Van Louse the Landlord, Nero the Fiddler, Count Nibbleneck, Frank & His Little Friend Stein, Kid Rotten the Gunslinger, Jeremy Swash the Pirate, Dr. Deranged the Mad Professor and Lucretia the Witch, with time to spare, this feat paid a whopping $25,000.

If you understood all that, you qualify as a potential fan of the show. It limped along for six months before adding celebrity partners to the game, which actually made the rules of the game even more complicated. That didn't help, and on May 30, 1980, *Whew!* ran out of breath.

A fan once asked Tom Kennedy why he thought the show fizzled and he remarked that he thought the show had an "identity crisis." The clues were frequently puns, and with the cartoony villains surrounding the players, it looked an awful lot like a comedy game. And yet, it was a race against the clock, which meant high suspense. The humor was missed or the suspense was missed; neither element could stand out as a selling point of the game.

But *Whew!* lovers have never seemed fazed by any identity crisis. They still fire up those old episodes that were preserved by fans with foresight during the show's run (it has never aired in reruns) and get a case of the warm fuzzies from the moment that Rod Roddy declares that they're about to see a game of: "Close calls! Narrow escapes! Split-second decisions! And $25,000 in cash! A combination guaranteed to make you say....WHEW!"

April 24

1978 - *Card Sharks* Premieres

Jim Perry wants to give the players a hand on *Card Sharks*.
(Author's Collection)

Aces high!
Deuces low!
Call it right!
And win the dough!
Oooooooooooooooon Card Sharks!

Nobody was better at squeezing golden eggs from a goose than Goodson-Todman. In the '50s, they had a hit with *What's My Line?* and got right to work developing more panel shows. In the '60s, the success of *Password* led them to crank out additional word games. It should come as no surprise, then, that when *Family Feud* soared in 1976, the company looked for a new game based on surveys of public opinion.

The game they whipped up, *Card Sharks*, was one of the most beautifully simple games ever devised. Hosted by Jim Perry, a veteran emcee in Canada but a fresh face in his native USA, *Card Sharks* pitted two contestants against each other, each with a standard deck of playing cards. Jim would ask the contestants a question that had been posed to a survey group. Unlike *Family Feud* and its open-ended questions targeted to a general audience, *Card Sharks* depended on compelling questions that had been posed to specific groups of people and had only two possible answers, often "yes" or "no."

· We asked 100 police officers: "Do you think marijuana should be legalized?"
· We asked 100 women who own pet pigs: "Who's messier, the pig or your husband?"
· We asked 100 high school teachers: "Have you ever had a student who didn't know where babies came from?"

- We asked 100 millionaires: "Right this moment, do you have a diamond somewhere on your body?"
- We asked 100 people in the studio audience at *Saturday Night Live*: "Have you ever seen a UFO?"
- We asked 100 people in the studio audience at *Card Sharks*: "Would you be a better host for this show than Jim Perry?"

To determine who got to play their cards first, one contestant decided on a number between one and one hundred and their opponent predicted if the correct answer would be higher or lower. Shown a sequence of five cards one at a time, the contestant predicted whether the next card shown would be higher or lower than the card that preceded it. That's all. Naturally, you'd say "higher" if you saw a three or a four, and of course you would say "lower" on an ace or a king. At times the cards were bound to work out against the odds and, besides, what call should a player make for the card following a seven or an eight? In that case, the contestant frequently chose to "freeze," which triggered a new question. If the contestant won and returned to that line of cards, the frozen card could be replaced with a fresh one.

It's easy to see why the game was a hit. The game had high suspense and low complexity, and those human interest questions were endlessly thought-provoking. The contestants were encouraged to talk out their answers, and some revealed wild logic in their explanations. One elderly man, faced with a question that had originally been posed to a group of strippers, said that some of them don't do certain things in their act because "they just don't have the shake in them." During a special celebrity week, Bill Cullen was asked how many audience members had brought binoculars to the Miss Nude USA pageant, and he reasoned that the answer was probably a low number because "binoculars would ruin it; you could only see a little bit at a time."

The first contestant to clear the row of five cards won the game, with two out of three winning the match and proceeding on to the Money Cards. Staked with $200, the player had to clear seven more cards, betting money on each card and predicting higher or lower. An additional $200 was awarded after the third card. With correct predictions, risking everything and doubling the cash each time, a player stood to win $28,800. Amazingly, it happened only once, to a bold contestant named Norma Brown.

The game performed reasonably well for three years, although Goodson-Todman proved unsuccessful when they attempted to launch a second version for nighttime viewing. Three years and more than $3 million in cash prizes later, *Card Sharks* came to an end on October 23, 1981.

Just under five years later, *Card Sharks* was back in business when CBS called upon Mark Goodson for another "big money game" to add to a daytime line-up that featured *Press Your Luck*, *The Price is Right* and *The $25,000 Pyramid*. Clearly, the network was fond of big money games.

With Jim Perry tied up at NBC on *Sale of the Century*, Goodson turned control of the cards over to Bob Eubanks, who auditioned several times and eventually beat out Patrick Wayne to earn the job. Eubanks was a mischief maker behind the scenes and didn't exactly endear himself to his employers after a prank he played early in the run. *Card Sharks* occupied the same studio as *The Price is Right* and, pressed for space, Bob Eubanks shared his dressing room with Bob Barker. Eubanks noticed a sign on the dressing room wall reading "WGMC" and asked what it meant. A staffer explained that the sign belonged to Bob Barker, and the letters stood for "World's Greatest Master of Ceremonies." Eubanks

Card Sharks, hosted by a real card. Bob Eubanks helmed the '80s version for CBS. (Fred Wostbrock Collection)

went back to the dressing room, pulled the sign off the wall and hid it under the couch. The following day, Mark Goodson's son Jonathan called him, saying that Bob Barker was in a snit because the sign was missing, and he was refusing to start that day's taping until it was returned.

Eubanks' response: "What sign?"

The game was substantially the same, although it added two new types of questions—the Educated Guess question, which was based in fact instead of on a survey, and groups of ten. The latter survey involved ten people—wrestlers, beauty queens, lottery winners—who were present in the audience, and Bob would frequently chat with them about the answers they gave. He arm-wrestled a female bodybuilder, and he fell victim to a frightening lift when women wrestlers were asked to predict whether they could hold him over their heads.

The Money Cards was substantially the same, except that the payouts were tweaked to offer the contestants a shot at a rounder total figure of $32,000; top dollar was never awarded on this incarnation, however. Jokers were also mixed into the deck for use during a game added after the Money Cards, called Car Cards. For this game, seven more cards were brought onstage. One card hid the word "CAR"; the rest simply read "No." The contestants would place their jokers on whichever cards they wanted—the jokers were those that they'd uncovered in the Money Cards plus one joker given to them for free at the beginning—and had a chance at driving home a new car.

In the fall of 1986, a nighttime version finally went to air, with host Bill Rafferty. This version had yet another new twist. Five extra cards were mixed into each player's deck, each bearing a different prize. The winner of the match won all of the prizes that contestant had uncovered. It didn't catch on with prime time audiences, and was gone in one season.

The daytime show continued on, weathering some major backstage drama when one of the card dealers, Lacey Pemberton, got married. Mark Goodson, who had not so subtly spent the previous year showering Lacey with gifts, was irate and tried to fire her. When she threatened to sue for wrongful termination, Goodson backed down and the show dodged a potential scandal.

The show ended, perhaps prematurely, in 1989. Eubanks suspects that CBS's head of daytime programming regretted the move in hindsight. In his memoir, he looked back on his time at *Card Sharks* with extreme fondness. "*Card Sharks* was a host's dream...hands down, *Card Sharks* was my favorite game show of all time."

In 2001, the show returned in syndication with a revamped game that involved contestants trying to predict the outcome of hidden camera segments. Audiences ignored it, and it disappeared with barely anybody noticing after one season, an ignominious end to a show that seemed fail-proof in its original design.

April 25

1997 - *Idiot Savants* Comes to an End

For all the complaining that viewers do about seeing the same old stuff on television, the fact is that it's hard for "new" things to break through. The familiar is often comforting. So it was a gutsy move when MTV took a drastic left turn on December 9, 1996, by introducing a hard quiz show titled *Idiot Savants* that tested its contestants in ways that *Trashed* and *Singled Out* never attempted.

Idiot Savants pitted four contestants against each other through an entire week of shows. To start each game, host Greg Fitzsimmons would announce the category of that day's "Control Question," and the contestants would press their buzzers to give the correct answer; more often than not, the correct answer turned out to be the name of the category. On another occasion, though, the Control Question was a truly inspired one. Fitzsimmons asked the players, "Who was the first contestant to ring in?"

The contestant who gained control chose one of eight categories and played questions worth one hundred, two hundred and three hundred points. At the end of the round, the low-scoring contestant was removed from that day's game and sent to the dunce's corner. One week, when a contestant did particularly poorly and kept going to the dunce's corner every day, the show played his woes to the hilt, having a pizza delivered onstage for him while the game was still in progress.

For Round Two, Greg's assistant, "Brain"—a man's face on a monitor inside a giant fake brain—chose the categories and all were worth double point values. The questions were every bit on the level of *Jeopardy!* A category called "Stuff Girls Read" was about literature. For another category, a contestant was given mish-mashed names like "Harry Truman Capote" and "Jason Alexander Haig" and had to briefly explain each dual identity.

The two remaining players competed in a 45-second "Brain Storm," rapid fire Q&A. For example, Fitzsimmons might give a number, and the players had to ring in and calculate how many times that number was evenly divisible by four. The winner would advance to the Cylinder of Shush, a soundproof cone where a bonus prize would be offered for answering ten questions about any area of expertise—physics, *The Godfather*, golf—that the contestant had selected in advance.

On Friday, the scores the players had accumulated throughout the week were added together to form their starting score for that day, and the point values for the entire half-hour were doubled. The top scorer at the end of the week earned a car or a dream vacation.

The big winner went home a little happier and, by virtue of being called a dunce or tested by grueling trivia, possibly a little traumatized. Recounting his humiliating week as a "savant," *Time* columnist Joel Stein devoted his November 22, 1999, column to discouraging readers from taking the phone test for *Who Wants to be a Millionaire?*

Stein confessed to having an itchy buzzer finger. All Fitzsimmons got out was "Steve Martin played a wild and crazy..." when Stein eagerly rang in and answered, "Somewhere near Romania." Fitzsimmons started to ask another question and only said "Venus flytrap..." when Stein rang in and drew out the syllable "reeeeeee" for several seconds as he unsuccessfully struggled to remember the name of Tim Reid, who played Venus Flytrap on *WKRP in Cincinnati*. After the buzzer sounded, Fitzsimmons finished the question, which turned out to be about plant life.

"Seeing this on videotape," Stein wrote, "cemented my decision never to have children."

To the chagrin of viewers everywhere who enjoyed a fresh challenge from an unlikely source, *Idiot Savants* ended after only five months. To the chagrin of Joel Stein, the games he taped managed to see the light of day in that time frame.

April 26

1985 - *Time Machine* Runs Out of Time

"Imitation is the sincerest form of television." —Fred Allen

One of the remarkable things about the success of *The Price is Right* is how few game shows have attempted to duplicate its format of many recurring small games contained within a single show. One that did was an ambitious effort from NBC titled *Time Machine*, which premiered on NBC on January 7, 1985.

Each day, three contestants, not called to "come on down" from the audience, simply strolled onto the space-age set where they were greeted by host John Davidson. Each contestant had a chance to win some fabulous prizes by playing a small game based on twentieth century history. Some of the games featured included:

AS TIME GOES BY – The contestant saw three photos of the same person and had to guess, within five years, the year in which photo was taken in order to earn a "spin." Facing away and unable to see a clock with a giant spinning hand and the 12 o'clock hour highlighted in red, the contestant stopped the spinning hand with a button. If the hand stopped on 12 o'clock, the contestant won some fabulous prizes.

BEFORE OR AFTER – A contestant was shown a year followed by a series of four noteworthy events. The contestant had to decide whether each event came before or after the given year.

MAIN EVENT – A year was announced, and the contestant faced a board of five categories. The contestant could capture each category by correctly answering a question in that category. The categories also hid clues to the identity of a famous event that took place in the designated year. After the contestant answered the five questions, the clues hidden behind the categories were revealed, and the contestant could win up to $5,000 by identifying the event from the clues.

SWEET SIXTEEN – This one resembled Lucky Seven from *The Price is Right*. Given sixteen $100 bills and shown four historical events, the contestant had to guess the year in which each event took place. For every year away from the correct year, the contestant handed back $100. If any cash at all was left at the end of the round, the contestant won a bonus prize.

3 IN A ROW – A tic-tac-toe board with nine years was displayed. To start, the player had to place three "poison cards" in a row. The player was then shown a list of nine events and chose them one at a time to light up the matching year. Lighting up a tic-tac-toe won a prize, while lighting up all three "poison" years lost the game. The poison cards were later eliminated, and the contestant lost by getting three in a row diagonally instead of vertically or horizontally.

THE TUBE GAME – A prize was hidden behind one of three TV network logos—NBC, ABC or CBS. For each network, the contestant was shown a pair of publicity stills from different TV shows. The contestant had to choose which show aired on each network in a designated year. Selecting the right show captured that network as well as the prize if it was hidden behind that network.

The show had its own Showcase of sorts, the Time Capsule. The players were shown a fabulous prize package and given a series of historical events. They each secretly locked in their guess at the year, and whoever came closest to the true year answered one final question to capture those prizes.

Before long, the format was overhauled. Contestants competed against each other in a series of games for the right to face that day's returning champion in a final game. Despite John Davidson's assertion that the change helped—he claimed in a March 1985 interview that ratings were climbing—NBC was unimpressed, and just a month after Davidson's optimistic proclamation *Time Machine* was history.

April 27

1930 – Casey Kasem's Birth

Casey Kasem is prominently known as the king of the Top 40 Countdowns after decades of spinning records and urging his listeners to "keep your feet on the ground and keep reaching for the stars." In 1999, he hosted a game show for the only time in his career. It was called *100%* and if you don't remember it, don't feel too embarrassed. It's hard to watch a game show that aired in only four cities.

100% was intended to have a longer run on more stations, but its test run bombed and it fizzled in a matter of weeks. It was one of the simplest games ever devised, but in this case, that wasn't a good thing. Casey asked three contestants one hundred multiple choice questions. The contestants pressed buttons on their podiums to select the correct answer. A right answer earned one point. Highest score after one hundred questions won ten bucks per point. In the event that hell froze over and a contestant answered all one hundred questions correctly, a $99,000 bonus would be awarded. Unsurprisingly, the grand prize was never paid out.

The game is worth discussing, though, because of one particular quirk about Casey Kasem's performance on the show. You could hear him, but you couldn't see him. As far as the viewer at home was concerned, those questions were just asked by some disembodied voice. When *100%* originally premiered in the United Kingdom, it was touted as "the game show without a host." It was the first game to be presented this way. Amazingly, it wouldn't be the last.

In 1998, America's Game Show Network unveiled a similar show called *Inquizition*, hosted by a man identified only as "The Inquizitor." He was only seen in brief glimpses in the opening titles; long white hair, a beard, and a black suit. Only the back of his head was visible during the game, and per his contract with Game Show Network, his name was never revealed. To this day, the identity of the Inquizitor has never been revealed.

Inquizition, while similar, set out for a creepy atmosphere. The chroma-keyed set resembled an abandoned warehouse. Eerie music underscored the entire show. The Inquizitor addressed the contestants as Mister or Miss, frequently insulted them, and bellowed "You have failed" to contestants as they were gradually eliminated from the competition.

April 28

1963 - *Alumni Fun* Ends Its CBS Run

College Bowl was still going strong after two years on radio and four years on the tube, just about the only hard question-and-answer game to survive the quiz show scandals intact. It was on the level, it was for a noble cause—the prize was money for scholarship funds—and the audience kept tuning in.

Producer Don Reid introduced a spin-off, *Alumni Fun*, in which the students stepped aside and prominent graduates played the game, dealing with questions in seven categories: Arts, History, Business, Sports, People, Places and Literature, all displayed on the Tree of Knowledge. Each season was structured as a tournament, with the winners earning $15,000 in scholarship funds for their alma mater, and second place earning $10,000.

Alumni Fun showcased a strong roster of players who otherwise probably never would have set foot anywhere near a TV game show. Notable players included:

COLGATE—Rep. James C. Cleveland (R-NH)
COLUMBIA—Publisher Bennett Cerf and Pulitzer Prize winner Marguerite Higgins
DARTMOUTH—Former NBC President Sylvester "Pat" Weaver, actor Robert Ryan and Representative Thomas B. Curtis (R-MO)
GEORGE WASHINGTON—Football pro Eddie LeBaron, US Mint director Eva Adams and executive Jacob Rosenthal
THE OHIO STATE UNIVERSITY—Olympian Jesse Owens and columnist Earl Wilson
OHIO UNIVERSITY—Bandleader Sammy Kaye, philanthropist John Galbreath,
PURDUE—Pitcher Bob Friend, astronaut Virgil "Gus" Grissom and broadcaster Durwood Kirby
TULANE—ABC commentator Howard K. Smith, tennis star Ham Richardson and historian Charles Dufour
UNIVERSITY OF CINCINNATI—Pitcher Sandy Koufax and actor Lee Bowman
UCLA—Actor Lloyd Bridges and baseball pioneer Jackie Robinson
UNIVERSITY OF KANSAS—Rep. Robert Ellsworth (R-KS), oil executive Stanley Learned and columnist Doris Fleeson
UNIVERSITY OF MINNESOTA—Dr. Charles Mayo, Sen. Hubert Humphrey (D-MN) and actress Arlene Dahl
UNIVERSITY OF THE PACIFIC—Actress Janet Leigh and UN representative Richard Pederson

UNIVERSITY OF ROCHESTER—Sen. Kenneth Keating (R-NY) and TV critic Harriet Van Horne
UNIVERSITY OF SOUTHERN CALIFORNIA—Football star Frank Gifford and columnist Art Buchwald
UNIVERSITY OF TEXAS—Gov. Allan Shivers and actor Rip Torn
UNIVERSITY OF WISCONSIN—Los Angeles Rams GM Elroy Hirsch, businessman B.W. Murphy and David Susskind.

Even the hosts of the show were a little intimidating. Originally at the helm was John K.M. McCaffery who, prior to his hosting career, earned a B.A. at the University of Wisconsin and an M.A. from Columbia. When the show jumped ship to CBS, returning to the airwaves on January 4, 1964, the new host was author, lecturer, educator and Encyclopedia Britannica editor Clifton Fadiman. Fadiman was eventually replaced by actor Peter Lind Hayes.

The show's strength of brainpower was also its weakness as, apparently, these lofty reputations were too much to risk. Alert TV critic Cynthia Lowry noticed a stark difference in the difficulty of questions one week between *Alumni Fun* and *College Bowl.* The students of *College Bowl* were asked how fast a stone would travel three seconds after being tossed from the top of the Leaning Tower of Pisa. The grads of *Alumni Fun* were asked who once said, "Let them eat cake." The game stayed on the air for four years, while *College Bowl* would survive through 1970 and return to radio for another three-year run. There was just no topping the original.

April 29

1977 – *Double Dare* Ends

Alex Trebek dares you not to tune in! (Author's Collection)

Any child of the '80s or '90s who remembers a pie-flinging, slime-slinging game show on Nickelodeon could be in for a surprise. That wasn't the first time a game show called *Double Dare* was on the air. The original series was a totally unrelated tough quiz for adults on CBS.

Originally premiering on CBS on December 13, 1976, as a replacement for *Gambit*, *Double Dare* was a Goodson-Todman game hosted by a man who eventually became very familiar with tough quizzes for adults: Alex Trebek, fresh off his stint on *High Rollers*. The man in charge behind the scenes was Goodson-Todman staffer Jay Wolpert, who earned a rare "created by" credit from his bosses for this show.

The game pitted two contestants against each other. In a twist that must have made viewers wonder if they were in a time warp, both players were placed in isolation booths for the duration of the game. The contestants would see a series of clues to the identity of a person, place or thing. When a player rang in to answer, the opponent's booth was further isolated with a loss of audio and a curtain drawn around it, obstructing the view.

A player who gave a correct answer received $50 and could win bonuses of $100 and $200 by "daring" the opponent to give the correct answer on upcoming clues. Racking up $500 won the game and a chance to face a team of three villains called "the Spoilers," who each held a Ph.D. After Alex showed the contestant the correct answer and a series of eight clues to it, the contestant selected four clues to give to the Spoilers. The contestant could win $5,000 if at least one Spoiler was stumped by all four clues.

Originally, the game was straight-laced and serious in its presentation. As the series progressed, the clues got more salacious and silly, although the game stayed just as tough. See if you can guess the subjects from these clues actually used on the show.

1. THING – In Syria, girls ready for marriage hang theirs out the window.
2. ACTIVITY – In *A Hard Day's Night*, the Clean Old Man notes that a woman's enormous cleavage would help support her in this activity.
   Although sensual and pleasurable, many people are traumatized for life by their first attempt at this activity.
   Some people find this activity more relaxing lying on their backs, but most people prefer to do it facedown.
3. THING – A seventeenth-century manual notes that to use one, "Produce your rammer, open your pouch, place the instrument within, ram and withdraw."
   The ones of men in the south Pacific are eighteen inches long and are said to have a staggering effect.
4. THING – "In Brooklyn, NY, it is illegal for a donkey to sleep in one."
5. ACTIVITY – Henry VIII used to tax the methods of doing this, which were known as "Logating in the Fields" and "Sliding the Shrove Groat."
6. PERSON – "When Lady Astor said, 'If you were my husband, I'd poison your coffee," this man replied, "If you were my wife, I'd drink it."
7. THING – A California woman once tried to get her dog to grab hers by flavoring it with beef.
   Parts of these include the nipple, the navel, the Bump of Boggio and the Slope of Shultz.
8. THING – In France, some people about to go to the guillotine would reduce tension by playing theirs.
   Reportedly, Marlon Brando held his at his first screen test.
9. THING – In *How to Marry a Millionaire,* Marilyn Monroe plays a woman ashamed to reveal hers.

Generally speaking, the more pronounced the curve of their working parts, the more their owner relies on them to get by.

10. THING – The more horizontal this thing is kept while in action, the more likely you'll get what you're after.
    To use one properly, grip it firmly with three fingers at the curve near the tip.

April 30

1945 – *Queen for a Day* Premieres

Jack Bailey crowns another queen. (Author's Collection)

"On this show, housewives stand on a stage in front of a studio audience, most of them sobbing pitifully, and tell about their deformed children, their tubercular husbands, or their blind mothers. The one with the most pitiable story gets laden with TV sets, trips to Europe, electric ranges and heaven knows what else." –John Crosby, newspaper columnist and TV critic

Queen for a Day, the self-proclaimed "Cinderella show," was a mawkish, maudlin, sentimental, tear-jerking spectacle, and millions of radio listeners and television viewers wouldn't have had it any other way. For nineteen years, four women a day stood before host Jack Bailey and shared their plights and their wishes, with the studio audience voting on which one was most deserving to be *Queen for a Day*. That woman spent the remainder of the half hour being bombarded by prizes and money beyond her imagination.

The show was an overnight sensation. It began going on tour, filling auditoriums and arenas all over the country with women hoping to be selected as the Queen of her hometown. In a typical episode, the four competing to be named Queen were: a woman who had to stop working because of an injury and had a wheelchair-bound son to care for; the mother of a child who was in and out of the hospital; a woman who had lost both parents, both children, her husband and an elderly friend all within a short time period, and a mother who was overwhelmed by all the sailors that her sons, both Navy men, brought home when they dropped by for weekend stays. All shared their stories fearlessly with Jack Bailey in front of the captivated audience.

The big winner was the first woman, who received a new wheelchair and special bicycle for her son; an evening of entertainment at a nightclub featuring Bob Newhart as a headliner; a new camera and projector; a vacation at the Jamaica Inn; gift certificates; a new kitchen and appliances; a sewing machine; a dishwasher; a month's worth of frozen food, and a wad of cash for herself and her son.

Another big winner was the mother of a paralyzed three-year old; by day, Mama was the editor of a Los Angeles newspaper. Another day, the coronation ceremony was held for a widow who lived with her two children in a converted chicken coop.

Sob stories shared the stage with good works. One woman was voted Queen because the audience was touched by her story of turning her apartment over to a homeless veteran, and a special series of episodes called "Queen of America" permitted listeners to nominate potential queens based on the contributions they made to their community. The big winner was a nurse who specialized in care for underprivileged families.

Regardless of how exploitative or tasteless the show may have seemed to some, it generated great stories. After the show arrived on television in 1956, Jack Bailey welcomed a Yugoslavian immigrant named Melitta Real, who had given birth in a German prison camp and was told by doctors that the baby had died. She came to the show seeking a trip to Europe, because she had just learned that the child was still alive and residing in France. The audience declared her Queen without much debate, and mother and son were happily reunited in Paris.

Even on *Queen for a Day*, humor had its place. Jack Bailey once asked a woman why she should be Queen, and she explained that she had expensive repairs to make after accidentally driving her car through a wall of her house. Jack asked, "What did your husband say when he saw what happened?" and then hastily yanked away the microphone when he realized that she was about to quote something unfit for broadcast.

Typically the women volunteered their own stories, but

periodically *Queen for a Day* held special contests for people to nominate deserving women in their lives. For example, when the show held an essay contest to find America's best mother-in-law, 3 million men across the country wrote in singing the praises of the special woman in their special woman's life. The big winner received a $35,000 haul. Another special contest saw to it that any baby could be born with a silver spoon in his mouth when the show awarded a selection of silver gifts to the mother of each baby born on New Year's Day, 1951.

The show grew so popular that it became adapted in ways unheard of for a radio giveaway show. A comedic play based on the show toured the country in 1948 and, in 1951, a *Queen for a Day* movie was released.

Why was this show a hit? Rather than offering some spin about celebrating the human spirit and rewarding deserving human beings, producer Howard Blake wrote an unabashedly cynical explanation for the show's popularity in the appropriately named *Fact* magazine.

"Sure, *Queen* was vulgar and sleazy and filled with bathos and bad taste...That's why it was so successful. It was exactly what the general public wanted...We got what we were after. Five thousand Queens got what they were after. And the TV audience cried their eyes out, morbidly delighted to find there were people even worse off than they were, and so they got what they were after."

Host Jack Bailey was conclusively linked with the show, hosting it for most of its two-decade run, although sharp-eared Disney fans probably recognized his voice for another job he did. Once upon a time, Jack Bailey was the voice of Goofy. He spent his lifetime in pursuit of a big show business career, dancing throughout high school before studying drama at Drake University. At the 1933 World's Fair in Chicago, Bailey worked as a barker and spent the

Jack Bailey's career crossed from cartoons to coronations.
(Fred Wostbrock Collection)

remainder of the decade directing musical revues and comedies throughout the Midwest before moving to Hollywood in 1940.

Why move to Hollywood? It was a whim. His obituary noted that his widow recalled somebody suggesting that Jack try his luck working in Hollywood, and with that challenge he moved out west almost immediately. *Queen for a Day* was originally a temp assignment for him. When the show premiered, the host was Ken Murray, and the show aired in New York. A matter of months later, the program relocated to Hollywood, Ken Murray stayed in New York and Jack Bailey got a career-changing booking as a two-week temporary host while the show searched for a new host.

Jack Bailey proved to be perfect, and the temp assignment became permanent by the end of that two weeks.

Queen for a Day returned in 1969 for a syndicated run hosted by Dick Curtis, but it didn't last more than a season. Times were changing, social attitudes regarding women were changing, and it was apparent that *Queen for a Day* was very much a product of its time. In today's era of reality TV, it would probably seem too tame.

May 1

1924 – Art Fleming's Birth

Art Fleming emerges from the shadows to host a venerable game. (Author's Collection)

> "Mr. Fleming, who had the carriage of a gentleman soldier and the manner of a benign schoolmaster, seemed just the sort of host who wouldn't be resented for knowing, say, that it was Henry of Navarre who thought Paris well worth a mass in 1593."
>
> –*New York Times* obituary, April 27, 1995.

Possibly the most likable intellectual ever to be welcomed into America's living rooms, Art Fleming humbly credited his depth of knowledge to a "jack-of-all-trades" background. He was born into a show business family. His ancestors included circus performers; his grandfather was an opera conductor; his parents were an Austrian dance team who moved to New York to wow American audiences. Little did they realize their son would beat them to the punch.

At the age of four, Art made his Broadway debut and kept performing until taking time off at age seventeen for military service and college. He served in the Navy during World War II and was captain of the football team at Colgate University before transferring to Cornell, where he earned a Bachelor of Science degree.

In 1945, he moved to North Carolina to begin a broadcasting career. He spun records in Rocky Mount and Raleigh before moving to Akron. By 1950, he had worked his way up to the ABC television network, serving as a staff announcer and doing commercials for RJ Reynolds, telling viewers that "Winston tastes good like a cigarette should."

He made his game show debut as one of the roving assistants wandering the audience to round up contestants for *Dr. I.Q.* in 1953, but briefly broke away from broadcasting for a surprising

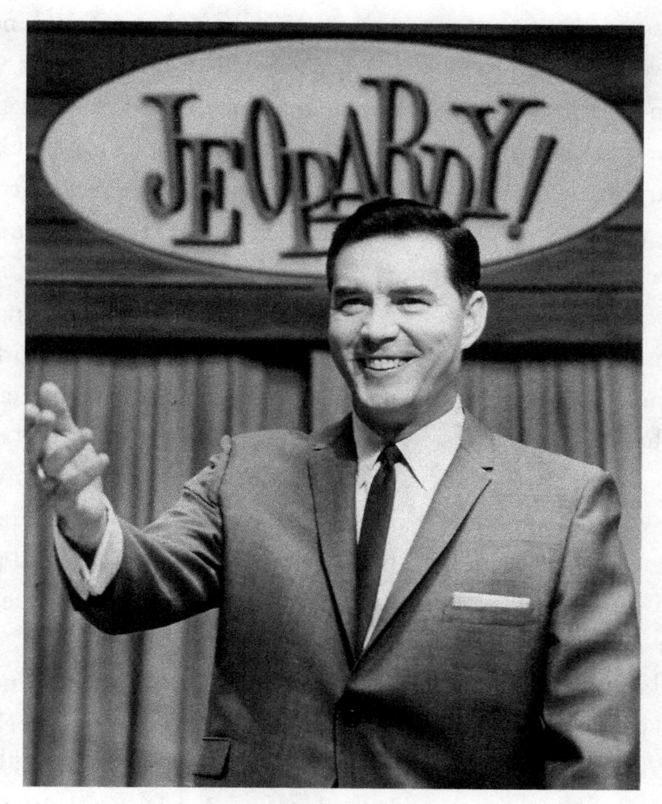

A class act on a classic show, Art Fleming and *Jeopardy!*
(Author's Collection)

career switch. He became a stuntman. He worked on numerous shows before becoming a featured actor on a western, *The Californians*, and the star of a short-lived series, *International Detective*, in 1959. Although that show lasted only one season, it was a job that Art relished. He lived in England when the show was in production and amassed an impressive collection of British military relics, including swords and medals.

When the show was canceled, he moved back to New York and tried to start a film career but won only a few roles and minimal success. He became the anchor for WNBC's eleven o'clock news and went back to work doing commercials. Merv Griffin's wife Julann spotted him in a TWA ad and thought he'd be perfect for the new game show her husband had just developed for NBC.

Art recalled later, "I did it out of curiosity, thinking it was going to last three months. I had no idea I would end up spending thirteen years with the show."

Jeopardy! became more than just a hit for Art Fleming; it became his identity. Every weekday at noon, housewives, workers on their lunch breaks and college students between classes switched on their TVs to watch the hard quizzer with the soft-hearted host. Art smiled like a proud father at contestants who came up with particularly difficult correct responses, encouraged those who were faring poorly to "get out of that minus!" and preemptively thanked the viewers for sticking around each time the game was paused for a commercial.

The show brought him a great deal of joy, and he was never bored by it. He told reporter Frank Swertlow, "It's a different show each day, a different audience, different answers. It's not like a Broadway show where you have the same dialogue and the same characters day after day. What can I say, I enjoy it."

Being a staple of daytime TV had its benefits. Art and his wife enjoyed the good life in their Fifth Avenue penthouse, which they loaded with antiques and a massive book collection. Art spent most of his time at home cooking. He was a master chef and happily welcomed friends to the apartment to enjoy a gourmet meal at the dining and eating counter that he built himself from a slab of polished pine. Each meal also came with a generous serving of wine and, if asked, Art was always able to tell friends its vintage, its locale, the soil used for growing the grapes and the weather conditions during the year it was made.

Art Fleming celebrates a show anniversary with a production assistant. (Author's Collection)

Being the star of *Jeopardy!* was also the source of some pressure. He was frequently called upon by strangers who recognized him to help settle factual arguments because, surely, Art Fleming would know the answer to whatever was puzzling them. As a guest on *The Hollywood Squares*, Art found himself in the Secret Square with $11,000 at stake when Peter Marshall asked him who won the 1938 Wimbledon women's title. It turned out Art had an Achilles' heel. He didn't know anything about tennis. He took a shot in the dark, probably hoping the contestant would disagree with his choice of Helen Wills Moody.

The contestant smiled and said, "Art Fleming wouldn't lie! He's right!"

Art's blind guess turned out to be right, and the contestant took home the jackpot.

Art Fleming had the answers. Could you give him the questions? (Author's Collection)

Away from *Jeopardy!*, Art became a deacon in Manhattan's Marble Collegiate Church. He explained, "I was brought up a Catholic, but I felt I was a spectator. I wanted to be a participant."

As a deacon, Art co-founded a crisis center to offer ministry to callers year-round. "It's somebody you can talk to. And it's religion coming out to the people rather than forcing them to come to religion."

Jeopardy! came to an end in 1975. A brief revival in 1978 fizzled and Art Fleming said goodbye to the show in 1979 after a total of 2,858 games. He didn't do much television after that. He was frustrated by what he called the medium's "herd mentality." Instead of a vast array of original shows, he saw carbon copies all over the place because the concern was duplicating whatever ideas already worked.

Art went back to radio, acting as quizmaster for a CBS revival of *College Bowl* that toured the country each week. Although he may have professed to dislike cookie-cutter programming, Art understood the popularity and—at the time—mass saturation of game shows.

"It's a form of gaining knowledge that isn't demanding and doesn't take time because it's done as a relaxation," he told *The Pittsburgh Press*. "People are intrigued with information and like to show off what they know. People like to say, 'Did you know the water on earth is recycled, so that we could be drinking the same water the Pharaohs of Egypt drank?' Or they like to ask tricky questions, such as 'How many twenty-five-watt light bulbs equal a one hundred-watt bulb?' Believe it or not, it takes six."

When Art arrived in Huntington, West Virginia, to host *College Bowl*, he stopped by a local radio station to do an interview promoting the show. The interviewer was a lifelong game show

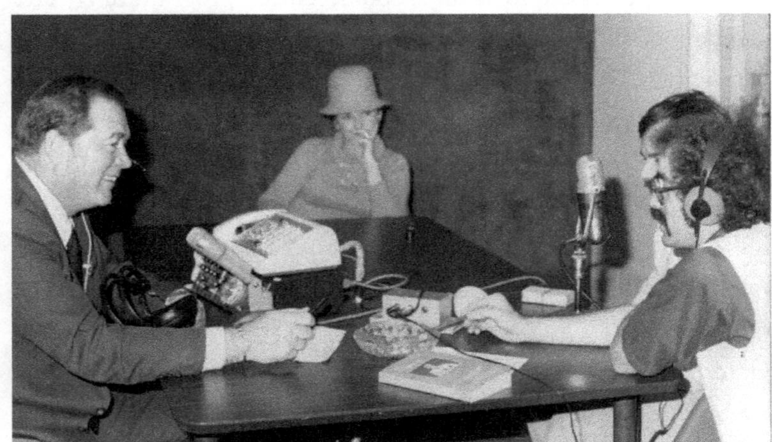

Art promotes *College Bowl* during a personal appearance in Huntington, WV. (Ernie G. Anderson Collection)

fan known on the air as Ernie G. It was a thrilling assignment for Ernie, and Art left a lasting impression on him.

Ernie recalled, "He was much taller than I imagined. He was so kind, gracious, great smile; his wife, Becky, was with him. She was cordial, too. He told me I did a good Don Pardo imitation…It was like meeting an old friend whom you admired, and he was as nice in person as he appeared on television—no ego, no 'don't you know who I am,' very approachable. He seemed like an everyday guy, not some 'I'm better than you' person."

Art was so taken by meeting a sincere fan of his work that after the interview he volunteered to stay in the studio and record some promos for Ernie, speaking off the cuff as he recorded the messages telling listeners that he would consider it a personal favor if they listened to Ernie's show. Ernie marveled, "It's Art Fleming from New York and *Jeopardy!* doing something nice for a game show freak like me and seeming to enjoy adding to my excitement of the moment of getting to meet a TV icon!"

After *College Bowl* wound down, Art moved to St. Louis to host a radio show that included a daily trivia competition between callers. He made appearances playing himself in two films, *Twilight Zone: The Movie* and *Airplane II: The Sequel.* Most famously, he joined Weird Al Yankovic in the music video for "I Lost on Jeopardy!"

In 1984, *Jeopardy!* went back on the air and, to the surprise of many, Art wasn't considered for the job. Alex Trebek got the assignment. Art revealed years later that the loss of his most famous job didn't upset him very much, because several rule changes in the new version rubbed him the wrong way. Although he openly expressed that opinion, he had nothing but positive words for the host, speaking highly of Alex Trebek's performance when asked about it in public.

Art didn't completely move on from *Jeopardy!* though. He made a lucrative living renting himself out to corporate functions and conventions to host specialized games of *Jeopardy!* When the show released a special Twenty-Fifth Anniversary commemorative box game, Art toured the country making public appearances to promote it.

After wrapping up his show in St. Louis, Art moved to Florida, where he spent his remaining years doing volunteer work and briefly hosting a newsmagazine show aimed at senior citizens. He kept working on the show right up until he was diagnosed with pancreatic cancer. He died within weeks of the diagnosis, on April 25, 1995. Today, he's largely remembered as the answer to a trivia question: "Who hosted *Jeopardy!* before Alex Trebek?" But to a generation of TV viewers, Art Fleming was *Jeopardy!* And he was a friend, too.

(Author's Collection)

May 2

1984 – Jack Barry Dies

A radio arcade card, promoting Jack's early work in broadcasting. (Author's Collection)

Jack Barry's show business career was a three-act play: the greatest heights of success, an almost-overnight nosedive to rock bottom, and then redemption.

The man born Jack Barasch on March 20, 1918, in Long Island didn't anticipate a long, controversial and storied career in entertainment. He didn't envision *any* career in entertainment. Jack graduated from college with a degree in business and went to work for his father, selling handkerchiefs.

When he got bored with handkerchiefs, he looked for something else to do with his life, but he had no sense of direction until he went to a party where several friends marveled at his voice and suggested he try breaking into radio. That's exactly what he did, and he would never look back. In his first year as a radio announcer in New Jersey, his weekly salary jumped more than thirtyfold; he moved on to New York, where he became the announcer for *The Uncle Don Carney Show*, a children's show where he met and befriended the production manager, a former radio engineer and Signal Corps member named Dan Ehrenreich.

Part of Jack's duties as announcer was warming up the audience of children before each broadcast; he would ask them tricky questions and get into conversations and debates with the youngsters that delighted him so much that it gave him an idea. Dan Ehrenreich teamed up with him to turn the warm-ups into an entire show.

> "A barrelful of bright little monkeys—and sometimes as much fun...One of the funniest shows on the air." –*Time*

The show, called *Juvenile Jury*, premiered on the Mutual Broadcasting System in 1946. Each day, Jack sat with a panel of bright young children and put them on the spot with the problems of listeners who had written in seeking advice. The kids gave answers that were honest, adorable and just plain funny.

"Should an eleven-year-old girl wear lipstick?"
Ten-year-old Buddy: "No, they look ridiculous."
"Who should spank the child, the mother or the father?"
Seven-year-old Maryann: "The mother should do it…she can spank more lighter than the father."

The show was a smash with listeners; the children were carefully cast to weed out smart alecks and prodigies, and the gathering of a group of real kids trying to sound like adults but instead just sounding like real kids delighted the audience. It received overwhelming critical acclaim, not just for the kids, but for Jack Barry's impressive job handling all of them. One critic, Robert Fleming, said Jack had "an interested, understanding, yet self-effacing attitude that makes the show click."

The show was such a smash that NBC snapped up the program from Mutual and added a prime time television edition. Premiering in 1947, the video version of *Juvenile Jury* was the first commercial-sponsored program on the fledgling NBC TV network. It stuck around for seven years.

In 1948, Barry and his partner, who by this point had changed his professional name to Dan Enright, launched a spin-off of *Jury* that went to the opposite end of the spectrum. *Life Begins at 80* featured a panel of octogenarians fielding questions from listeners. Barry & Enright had another hit and, just as with its sister show, *Life Begins at 80* made a successful move to television, arriving in 1950 and lasting six years.

The next logical step was fusing the two: *Wisdom of the Ages* featured panelists of all ages trying to solve problems, but the hybrid survived only one season on the Dumont network.

In 1953, Jack became the host of a successful and critically acclaimed Saturday morning kids' show, *Winky Dink and You*, a show that was heralded by teachers and parents' groups for teaching children how to draw and encouraging self-expression and interaction rather than passive viewing. Jack served as the narrator while Winky Dink, a pixie-like character, got into a series of predicaments. With the aid of the "magic screen," a plastic shield that parents could purchase for fifty cents and attach directly to the TV screen, the kids used crayons to draw simple objects, like a bridge or a rope, that Winky Dink needed to get out of trouble. Jack would usually encourage the kids to modify the drawing however they wanted, to really make it their own drawing.

He told reporter Jack Gaver, "I consider it as a program that brings 'audience participation' into the home, making it unnecessary for children to go to a TV studio to get into the act."

Jack's first foray into big money quizzes was the short-lived *The Big Surprise.* (Author's Collection)

In 1955, he finally made the move to hosting a game show, NBC's big-money answer to *The $64,000 Question*, from the same producer, Steve Carlin. It was titled *The Big Surprise* and offered a $100,000 payday to a contestant who could go all the way. Jack told reporter Hal Boyle about how much he enjoyed his new job.

"The tension builds up in you, because you sometimes get as deeply involved emotionally with the contestants in the twenty minutes you deal with them as you would if you had known them for twenty years. When they win, a wave of excitement hits you, too; a feeling which lasts until you suddenly realize it is really somebody else who won the money and not you."

It seemed like Jack could do no wrong as a host; he received praise from critics for his job on *The Big Surprise*. Boyle called him "the new type of television emcee, who is brightly eager to shower you with cash if you can show your head holds even the smallest nugget of knowledge. This contrasted with old-style emcees, who often had a different aim—to minimize the amount of the sponsor's money that was given away."

Not everybody shared the sentiments of the critics, however. Barry was fired from *The Big Surprise* in March 1956; the reason cited was that he was too dull as a game show emcee. The slight irked Jack, who complained to an interviewer that his dismissal was "unethical." Producer Steve Carlin was furious about Jack's view of the firing, retorting, "One sponsor became dissatisfied with Jack almost from the start...couldn't get rid of Jack fast enough... was willing to replace Jack with practically anybody."

Jack picked himself up, dusted himself off and got to work with Dan Enright developing and producing their own big-money quiz show. They mounted a pilot for CBS titled *Twenty One* and, when that network passed, NBC picked it up. The show premiered in

The show that would make, then break, Jack Barry, *Twenty One*.
(Author's Collection)

the fall of 1956. What followed was a two-year-long roller coaster that made many people wealthy and then destroyed them.

After a disastrous premiere broadcast, when the order came in from the execs at sponsoring Pharmaceuticals, Inc., that they never wanted to see an episode that bad again, the decision was made to start rigging the show. How much Jack actually knew about the rigging was up for speculation. One of the show's most infamous contestants, Herbert Stempel, said in interviews that he suspected that Jack didn't know the show was rigged at all. Barry & Enright staffers maintained that he did. Jack's own account was that the truth lay somewhere in the middle. He claimed that he knew the show was rigged but chose to be kept in the dark about the scripted fates of the contestants because he felt he wouldn't do a convincing job building suspense if he knew who would win.

Stempel, embittered about the wealth and fame showered

upon the contestant who defeated him, Charles Van Doren, and irate that Dan Enright reneged on a promise to use Stempel for a panel show, *High Low*, that Barry & Enright launched a few months later, went to the New York District Attorney's office. An investigation eventually turned up evidence of deception. An incident involving a contestant on *Dotto* (see August 15) brought forth concrete evidence that quiz shows were fixed, and Stempel came into the limelight with his story. Whereas he couldn't get the papers to listen when he had earlier tried to break the news, now they wanted, and eagerly printed, every detail.

When the news broke, the bottom dropped out immediately. *Twenty One* lost sixty-six percent of its audience in the Trendex ratings, and subpoenas began trickling out. In October 1958, Barry & Enright asked NBC to relieve them of their duties as producers so they could devote their time and energy to fighting the charges. NBC immediately canceled *Twenty One*; replaced Jack with a new host at *Tic Tac Dough;* and took over control of the production of *Concentration* and *Dough-Re-Mi.* Barry & Enright continued the fight for their reputation. The fight was a losing battle, for the simple reason that the accusations were true. They had rigged their shows.

Many former contestants perjured themselves when giving testimony to grand juries, the New York County District Attorney's office and a Congressional subcommittee, but a few, like Stempel and James Snodgrass, willingly spoke up about participating in the rigging. Even the golden boy of *Twenty One*, $129,000 winner-turned-*Today* correspondent Charles Van Doren, eventually cracked and admitted that he was involved.

NBC hastily plugged the vacancy left by *Twenty One* with a prime time version of *Concentration* at the helm, but viewers were angry. They didn't want to see a game show hosted by Jack Barry.

They had just spent two years being deceived by such a program, and the nighttime version of *Concentration* was gone after just four broadcasts.

Jack tried to pick himself up and dust himself off after the quiz show scandals. This publicity photo circulated to promote several of his efforts as a stage actor. (Author's Collection)

The producers were in ruin. Enright was blacklisted in the U.S. for his involvement and moved to Canada to produce shows for the next decade. But at least he was somewhat employable. Jack's fate proved more severe. The sudden and drastic effects of unemployment took their toll; his marriage fell apart and he was divorced in 1959. (He would eventually remarry, to a *Concentration* production assistant.) He got out of television altogether for a position as executive vice-president of a chemical firm, but before long he tried to rebuild his TV career. He attempted to mount a new version of *Juvenile Jury* titled *Kidding Around*, but couldn't get it picked up by more than one station; it was gone in six weeks.

In 1962, Jack moved to Los Angeles and started to get the ball rolling with his career again, hosting and producing four game shows and hosting a talk show for local station KTLA. But just when things looked promising, Jack had the rug yanked from under him. One of the games he was hosting, *You Don't Say!*, got picked up by NBC, but NBC wanted nothing to do with him, and Tom Kennedy got the nod to host the series. KTLA was sold a short time later, and the new owner fired Jack.

Jack developed a drinking problem. *Concentration* producer Norm Blumenthal recalled visiting him and noting how dejected he seemed. Jack told *TV Guide* years later of friends crossing the street to avoid him. On the rare occasions that he found work in game shows, it was only as a consultant, and he had to leave his name off the credits to avoid tainting the show. He got a job with Mark Goodson-Bill Todman Productions but quit almost as quickly as he arrived because he clashed with his bosses about how to go about producing a pilot.

By the end of the 1960s, things began to turn around very gradually for the falling star. The FCC, which had previously forced him to sell a radio station in Hollywood, Florida, because of his checkered past, granted him permission to buy a radio station in Redondo Beach, CA. Word spread throughout show business that the FCC had "forgiven" Jack through this gesture, and work began trickling in. He got a job hosting *The Generation Gap*, a prime time game show that lasted only a few weeks. Next came a short-lived movie quiz called *The Reel Game*. He even got *Juvenile Jury* back on the air, for a single season in 1971.

Jack Barry, kidding around with the kids and Marty Allen on the 1971 version of *Juvenile Jury*. (Fred Wostbrock Collection)

One aspect of this comeback still eluded him: Jack still wanted to be a producer. He came up with an idea for a quiz show involving a slot machine during his brief stint at Goodson-Todman. When he left, he mounted a series of pilots under the title *The Joker's Wild*, hosted by Allen Ludden, in 1969. He couldn't get it sold. He tried again as part of an ambitious idea he had for a ninety-minute game show format called *The Honeymoon Game*. The pilot, hosted by Jim McKrell, was produced in 1970 and didn't get picked up.

In 1971, KTLA finally picked up *The Joker's Wild*, so Jack at least got it on the air locally—and it turned out to be a hit, so much so that when CBS, which had been out of the daytime game show business for several years, decided reintroduce games to the

Jack is back! *The Joker's Wild* restored his reputation in the early 1970s. (Author's Collection)

1972 lineup, *The Joker's Wild* got picked up for a national run. On September 4, *The Joker's Wild*, *Gambit* and *The New Price is Right* all premiered on CBS, and all were hits.

The Joker's Wild enjoyed a three-year run on CBS with Jack as host and producer, finally giving him the vindication he was seeking. The game was totally on the level and provided plenty of excitement and big winners without having to sink to alternate means. Still, it's interesting to note that for all the trouble the scandal had caused him, Jack was remorseless about what he had done in the 1950s.

He said in an interview, "Everybody was doing it, not just Dan and I. Every quiz show was feeding contestants the answers…I felt then and I still feel now that I was being punished for the sins of others."

Jack considered his primary duty as carrying out entertainment in whatever form was deemed acceptable. When rigging a quiz show in the name of making it interesting became common practice, that was what he did. When it turned out that the audience insisted on a truthful show, that's what he provided.

Over the next few years, Jack came back into demand as a producer. He created *Hollywood's Talking* for CBS and *Blank Check* for NBC. When *The Joker's Wild* ended its CBS run in June 1975, Jack held back some emotion as he thanked the audience on the final show and declared that the past three years had been "the happiest and most productive of my entire life."

The following year, his old partner Dan Enright returned to the states and they were back in business together, developing new shows for networks and syndication. They introduced a Saturday morning kids' show, *Way Out Games*, on CBS in 1976. In the coming eight years, they established an unusual pattern for launching new shows. Many of their games seemed to borrow elements of popular game shows from other producers and simply tweaked them until they were new games. *Break the Bank* (see April 12) was clearly inspired by *The Hollywood Squares*. A 1977 syndicated game, *Hollywood Connection*, looked a lot like *Match Game*. *Hot Potato* (see January 23) strongly resembled *Family Feud*. Jack even borrowed from his own shows. A 1980 offering, *Bullseye*, was jokingly referred to by members of his staff as "Son of Joker" because of how closely it resembled *The Joker's Wild*.

The Joker's Wild proved to be a venerable show for Barry & Enright. A year after it left CBS, the duo sold reruns of the final year to a handful of local stations, and the strong ratings for the reruns suggested that perhaps the cancellation was premature. In 1977, the reruns were gone and new episodes of *The Joker's Wild* were produced. Again, it was a hit. The following year, they dusted off another old gem, *Tic Tac Dough*; in most markets, the two shows aired back-to-back, and audiences loved them.

Jack is ready to dole out the dough during the bonus round on *The Joker's Wild*. (Author's Collection)

In 1979, Jack spun off *The Joker's Wild* into a Saturday morning series, *Joker, Joker, Joker* in which children played the game. Jack spent a little more time getting to know the kids than he typically got to know the adult contestants, recapturing some of that old *Juvenile Jury* magic.

As the new decade rolled around, Jack sought to expand his empire, with mixed results. Barry & Enright launched a films division that released three major titles, the most successful of which was a teen sex romp titled *Private Lessons.* On TV, a talk show called *Soap World* and a sitcom called *Mama Malone* took the company beyond game shows. Jack established his own cable provider, the immodestly named Jack Barry Cable Company, to provide service to viewers throughout southern California. As cable TV became a more and more viable alternative, Barry & Enright revived *Juvenile Jury* with a new version produced for BET, hosted by Nipsey Russell.

Jack can't believe the check he's writing for this lucky winner. (Author's Collection)

The demands of running a growing and thriving empire were taking its toll on Jack Barry, who couldn't fight the effects of the aging process. His doctors had placed him on a strict exercise regimen after his blood pressure reached dangerous levels, and Jack began swimming and jogging daily to keep his body functioning normally. The exercise proved so rigorous that he lost forty pounds. By 1983, taping five episodes in one day was standard procedure for game shows, but that one day proved a bit too demanding for Jack, so the sixty-five-year-old host began alternating weeks as host of *The Joker's Wild* with Jim Peck. The long-term plan was for Jack to pass the torch to Jim, retire from hosting and remain behind the scenes as a producer.

But before that plan could come to fruition, fate intervened. On a New York vacation on May 2, 1984, Jack suffered a heart attack during his daily jog and was pronounced dead on arrival at Lenox Hill Hospital at the age of sixty-six. It was a sadly abrupt end to the life of a man who had accomplished so much in the span of a second chance.

(Author's Collection)

May 3

1955 – *Twenty Questions* Ends

Before there was *What's My Line?*, before there was *I've Got a Secret*, before there were even televisions or radios, there was a simple parlor game called *Twenty Questions*. One player would come up with a topic, and the other players, starting by establishing "Animal, Vegetable, or Mineral?" would ask twenty yes-or-no questions to try to identify the mystery subject.

Radio was already loaded with national and local shows that encouraged listeners to interact with experts, so it was only a matter of time before somebody got the bright idea to turn the game into a radio show. That somebody was Fred Van Deventer, an Indiana-born newspaper writer who had moved to radio news in the 1940s before hitting it big with *Twenty Questions*.

The show premiered on the Mutual Radio Network in 1946. Each program featured five panelists. Fred Van Deventer and his wife, Florence Rinard, were regulars, along with the show's producer, Herb Polesie, and a teenager named Johnnie McPhee. They were joined each week by a guest panelist and, together, they would grill moderator Bill Slater for hints in the form of yes-or-no responses to their questions. The subjects to be identified were all submitted by listeners; any listener whose subject was used by the program received a prize. If the subject stumped the panel, an encyclopedia was awarded as a bonus.

Parkersburg, West Virginia native Bill Slater previously had been the announcer for NBC's first game show, *Uncle Jim's Question Bee*, but was largely known as a sportscaster. *Twenty Questions* proved so successful for him that he would spend the remainder of his career hosting game shows. As host of *Twenty Questions*, he had possibly the least desirable job in broadcasting. He had no experts to speak of assisting him in answering the questions; he was on his own to provide the yes-or-no responses.

Audiences flooded the show with so much mail nitpicking some of his responses that *Twenty Questions* eventually hired a staff with the sole responsibility of answering complaint letters from listeners. One week, the subject was "Canadian Mounties," and when the panel asked, "Are they American?" Bill answered, "No." The name of the continent where Canada is located inspired a great deal of feedback. On another occasion, the panel was trying to zero in on "Martin Luther" and asked, "Is he famous for his musical abilities?" Slater answered "No," leading to an avalanche of mail pointing out that Luther had written numerous hymns. A debate about whether Casey Jones was real or fictional also drew a lot of ire.

But those audiences kept coming in and, in November 1949,

Twenty Questions made the jump to television. It premiered on NBC and pinballed back and forth between NBC, Dumont and ABC over the next six years. Bill Slater departed in 1953, replaced by Jay Jackson. Johnnie McPhee left the show and was replaced by Dickie Harrison, and later by Bobby McGuire. In a not-terribly-amazing coincidence, McGuire was the son of Fred Van Deventer and Florence Rinard.

May 4

1987 – *Classic Concentration* Premieres

Alex and model Diana Taylor chat on the set of *Classic Concentration.* (Author's Collection)

Nearly three decades had passed since NBC first unveiled *Concentration.* A generation of children who had grown up mesmerized by the simple game, the mechanical puzzle board, and those elaborate rebus puzzles had grown up and finally got their chance to be contestants when NBC teamed up with Mark Goodson to unleash a new version of the old favorite. When viewers first saw the lavish neon set with eight gorgeous cars sprawling across a silver staircase, it was clear that this wasn't your father's *Concentration.*

The game was a fusion of old and new, with quite a few changes that made fans of the original version scratch their heads, but certainly had no trouble pulling in a new audience. The game was arguably easier; the board was reduced from thirty squares to twenty-five; there was an extra wild card up there, and many games began with squares, sometimes one but up to four of them on some occasions, being revealed right away as a head start. If time was short, the contestants even had lock-out buttons and could ring in to solve the rebus as the puzzle pieces were revealed one at a time.

The show unveiled a new bonus round, plainly called the Car Game, in which a contestant faced a board of fifteen numbers. Behind them were seven matched pairs of cars, plus one extra car with no match, that was there just to trip up the contestant. The contestant had thirty-five seconds to match all seven pairs; if they succeeded, they won the last car they matched. If they failed, five seconds were added to the clock for the next Car Game.

Perhaps the most startling change for this incarnation is that the famous mechanical board that was such a hallmark of the original series was gone. *Classic Concentration* was high-tech *Concentration.* The game board was computer-generated. The contestants faced a monitor as they played the game, and after

Alex Trebek along with the boss' daughter, Marjorie Goodson, and one of the famous rebus puzzles designed by Steve Ryan. (Fred Wostbrock Collection)

each game, when host Alex Trebek interpreted the symbols in the puzzle, he stood in front of a green screen, looking not unlike your local weatherman as he gestured from corner to corner of the screen.

Alex Trebek, already three seasons into *Jeopardy!* when this series started, saw his stock rising as a master of ceremonies after fourteen years on American TV when *Classic Concentration* became a hit. He was such a success that in 1990, he found himself in the bizarre position of winning the Emmy for Best Game Show Host, and defeating himself in the category.

Joining Alex each day was model/daughter of the boss Marjorie Goodson, who frequently brought along her dog, Pokey, to help show off some of the prizes up for grabs. The show's regular announcer was Gene Wood, although Art James was pressed into service for several tapings, and it proved to be an interesting full-circle moment for Art. His first national television job was announcing the original version of the series in 1958. After more than thirty years of hosting and announcing, his brief stint sitting in for Gene Wood would be his final national TV job. He began and ended his career with the game of puzzles and prizes.

The show chugged along just fine for more than four years. In late 1991, NBC made the strange decision to end production, but keep it on the daytime schedule. Reruns of *Classic Concentration* aired for two more years before disappearing in 1993. *Concentration* hasn't been seen since in new episodes or reruns, but the game stays just as popular as ever. New *Concentration* board games have been printed; there's been a *Concentration* handheld game and a PC game as well. You may not be able to watch *Concentration* anymore, but it appears that a devoted fan will be able to continue playing it for years to come.

May 5

1949 – *Blind Date* Jumps to Television

In the 1990s, MTV aired *Singled Out*, a game show on which bachelors and bachelorettes tried to sweet-talk potential mates and win them over without being able to see each other. Game show fans at the time may have yawned, "It's been done," thinking of Chuck Barris' legendary *Dating Game*.

Here's the surprise, though. When *The Dating Game* arrived in 1965, there may have been game show fans at that time yawning, "It's been done." The original matchmaking game show was called *Blind Date*, a forgotten first in the genre's history.

The host was another first: Arlene Francis, best known for her years on *What's My Line?*, became the first female game show host when *Blind Date* enjoyed a three-year radio run beginning July 8, 1943. Each day, six men stood on one side of a wall and took turns speaking via telephone to the beautiful model sitting on the other side of the wall. The lovely lady picked out the sweetest of the sweet talkers, and the prize was an evening on the town together.

In 1949, the series was revived for television, airing in prime time on ABC. Arlene Francis returned for the TV version, which tried to make use of the new medium by having the potential suitors perform in silly skits or hypothetical situations. The woman in question, wearing a blindfold throughout, would join them on stage for the play-acting and sometimes base her decision on how each man handled the situation. Every now and then, the producers would mix up the show with themes like "Father's Night," during which either the men would try to win over the model's father or the model would grill the boys' fathers.

The show bounced from ABC to NBC to Dumont over the next four years, and Arlene Francis eventually moved on. The hosting duties were turned over to Melvyn Douglas for three weeks, and later to Jan Murray. A few years after that, Jan Murray hosted another game show subsequently borrowed by Chuck Barris (see August 13).

May 6

1955 – Tom Bergeron's Birth

Broadcasting renaissance man Tom Bergeron.
(Author's Collection)

Tom Bergeron is possibly the closest thing this generation of television has to Bill Cullen, yet, he's not really a game show host. Oh, he's hosted a game show, but he's more accurately a jack-of-all-trades, a pure broadcaster who simply goes where he's needed, be it a game show, morning news, a dance contest, or videos of children injuring their parents with whiffle bats.

He sought to be a broadcaster with personality; he grew up idolizing radio stars like Jean Shepard, who spun yarns so effectively during his broadcasts that some of his stories were cobbled together to make the film *A Christmas Story.* Tom got his chance at age sixteen by becoming a disc jockey at WHAV, an AM station in his hometown of Haverville, Massachusetts.

He probably would have stayed there—he got promoted to morning drive host in a relatively short time—if it hadn't been for his boss. Seeking to motivate Tom, his boss threatened to fire him unless he signed up for college courses. He was concerned that this young kid was settling into a rut too quickly in life. Tom signed up for a few courses, among them, a class in pantomime. He gradually parlayed that into gigs performing for children, and a sketch comedy routine for adult audiences. His signature sketch for adults was one in which he played Pinocchio and turned himself into a real boy by learning to disco dance.

Early on, he revealed himself as a broadcaster with a flair for humor and inventiveness. It served him well. After sending out his resume in the form of a lavish comic strip, he landed the job at station WHEB, where he built his reputation with a thirty-day radio series in which he hitchhiked from New England to San Francisco with radio equipment in tow to file reports from wherever he wound up.

Before long, he was hosting a local talk show for adults, *New England Crossroads*, and one for children called *Super Kids.*

Meanwhile, he was on the radio airwaves six days a week. He eventually made his way to a syndicated talk show, *People Are Talking*, where a particularly funny interview with Jimmy Carter grabbed the attention of executives at Fox.

Fox was launching a new cable network, FX, and wanted a co-host for *Breakfast Time*, its morning show to compete with *Today* and *Good Morning America*. Tom and his co-host, Laurie Hibberd, led an equally imaginative behind-the-scenes crew to produce a surprisingly inventive two-hour block each day. They took Bob Barker to the streets of New York to play "Hard Hat Price is Right," spontaneously asking construction crews to bid on their own equipment. A Thanksgiving Day Street Crossing Parade was arranged to compete with Macy's extravaganza. A few celebrity guests simply crossed the street near the studio for the tongue-in-cheek event. A puppet named Bob assisted with some segments and grew to be quite popular; when a rock band was booked to perform and gave an ultimatum that the puppet couldn't be on the show with them, Tom gave out the show's fax number and e-mail address and told viewers to voice their opinions. After receiving some overwhelming feedback, Tom, on the air, told the band to leave.

The show grew so popular that it was moved from cable to broadcast TV, in Fox Network's first bid to launch a morning show. Too many executives spoiled the broth, though, and Tom was so unhappy at the revamped format that the network demanded after the show moved that he quit.

Still, he had made one friend in high places during his time there: Whoopi Goldberg. She was a guest early on and was so delighted by Tom that in 1998, when she signed to become the Center Square for the new version of *Hollywood Squares*, she personally recommended Tom for the host's spot.

"Here's how we play the game: First, we don't alienate the Center Square." –Tom explaining the rules of the show, 1999.

Tom got the job and immediately slipped into the big shoes of Peter Marshall very comfortably. In 2000, he bagged the Outstanding Game Show Host trophy at the Emmys. It was the highlight of a memorable six-year run at the helm of *Squares*. Whatever critics and viewers thought of the overall show, praise was overwhelmingly positive for the master of ceremonies.

"The idea of being a game-show host was something I had to shake off a bit...But this is a special animal."

So was Tom. He had years of experience being himself in front of the camera, and himself was a witty man who happened to be secure enough to let other people get the laughs and the adulation when he was onstage. He attributed his laid-back nature and smooth performance to meditation. He engaged in it twice a day and for twenty minutes before any occasion where he was about to go on the air.

With *Hollywood Squares* rolling along, Tom added *America's Funniest Home Videos* to his resume before finally going prime time as host of ABC's *Dancing with the Stars* in 2005. Virtually every assignment with Tom in charge has turned to gold, but no matter how many accolades or hits he racks up in his career, he prefers to credit that success to dumb luck.

"The thing about it, for me, it's never been a plan, it's all sort of been accidental," he said in 1998. "My career has been happening in spite of me."

May 7

1946 – Sony is Founded

There's so much that could be covered about Sony. Game show adaptations have been released on every incarnation of the Playstation. For a time, Sony Picture Studios served as the taping location for *Wheel of Fortune* and *Jeopardy!* They've had ownership stakes in Game Show Network/GSN. But perhaps Sony's most important contribution to TV game shows is their development of the Sony ECM-51. Even if you had no idea what it was called, the long, skinny microphone is an unmistakable staple of the great game shows of the past.

Gene Rayburn on *Match Game* (Mike Klauss Collection)

Bob Barker on *The Price is Right* (Author's Collection)

Alex Trebek on *The $128,000 Question* (Author's Collection)

Mike Darrow on *The $128,000 Question*.
(Fred Wostbrock Collection)

Jim Peck on *You Don't Say!* (Fred Wostbrock Collection)

Jack Barry on *The Joker's Wild* (Author's Collection)

Tom Kennedy on *Whew!* (Author's Collection)

Bill Cullen on *The Joker's Wild* (Author's Collection)

Geoff Edwards on *Hollywood's Talking* (Author's Collection)

May 8

1978 – *Family Feud* is Ready for Major Network Prime Time

Family Feud had a Midas touch. Arriving on ABC in 1976, it quickly bested the opposition to become tops in its timeslot. Within two years, not only was it the number-one game show on television, but a weekly prime time version had launched in syndication and it, too, was a sensation.

Seven years after ABC had completely exited the prime time game show business, the network gave *Family Feud* a shot with an hour-long prime time special. The results were so positive that the specials kept coming for six more years.

The first special was a mini-tournament, featuring the casts of *The Love Boat*, *Eight is Enough*, *Soap* and *Three's Company* playing for their favorite charities. Anyone who had never seen *Family*

Feud until this special immediately got a crash course in what made the game fun. The stars eagerly played the game; there was no concern about a bruised ego because there was no such thing as a wrong answer. The stars merely had to guess how ordinary people responded to a survey's simple questions.

And yet, when the players gave answers that hadn't made the survey, they were whoppers. Asked to "name a part of the body where people dab perfume," Dick Van Patten bewildered Richard Dawson by guessing, "The tip of the tongue." Susan Richardson had to "name an Italian singer" and guessed that old favorite, "Nina Fettuccini." In trying to name a rating used for movies, Norman Fell suggested, "PR." Bernie Kopell had to name something men wear to bed and answered "socks," leading Richard Dawson to warn him, "I hope you never need the charity you're playing for."

The special was a hit. During the next few years, the stars of virtually every successful prime time network TV show took a turn feuding. *Barney Miller*, *Welcome Back Kotter*, *All My Children*, *General Hospital*, *The Ropers*, *Angie*, *The Waltons*, *The Dukes of Hazzard*, *Dallas*, *The Jeffersons*, *Dynasty*, *Knots Landing* and more had their chance to rack up some Fast Money for worthy causes.

The specials were so popular that the other versions of *Feud* airing in daytime for ABC and in syndication began adding more specials. It would have been off-putting to keep plugging in so many specials if it weren't for the fact that the audience simply loved *Family Feud*. By 1980, the weekly syndicated version expanded to a Monday-through-Friday show. *Feud* was airing ten times a week.

There was the Celebrity Championship, with celebrities and their real-life family members; "Singing Stars" week; plenty of soap opera showdowns; All-Time Favorites Week, with *Batman*, *Lost in Space*, *The Brady Bunch*, *Your Hit Parade*, *Leave It to Beaver* and *Gilligan's Island* squaring off; Commercial Stars; Super Teens; World Series week; NFL Stars vs. Cheerleaders; American Beauty Queens, Hollywood Walk of Fame week, and Olympic Medalists week.

By 1984, *Family Feud* was slowly fading, and the specials came to an end after a "Battle of the TV Crimefighters" on May 20. In 2006, NBC dusted off the idea with a series of "Celebrity Family Feud" specials hosted by Al Roker and featuring the casts of *The Girls Next Door*, *The Office*, *American Gladiators*, *My Name is Earl*, *American Chopper* and others. The six-episode series ranked among the top twenty shows throughout the summer.

May 9

1918 – Mike Wallace's Birth

Mike Wallace on *The Big Surprise* in 1956. (Author's Collection)

Mike Wallace would probably rather not be in this book. In Geoff Edwards' words, "he's had the fact that he was a game show host erased from his resume." He'd rather be remembered for his hard-hitting interviews and investigations as a journalist. He will be. That doesn't change the fact that once upon a time, Mike Wallace was deeply involved in game shows.

Wallace made his broadcasting debut on *Information Please* in 1939 and spent years plying his trade as a radio announcer, narrating action shows and even calling play-by-play for professional wrestling. By the end of the decade, he was back to game shows, announcing the commercial messages for *You Bet Your Life*.

For a time, Mike resisted television because he had pockmarked skin and figured nobody would want him on camera. Besides, he had heard horror stories about the lights used for television; indeed, early television lights became extremely hot and could be blinding to a first-timer. When he finally made his television debut, it was a miracle that he came back for more. He did the commercial announcements for a televised circus. A group of five elephants defecated simultaneously during one performance, and then Mike had to do a commercial with a small child. As Mike extolled the deliciousness of Peter Pan Peanut Butter (the same brand that would give Art James trouble years later—see March 28), the camera fixed on a shot of the child trying to bite into a peanut butter sandwich, sobbing uncontrollably because he couldn't stand the smell in the studio by that point, and then running across the stage to get away from it, losing his footing as he ran and falling into one of the piles.

Despite that experience, with a growing family to support, Mike stuck with game shows for most of the decade. He was a regular panelist on *The Name's the Same* for a brief period and hosted six games of his own: *There's One in Every Family*, *Majority Rules*,

Guess Again, *I'll Buy That*, *Who's the Boss?* and *Who Pays?* In 1956, he hosted a pilot for Mark Goodson-Bill Todman Productions titled *Nothing But the Truth*, but by the time the series was picked up, he had been replaced by Bud Collyer and the show was retitled *To Tell the Truth*.

In the late 1950s, he moved onto interview shows, conducting a series of hard-hitting and controversial interviews for ABC. He was threatened with a lawsuit by Joseph P. Kennedy when guest Drew Pearson accused John F. Kennedy for using a ghostwriter to pen *Profiles in Courage*. ABC aired a retraction and apology, which infuriated Wallace, who had stood by the story. A short time later, he interviewed gangster Mickey Cohen, who dished on so many high-ranking officials that the following week's program consisted entirely of Wallace and ABC Vice President Oliver Treyz apologizing for the show.

This created a bit of a problem because in the week between the Cohen interview and the apology, Wallace had been booked to be the Mystery Guest on *What's My Line?* The host of *What's My Line?* happened to be Mike's boss at ABC, Vice President in Charge of News, Special Events and Public Affairs John Daly. Daly threatened to walk if he was forced to appear on television with his troublesome employee, and Mike canceled his booking. He would never appear on *What's My Line?* or, for that matter, any other game show again.

Although Mike severed his connections to game shows, he retained some of the friends he made, particularly Bill Cullen. According to Bill's wife, Ann, Mike spent years trying to convince Bill to leave game shows and start doing serious journalism. Bill politely refused. It astounded Mike Wallace to think that somebody could be perfectly happy being a game show host.

May 10

1955 – Chris Berman's Birth

Catch phrase-spouting, nickname-loving sportscaster Chris Berman arrived at ESPN only one month after the network launched in 1979 and, frankly, it's hard to imagine ESPN without him. He's an institution at the network and, with a natural enthusiasm for sports combined with slick, professional broadcasting abilities, he was the right man for the job when ESPN expanded its horizons by introducing its first game show in 1988.

The cumbersome title of the show was *Boardwalk and Baseball's Super Bowl of Sports Trivia*. It took its name from the taping location of the program, the ill-fated Boardwalk and Baseball theme park in Florida, which opened the year before the show went on the air and closed down in 1990, the year after the final episode.

The game enjoyed a two-season run with a competition that resembled *College Bowl.* Two teams representing different colleges competed against each other. For the first two rounds, Chris would ask kick-off questions, with the team that rang in with the correct answer getting a chance to answer the extra-point question. In the third round, the teams tackled a series of four categories, and the game culminated with a one-hundred-second lightning round. Each of the two seasons comprised a thirty-two-team tournament, with the winners receiving $10,000.

ESPN has tried game shows off-and-on in the ensuing years, and for good reason. Every person knows somebody who's a walking sports encyclopedia. The network could potentially never run out of contestants. Here are some of the other games about games that the network has featured over the years. How many do you remember?

NFL Trivia Game (1988-89) – TV's Mister Kotter himself, Gabe Kaplan, was the unlikely host of this quiz. Teams competed against each other in four quarters. As long as a team kept giving correct answers, it stayed in control. Answering three in a row scored a touchdown and the right to play an extra-point question. Top scorers at the end of the day split $500.

Designated Hitter (1993-94) – *Press Your Luck* creator Bill Carruthers was the brain behind this game, hosted by Curt Chaplin. Contestants selected from the categories football, baseball, basketball and "Curveball" (other sports); each category had a $25 "single" question, a $50 "double," a $75 "triple," a $100 "homer" and a "pinch-hit," which carried a hidden sum. Accumulating three outs (wrong answers) cost a player $100. After two rounds, the winner played the Grand Slam, where a series of four questions could pay up to $3,000.

Dream League (1993-94) – Two teams captained by sports stars competed in a series of trivia questions. Each correct answer moved them along a football field. The faster a team answered, the more ground it gained. Scoring a touchdown gave the team an opportunity to earn an extra point by completing a physical challenge, such as shooting hoops or hitting a softball a certain distance.

Gaters (1994) – Taped in North Carolina, the show actually had very little to do with sports and was more or less *Beat the Clock* for small prizes—*really* small prizes, like t-shirts and hats, among other items typically not declared on tax forms.

The Perfect Match (1994) – Hosted by former *Remote Control* basement master Ken Ober, *The Perfect Match* was a battle-of-the-sexes game. On each episode, two teams of men would compete against each other in a game of sports trivia, and then two female teams would compete in a similar game. The winning teams then played a round against each other for a grand prize.

Sports on Tap (1994-95) – Bob Stewart's son Sande produced this show, distinguishable by a set that resembled a bar. Sportscaster Tom Green was the host/"bartender." Players took turns individually answering a series of questions for $50 each, and the third question gave them the opportunity to bet any or all of their cash. For the next round, the contestants competed head-to-head for questions worth $50 and a shot at a bonus question. The final round was the Play-Off, where contestants were gradually eliminated until only one remained.

2 Minute Drill (2000-01) – Kenny Mayne hosted this game in which contestants played a series of two-minute rounds answering a series of rapid-fire trivia questions from a celebrity panel.

ESPN Trivial Pursuit (2004) – Roger Lodge hosted this five-episode series. Two teams dealt with a series of six categories to fill wedges in their pie; filling all six wedges won the game and a chance to answer questions against the clock to fill the pie again for $5,000.

Stump the Schwab (2004-06) – Airing on sister networks ESPN2 and ESPN Classic, the game was a spin on *Win Ben Stein's Money* created by, and starring, ESPN statistician Howie Schwab. Stuart Scott was the host, in which three contestants competed against each other and against "the Schwab" trying to answer trivia questions that often involved statistics and lists. The top scorer faced Schwab one-on-one in a series of trivia questions. Any contestant who outscored the Schwab won $5,000.

Teammates (2005) – Teammates from pro sports teams played a game not unlike *The Newlywed Game*.

May 11

1954 – *Judge for Yourself* Ends

Fred Allen took a strange detour in the twilight of his career. He had been a prospering and popular comedian with a hit series, *The Fred Allen Show*, on NBC that conquered the ratings. And then, ABC introduced a game show, *Stop the Music*, to compete against him. In a matter of months, Fred Allen was off the air, having been soundly squashed by the sounds of *Stop the Music*.

In his memoirs, Fred Allen wrote this about give-away shows (as game shows were known in the days of radio): *Give-away programs are the buzzards of radio. As buzzards swoop down on carrion so have give-away shows descended on the carcass of radio. Like buzzards the give-away shows, if left to pursue their scavenging devices, will leave nothing but the picked bones of the last listener lying before his radio set…The networks that once vied with each other to present the nation's outstanding acting and musical talent are now infested with swarms of hustlers who are only concerned with the gimmick and a fast buck.*

Okay, this was clearly not a man eagerly looking for a lovely copy of the home game under his Christmas tree, and that's why Fred's career move in 1953 seems so odd. He became the host for a show co-produced by Mark Goodson—the co-producer of *Stop the Music*, the very show that had destroyed his once-dominant radio presence. The new show, *Judge for Yourself*, aired at New York City's Rockefeller Plaza, likely the site of some awkwardly silent elevator rides.

The show premiered on August 18, 1953, and Fred immediately rattled his new bosses when he opened the show by suggesting the audience turn to CBS and see what that network had to offer for the night. The show itself wasn't really a pure game show but more of a talent search with prize money and lucky contestants who could win that cash with little effort.

A series of acts, including singers, actors, and dancers, took to the stage and did their thing. Each performance was scored on a scale of one to three by two separate panels—a panel of three celebrities and a panel of ordinary contestants. The contestants could win $1,000 if their score matched the score given by one of the stars.

That format didn't work, so after the New Year a little tinkering had the contestants listening to new songs from established songwriters performed by a troupe of regulars. The contestants guessed which song the studio audience would like the most and received $1,000 if they were right. It still didn't work, so the show was cancelled in May.

Fred moved onto another effort for Goodson-Todman, becoming a regular on *What's My Line?* to replace Steve Allen, who was departing to launch *Tonight!* on NBC. Introduced on his first night by Dorothy Kilgallen as "Steve's youngest boy," Fred immediately established how much he was looking forward to playing the game by suggesting to the first contestant, "Why don't you just tell me what it is that you do and it'll save us both a lot of trouble?"

Fred wasn't the strongest player—he correctly guessed a line exactly once, and was so shocked that he fell out of his chair—but he was funny and he had marvelous chemistry with the rest of the panel. He remained with the show until his sudden death on March 17, 1956. The following night's broadcast closed with John Daly and the panel eulogizing Fred.

Arlene Francis: "Fred Allen was a great talent, but a great gentleman, and he shall be sorely missed."

Steve Allen: "Just a few months ago, sitting in this chair, I believe, Fred read a postcard a viewer had sent to *What's My Line?* asking if Fred Allen was Steve Allen's father, and Fred laughed at it. The answer of course was 'no,' but last night, when I heard the sad news, I couldn't have been any more depressed if the answer had been 'yes.'"

Bennett Cerf: "The half-hours that I spent with Fred Allen in the dressing room before *What's My Line?* every Sunday night meant a great deal to me. Goodbye, Fred. Like so many others who loved and appreciated you, we'll never forget you."

May 12

1951 – *Say It with Acting* Ends

Bill Cullen had carved out a cozy living for himself as a host and announcer for numerous radio shows by 1949, but television was clearly the wave of the future. Self-conscious about the possibility of having to walk on camera with his limp (see April 10), Bill was reluctant to move to television. However, if he wanted to keep working, there was no denying that he'd have to try TV eventually.

Bill took his first baby steps in the new medium with a game show, *Look Ma, I'm Acting*, that premiered on Dumont affiliate WNBT in New York on January 14, 1949. It was simply a game of charades contested between two teams of actors and actresses in current Broadway shows. There's no known film of the show. Some sources suggest the game included a segment in which Bill would call a home viewer, who could win prizes by accurately describing what was happening onstage at that moment.

On February 20, the show changed its name to the significantly less-stupid-sounding *Act It Out*, and on May 22 changed it again to *Say It with Acting*. The series stuck with that title all the way to the end of its local run on October 22, 1950.

On January 6, 1951, *Say It with Acting* went national, with a new version airing on NBC. Bill didn't join the national version, and the reins were turned over to Ben Grauer. The national show added team captains Maggi McNellis and Bud Collyer. Bud was far better known as an emcee and would continue to be known in that capacity for the rest of his life, but *Say It with Acting* was the only time that he ever played a game himself.

May 13

1975 – *We've Got Your Number* is Taped

Jack Barry had enjoyed tremendous success with *The Joker's Wild*, which in 1975 was winding up on CBS after three years of delivering mostly strong ratings and solidly rebuilding Jack's once-shattered reputation as a host and producer. Not yet eager to close out his career, however, Jack called on his ex-partner Dan Enright to revive their production company. Their first project was *We've Got Your Number*, a game of dice that didn't make it past the pilot stage.

We've Got Your Number was similar to *High Rollers*, setting up the Barry & Enright Productions pattern of developing shows by tearing down and rebuilding already established games. Two contestants competed against each other for a series of questions. A correct answer gave the contestant the right to roll the dice—well, not roll the dice, but press the button for the dice. *We've Got Your Number* used two eight-foot-high white slabs with lights in them to represent the dice. The dots in the dice shuffled around until the contestant hit the "stop" button. The object of the game was to roll the dice a total of four times and arrange the rolls in sequence from lowest to highest on a grid of four slots. A contestant could lose by rolling a number that couldn't be placed; for example, if a contestant rolled a seven and a nine, and placed them side by side on the grid, rolling an eight would lose the game since there'd be no place to put it.

Two out of three games won a lovely prize and a shot at a hefty sum of money. The ordinary set of the show made an elaborate transformation when it was time for the bonus round. A craps-style table rose out of the floor, the giant dice spun around to reveal two elegant mirrors looking like something from a showboat and a series of chandeliers descended from the ceiling. Even though the show didn't sell, fan should tip their hat to Barry & Enright for clearly investing quite a few bucks into their project.

In the bonus round, the contestant started with $200 and rolled the dice a maximum of seven times. As long as the dice didn't repeat any numbers, the money doubled, for a top maximum payday of $25,600.

Despite the disappointment in failing to get *We've Got Your Number* on the air, Barry & Enright stayed productive in the coming years with a syndicated version of *The Joker's Wild*, *Tic Tac Dough*, *Play the Percentages*, *Bullseye*, *Juvenile Jury*, *Hot Potato* and other games. They didn't bat a thousand, though; some efforts that didn't make it.

Several months after CBS cancelled *Joker*, Jack Barry hosted a pilot at Television City titled *Double Cross*. It was a rather familiar-looking game. The contestants spun a series of three wheels to determine what category would be played and how much each correct answer was worth. The twist in *Double Cross* was that two of the wheels contained crosses. Spinning a cross cost you a turn; spinning two crosses cost you a turn and all the money accumulated up to that point.

In early 1979, Barry & Enright produced a series of pilots for NBC titled *Decisions, Decisions.* Bill Cullen hosted the game, in which star-civilian teams would be shown a list of answers to a question and had to sort them. One member of the team would choose two answers from the list, and the partner would make the final selection as the better of the two answers. Success is never guaranteed; even with Bill Cullen hosting, and even with rising star David Letterman appearing as a player and cracking up Bill and the audience often throughout the pilot, NBC passed on the show. America was deprived of hearing the peculiar theme music whipped up for the show, an instrumental track of "MacArthur Park" accompanying a chorus of singers warbling, "Decisions, decisions."

In 1982, CBS was looking to beef up its daytime lineup with more game shows, and Barry & Enright stepped up to the challenge with an unlikely candidate: a revival of *Twenty One*, the show that had destroyed them nearly twenty-five years earlier. The new version was hosted by Jim Lange. In what may have been the producers' effort to silence whispers of rumors, the categories throughout the game were selected randomly. With stacks of cards arranged in a wheel in front of him, Jim Lange would blindly pick one stack for each round of questions. In an odd rule change, the maximum point value for a question was nine points, which meant it would take at least three questions to reach twenty-one points, but Jim Lange still asked contestants if they wanted to stop the game after the second question.

Unlike the original version of *Twenty One*, this one had a bonus round. The contestant used a remote control to stop a series of flashing numbers in a game that was essentially blackjack against the house. For each number, the contestant decided whether to keep it or give it to the house. Any contestant who could score 21 or force the house to bust won $2,000 and a vacation.

Like *Decisions, Decisions*, the most interesting part of the *Twenty One* pilot might have been the music. If the series had sold, it would have been the only game show credit ever for the Alan Parsons Project.

May 14

1951 – Ernie Kovacs's Network TV Debut

Ernie Kovacs was arguably the first comedian to take full advantage of the visual element of television. Many radio performers who had made the leap from radio to TV did so with minimal adaptations. Their TV shows were largely the same as their radio shows, the action fairly confined and straightforward. Ernie Kovacs wouldn't settle for that.

Ernie had made a name for himself with a bizarre TV morning show called *Three to Get Ready*, a local entry in Philadelphia that served as a predecessor to NBC's *Today* with news and feature stories between the hours of 7:00 a.m. and 9:00 a.m. Ernie became known for the stunts he would pull on the show, broad humor like pouring buckets of water on the weatherman if rain was in the forecast; putting on a gorilla suit and having the camera follow him while he ran through the streets of Philadelphia; introducing "The World's Strongest Ant", and using tricky camera angles to make it appear that a woman was walking on his arm.

The buzz around him became so strong that NBC offered him his own network series, *It's Time for Ernie*. In the coming years, Ernie's shows bounced around various time slots and networks, but the same eclectic mix of elements would always be featured —parodies, eccentric bits involving trick photography or other experimentation, and an army of original characters, including Percy Dovetonsils, Aunt Gruesome, Chef Miklos Molnar and the Nairobi Trio.

As was the case of virtually any rising TV star of the 1950s, Ernie caught the eye of game show producers. Through 1956-57, he appeared as a panelist on a dozen episodes of *What's My Line?* When Fred Allen's 1956 death left his seat vacant for guest panelists to fill, Ernie was among those given a shot. Mark Goodson handed him a list of rules to make sure he had a firm grasp on the game; Ernie promptly lost it, which didn't seem to bother him much.

He made a splash on his first night, though. The panel sat blindfolded, trying to solve the identity of noted industrialist Henry Kaiser. The panel had made it far enough to discern that he shared his name with an automobile when it was Ernie's turn to question.

"Now, this is just a wild guess—but could you be Abraham Lincoln?" Ernie deadpanned. The audience and the rest of the panel cracked up.

The following summer and fall, he returned for eleven more shows. A gossip columnist reported that the show's staff was annoyed when Ernie told people that he planned on taking the night off from the show any time that he felt like going out for a

Sunday dinner. Producer Gil Fates' memoirs paint a more benign picture of what happened: when offered a contract to become a regular panelist, Ernie leveled with them and said he didn't want to get tied down to a weekly gig when he had so many offers for other opportunities. Fates empathized, and Ernie departed for good from *What's My Line?*

In 1959, Ernie took his comedic talents in a unique direction: a panel show of his very own, titled *Take a Good Look*. It was a move that baffled many people, particularly after, according to one reporter, Ernie had rejected more than two hundred offers for other television projects. Ernie was allured by the idea of an eight-hour work week. Putting together a comedy-variety show of his own for several years had just plain worn him out, and hosting a panel game show gave him an opportunity to keep one foot in show business while spending the other six days of the week at home in Beverly Hills with his wife, Edie Adams, and their three children.

So revered was Ernie Kovacs at this point that the sponsor of *Take a Good Look*, Dutch Masters Cigars, conceded to a demand that most sponsors would consider ludicrous: the commercials on *Take a Good Look* would have no spoken dialogue. Ernie was annoyed by hard-sell talking heads on television and wanted to rebel against it with what he called a soft-sell approach. The commercials for Dutch Masters on his show were done in the style of a silent movie, using only visuals and maybe a little music to sell the product, without any voices heard.

Take a Good Look was a Kovacsian spin on *I've Got a Secret*. A contestant was brought out, with a secret revealed to the audience. The celebrity panelists would then be shown a skit, often with Ernie playing one of his signature characters. Buried somewhere in the skit would be a clue to the secret. The panelists would ask yes-or-no questions and, if they couldn't correctly guess the secret, the contestant earned $50. If the panelists remained stumped after a maximum of three skits for each secret, the contestant received a total of $200.

Premiering on October 22, 1959, *Take a Good Look* would enjoy a year and a half on ABC before coming to an end of March 16, 1961. Ten months later, on January 12, 1962, the unique and innovative comic's life came to a tragic end in a car accident. He was forty-two. He's survived by countless admiring performers, including Chevy Chase, David Letterman and Craig Ferguson, who have declared him an influence on their careers.

May 15

1954 – *Bank on the Stars* Moves to NBC

TV AND FILMS GO TOGETHER WHEREVER YOU LOOK. Old TV shows are turned into movies, and if you aren't seeing a movie or a trailer on television, you're seeing an actor or director on a talk show plugging an upcoming film. In the early 1950s, the relationship between the television industry and the film industry wasn't so cozy. In fact, it was tense.

TV changed how Americans sought out entertainment, and filmmakers were sweating. After all, why go out when you can be entertained in the comfort of your own home?

But 1953 was the year of peace offerings. It finally occurred to a few people that television could be used to promote films, and Ed Sullivan began airing movie trailers as part of his Sunday night extravaganza. That came to a quick end, however, when the sponsors objected and incoming mail suggested that the audience preferred live entertainment to clips of movies.

Another olive branch—one that lasted slightly longer—was a game show that premiered in prime time on CBS on June 20, 1953. It was titled *Bank on the Stars*. The host was up-and-comer Jack Paar. It was a memory game; a pair of contestants would be brought onstage and shown a clip of an upcoming film release, usually accompanied by assurance that the film was "exciting," "hilarious," "thrilling" or any other complimentary word that Jack could offer. After viewing the clip, the contestants were asked a series of questions about what they just saw. If both of them answered correctly, they received $100. If only one answered correctly, they received $50. If they both gave wrong answers, the game ended. As a consolation, both contestants were allowed to dip a hand into a barrel of silver dollars before they left.

At the end of the night, after three sets of contestants had played, the top winners returned for the Bank Night Bonus, where they would hear a clip but not see it. A correct answer paid $500.

The game lasted through the summer, ending on August 8. The following May, it headed over to NBC for another summer run. Bill Cullen took the reins, hosting ten episodes. Jimmy Nelson would take over on July 17 and finish out the series on August 21.

May 16

1990 – Jim Henson Dies

It seems unnecessary to devote a paragraph summarizing Jim Henson, the brilliant creator of the Muppets. Is there really anybody out there who doesn't recognize the name or his wild, colorful creations? They've touched just about everything on television—commercials, variety shows, sitcoms, music videos—so of course, they'd have their felt and furry hands in a game show or two…or more.

1 vs. 100 – Oscar the Grouch was a member of The Mob in 2006. Host Bob Saget accidentally referred to him as Grover at one point in the game. Oscar responded by calling Bob Saget "Howie."

Deal or No Deal – On Christmas 2006, the contestant, an ice cream man named Lamar Wilson, had his mother sitting in the audience cheering him on. His mother told a story about how her son had been afraid of Big Bird as a child. After Howie Mandel teased Lamar for a few moments about being afraid of a Muppet, Big Bird surprised Lamar by emerging onstage and hugging him. Big Bird remarked that Lamar reminded him of Snuffy, because Snuffy was afraid of him when they first met, too.

Family Feud – In 2001, The Muppets squared off against the Dixie Chicks in a special week for charity. Kermit the Frog, Mo Frackle, Sweetums, Dr. Phil Van Neuter, Pepe the King Prawn, Johnny Fiami, Bobo the Bear and Rizzo the Rat all joined in the fun during the week.

Years earlier, Richard Dawson had appeared on *Sesame Street* to host "Family Food." The Hungry Family had to name five foods that made a healthy meal. Their grand prize was a horse.

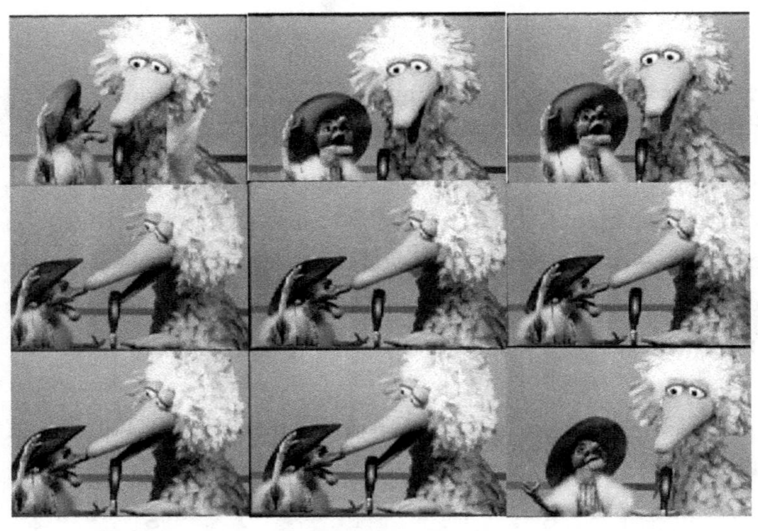

Big Bird meets Madame during an appearance on *The Hollywood Squares*. (Courtesy of Art Alisi)

Hollywood Squares – From 1976-80, Carroll Spinney appeared on fourteen weeks of the show, alternating his Oscar the Grouch and Big Bird alter egos throughout each week of shows. Behind the scenes, Carroll struck up a fast friendship with fellow panelist Gary Burghoff, who portrayed the teddy bear-toting company clerk, Radar, on *M*A*S*H.* Carroll took such a liking to him that he named Big Bird's teddy bear "Radar."

From 2001 to 2004, more Muppets appeared on the panel, including Miss Piggy, Kermit the Frog, Elmo, Gonzo and Bear in the Big Blue House.

Jeopardy! – In 2006, one of the featured categories was "Sesame Street Eats." Each of the five clues was a pre-taped segment in which Alex Trebek appeared on the set of "Sesame Street," every time with a different Muppet, including Elmo, Oscar the Grouch and Big Bird.

To Tell the Truth – Kermit the Frog was a panelist for a week, modeling a jock strap over his head for one game while dealing with a contestant who had invented a specialized form of one.

What's My Line? – Big Bird was the Mystery Guest on July 5, 1973. The audience couldn't contain their delight as the eight-foot-tall six-year-old struggled to sit down next to host Larry Blyden, and then looked at the panelists with wide-eyed curiosity during their questions. After the game, Carroll Spinney emerged without his costume and chatted with the panel about how one goes about operating a Muppet while standing inside it.

Jim Henson was a contestant on November 16, 1974, appearing with Kermit the Frog. The panel was blindfolded as they questioned Jim, who also brought along a variety of hats and wigs. For each question, he would put one on Kermit's head and perform with a different voice.

In return, *What's My Line?* was frequently the subject of

parodies on *Sesame Street*, featuring Arlene Frantic and Bennett Snerf among the panelists. There's even a stronger bond between the two shows that viewers may not realize. *What's My Line?* panelist Bennett Cerf's son Christopher composed much of the music for *Sesame Street*, while his other son, Jonathan, authored *Big Bird's Red Book*.

Wheel of Fortune – Kermit and Gonzo appeared in 1999 to promote the movie *Muppets in Space. Sesame Street* viewers were treated to "Squeal of Fortune" with host Pat Playjacks in one memorable segment.

Who Wants to be a Millionaire? – For a special celebrity edition in 2000, Kermit the Frog, dressed like host Regis Philbin, appeared in the audience as a guest of player Jon Stewart. When *The Muppet Movie* was the subject of a question for Drew Carey later in the night, Kermit helped him cheat a little bit to figure out the correct answer.

May 17

2011 - Ron Greenberg's Eightieth Birthday Party

JOURNEYMAN PRODUCER RON GREENBERG ORGANIZED what he called "a stag party" for his eightieth birthday, bringing in friends like Heatter-Quigley producer Art Alisi, announcer Randy West, host Mark L. Wahlberg, and all names in between. The high point of the evening was a videotape montage recapping Greenberg's entire career in television, showing clips of many of his shows, and even clips of pilots that didn't get picked up, each pilot clip accompanied by a buzzer and a flashing X. Friends and contacts from a fifty-five-year career came together for a nostalgic night to celebrate a friend.

When asked how good it felt to have his friends coming together to commemorate the birthday, Greenberg brushes it aside and says, "You know what was great about that party? There were people there who hadn't spoken to each other in twenty-five years. They had lost contact. And they were chatting and having a great time together. You know, in show business, you drift apart like that, and it was wonderful to see everybody come together again."

For the birthday boy, the greatest present was the chance to bring together old acquaintances. That, more than anything, sums up the spirit of Ron Greenberg, a jolly, outgoing, confident people person utterly devoid of pettiness or grudges. He considers himself a lucky man and looks back at his life without regret, but with excitement at all the things he got to do.

The lucky life of Ron Greenberg began on May 15, 1931 in Brooklyn, New York, but his father's work as a clothing salesman meant the family had to uproot and go wherever the work was; Ron's mother used to joke that all of the furniture was on dollies. Ron did most of his growing up in Brooklyn. He was fascinated by radio, listening mostly to *Captain Midnight*, *Jack Armstrong the All-American Boy*, and a quiz show, *Quick as a Flash*. He had a showmanship streak in him, which he manifested by putting together makeshift variety shows with his brother and performing them on the porch for the rest of the family. He also did magic shows, charging "five bucks and free lunch" per performance. In high school, he was on the basketball team. His interests in basketball and broadcasting led him to consider a career in sportscasting. He was a big fan of Marty Glickman, a former track & field Olympian who became an enduring presence behind the microphone for New York sports teams.

When Ron was in high school, the family moved to Brookline, Massachusetts, where only three houses in the neighborhood had television. Ron's first exposure to television was voyages down the street to watch *Texaco Star Theater* with Milton Berle, boxing, and wrestling matches at the neighbors' houses. He recalled, "TV was the most exciting thing. I don't claim to be clairvoyant, but you could see that something big was happening."

Ron eventually went to school at Boston University, where he earned his B.S. in Communications. He got to try his hand in broadcasting, providing color commentary for football games and even learning how to use the equipment...sort of. "I learned how to operate a wooden television camera. Boston U didn't even have real equipment yet, I learned how to be a broadcaster with fake cameras and fake boards."

After graduating from college, Ron made one more move with his family to New York City, where he promptly headed to an Army office to register for the draft. It was something of a family business. His mother had been a yeomanette, his father had served in the Navy and his brother had been in fifty-five missions in North Korea. Ron went to Fort Dix and got assigned to the Honor Guard in Washington, D.C. He performed ceremonial details, performed on the drill team, and even worked as a regimental announcer.

Once he got discharged, he still had an interest in broadcasting and show business, but his focus changed. Ron came to realize that Marty Glickman wasn't going to retire any time soon; besides, being a radio announcer required plying your trade in small town after small town and gradually climbing the ladder to get to larger broadcasting markets. Ron didn't have the patience for it, so he decided that he'd have an easier time finding work behind the scenes. He got a job at 30 Rockefeller Plaza as an NBC page, starting off as a "red braid," a part time page, where his duties involved delivering salami to Steve Allen so he could have a snack before *The Tonight Show*. He also seated the kids in the peanut gallery for *Howdy Doody* and performed various duties for Sid Caesar, Ernie Kovacs, Perry Como, and Eddie Fisher. He eventually got promoted to "blue braid" (a full-time page) and then "white braid" (full-time and entrusted with the keys to the complex).

His first break came from a game show producer, and the path for Ron Greenberg's life was set. "Bob Noah gave me my very first job in this business; he was the kindest, most gentle man, and I always had an affinity for him."

The job was at Jack Barry & Dan Enright Productions, at the time a white-hot entity with hits like *Tic Tac Dough* and *Twenty One* on NBC. He was charged with recruiting children to be contestants for special episodes of *Tic Tac Dough* and answering the office phones for the contestant line that viewers were encouraged to call if they wanted to take a test and try to be on the show.

Ron remembers, "When I answered the phone, I went by the name Leslie York. The reason for that was that Leslie York was a gender-neutral name, so anybody who was in the office that day could be assigned to answering that phone, and we all went by the name Leslie York for that part of the job. The funny thing was I had to use a device called a Hush-a-Phone (a small attachment that would amplify the speaker's voice so even a whisper could be heard loudly and clearly) because I would take the phone calls while somebody was sitting in the office right next to me taking the test."

The job worked out well for Ron and he eventually made his way to the studio to work as a production assistant on *Concentration* and *Dough Re Mi*, but when the quiz show scandal hit, the Barry & Enright empire fell apart and Ron had to leave and seek new work. He became an associate producer for "Charge Account," the game show portion of *The Jan Murray Show* and then went to work with Gil Cates, future Academy Awards ceremony producer, on *Camouflage* for ABC.

After *Camouflage* got cancelled, his wife took a vacation to visit her family in California and spotted an ad in the paper seeking a producer for *Seven Keys*, the popular ABC game show produced on the west coast. Ron applied and got hired, eventually leaving *Seven Keys* to go to work for Monty Hall on the staff of *Let's Make a Deal* in the early months of that series.

"I actually left the show before the contestants even started wearing costumes, that's how little time I spent there."

Ron had a positive relationship with bosses Monty Hall and Stefan Hatos, but he got a generous offer from Merv Griffin to move back to New York City and produce game shows for his company. At the time, Merv's pet project was a new idea in which contestants were given answers and had to supply the questions.

Ron hastily, and modestly, says, "*Jeopardy!* was a team effort for us, but for the record, I really had nothing to do with the show once it went on the air."

Ron worked with Merv Griffin for three years, producing *Word for Word*, *Let's Play Post Office*, and *Reach for the Stars* in that time. He quit to develop a game show of his own creation for NBC. When NBC was slow to pick it up, Ron found work producing *Dream House* and *Sale of the Century*. But by the end of 1969, NBC had picked up Ron's creation, *The Who, What or Where Game* (see December 29), and after a slow start, it turned into a hit. When the show went off the air, Ron teamed up with another producer, Don Lipp, and got two more shows on the air, *The Big Showdown* and *The Money Maze* (see December 23). He also produced numerous pilots, including *The Couples Race* with Mike Darrow, and *Word Grabbers* with Art James and Jim Lange, and *Wheeler Dealers* with "Cousin" Brucie Morrow, none of which didn't make it on the air.

The Big Showdown and *The Money Maze* were both short-lived;

about six months apiece. Even with the five-year success of *The Who, What, or Where Game*, Ron was still "the little guy" in the world of TV game shows.

He explains, "In 1975, there were a lot of game shows on the air and—I don't say this to complain, it's just true—all the clout was with Mark Goodson & Bill Todman, and Bob Stewart to some extent. So if I had a pilot, and those guys had a pilot, well, what are my odds? Even though I had faith in my shows and I knew I was doing good work, I felt like the junk man."

In the late 1970s, the game show business began migrating to California and Ron migrated with it after receiving a phone call from Jack Barry & Dan Enright, eagerly telling him that they were re-launching their old company. Ron helped rebuild the once-ailing company, acting as a key figure in getting *Tic Tac Dough* back in production and serving as executive producer for many Barry & Enright properties, including *The Joker's Wild* (which sometimes used "Who, What, or Where" as a category), *Joker, Joker, Joker*, *Bullseye*, and *Play the Percentages*.

In 1982, Greenberg received an offer from producer Alan Landsburg (*In Search Of...*, *Kate & Allie*) and joined his production company. He developed *The Pop 'N Rocker Game* as well as a comedy show, *The Mac and Jamie Comedy Hour*, which ran for two years. He also developed numerous pilots for NBC.

By the late 1980s, Greenberg was working on adapting Nickelodeon's hit, *Double Dare*, into a game show for adults, *Celebrity Double Dare*. A pilot was made, but it wasn't picked up. A former associate, Bob Synes, called him, seeking help developing a new game show for kids. Greenberg eagerly walked away from *Celebrity Double Dare* and helped bring *Fun House* to fruition. Ron received residuals from the series because so many of his ideas were used, but he only produced the pilot. By the time *Fun House* went to air, Ron had taken an offer from Dick Clark to co-produce game shows.

In 1990, he joined Dick Clark Productions and Buena Vista Television, a Disney company, to create *The Challengers* (see September 3), an updated version of *The Who, What or Where Game*. The group also teamed up with Monty Hall to revive *Let's Make a Deal* for NBC. For a variety of reasons, neither venture was successful, although Greenberg remembered it as a positive experience and speaks highly today of Monty Hall, Dick Clark, and many associates at Buena Vista.

In the coming years, he teamed back up with Don Lipp to sell game show formats overseas. In the late 2000s, Ron finally got a crack at being a master of ceremonies himself, hosting the radio game show *Anyone Can Play...But Don't Call Us, We'll Call You* for Shokus Internet Radio.

When asked what he enjoyed most about a fifty-year career as a respected and successful producer, Ron's thoughts are not of himself: he immediately and eagerly talks about the people he worked with as the greatest benefit. "I'm very lucky, I got to work with some of the nicest people. I never had one ounce of trouble with any of them. We were close, they were concerned, they cared, and we did great things together. I was proud to know all of them. That's not quite a great story...it's probably not what someone wants to hear, you know, when they say 'What's so-and-so really like?' They want some story from behind the scenes. And I just don't have stories like that. They were all wonderful people."

The feeling, presumably, is mutual.

May 18

1924 – Jack Whitaker's Birthday

Jack Whitaker is best known for a long career of sportscasting, calling the action and filing reports for CBS and ABC. He covered the Triple Crown, the Super Bowl, golf championships and just about everything in between. In 1966, Whitaker branched out a little bit by hosting a game show, *The Face is Familiar*.

Behind the scenes, *The Face is Familiar* will probably go down in history for jumping from developmental stages to series faster than any other game show in history. Goodson-Todman spent a decade refining *Tattletales* before it went on the air. Monty Hall prepared for nearly five years to get *Let's Make a Deal* off the ground. From conception to pitching the idea to the network, *The Face is Familiar* took about one hour.

Bob Stewart had just launched his own production company with a single show on the air, *Eye Guess*. Since his only show was a hit, he had an immediately credible name in the game show business. One day at 5 p.m., Fred Silverman, head of programming for CBS, called Bob out of the blue and said, "We need a summer replacement series. Have any ideas?"

"Sure," Bob lied. He didn't really have a new idea to show to anybody, but he figured it would be foolish to have a prime time opportunity dropped in his lap and pass it up.

Silverman replied, "Come on over."

Now Bob Stewart was in a bind. He probably figured the next step was booking a time for a meeting, and he would at least have a few days to conjure up some sort of new game. Silverman wanted it then and there. Bob bluffed about being tied up with something and said he'd be over in one hour.

Bob ran outside, grabbed a pair of scissors, and cut up some pictures in a magazine. He got to the meeting and described an idea where contestants would see a picture of a celebrity cut up into pieces, and had to figure out who the celebrity was.

Fred liked it, and *The Face is Familiar* went on the air on May 9. The finished product was a surprisingly high-tech game for 1966. The photo puzzles were displayed with a $10,000 device called Vismo, which had been developed by a team of employees at NBC. It used a series of lights and buttons to divide photos into sections and rearrange them on the screen in whatever order was needed.

Two celebrity-contestant teams competed. Facing a game board divided into seven segments, the four players took turns answering questions asked by Jack Whitaker. For each correct answer, the player picked a segment and saw a piece of a celebrity's photo. The seven pieces were jumbled, so even when fully revealed, the image could stump the players. If all the segments were revealed and nobody could figure it out, more questions were asked, and a correct answer permitted the player to select two puzzle pieces to switch places. The first team to figure out the famous face won the game and $150.

For the bonus round, "Three of a Kind," the players viewed three sets of eyes and were asked to choose the set that belonged to a specific star. A correct guess paid $50. They repeated the process with three sets of noses for an additional $50, and then with three mouths for a chance to double all of the money earned by that point, for a maximum payday of $500.

In Bob Stewart's own words, it was "a horrendous idea," but it got favorable reviews from critics, one of whom called the show "pleasant and involving." Despite that, after one month Bob retooled the game, eliminating the questions and simply having the players alternate picking and rearranging numbers. On September 3, the show left the airwaves, never to return. Bob Stewart instead focused his energy on less "horrendous" ideas.

BONUS ROUND

You're about to see three sets of eyes, three noses and three mouths. Can you identity the features of your favorite hosts?

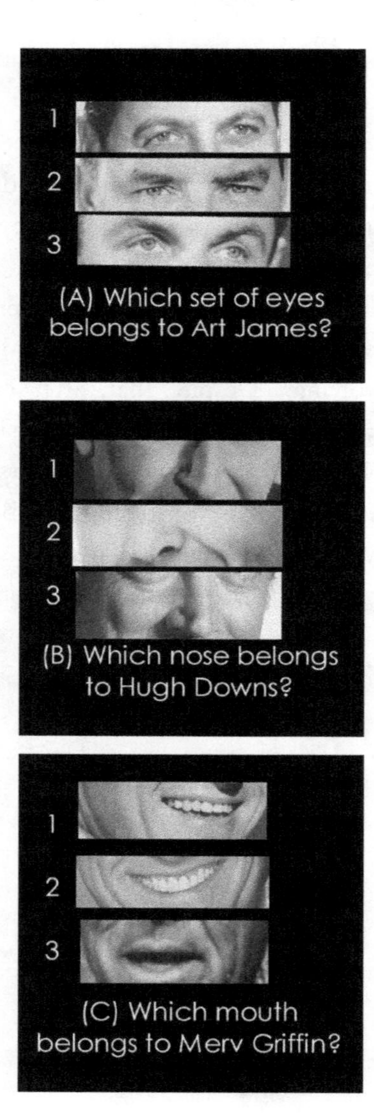

1
2
3
(A) Which set of eyes belongs to Art James?
1
2
3
(B) Which nose belongs to Hugh Downs?
1
2
3
(C) Which mouth belongs to Merv Griffin?

May 19

1984 – Big Bucks...*Very* Big Bucks

Peter Tomarken on the set of his signature show. The five lights at the bottom of his podium alerted the contestants when they were allowed to press their buttons to answer a question. (Jason Hernandez Collection)

In 1983, producer Bill Carruthers dusted off a short-lived show of his called *Second Chance* that had aired on ABC in 1977. He gave it a high-tech makeover and tweaked the rules a little bit, and voila! *Press Your Luck* debuted on September 19, 1983 on CBS.

The new game, hosted by Peter Tomarken, rejoined by his former *Hit Man* announcer, Rod Roddy, pitted three contestants against each other. To start the game, they'd listen to four questions, ring in and hope to supply correct answers earning "spins." Those spins were redeemed on the big board, a massive technological marvel for the time, consisting of eighteen squares that flashed a variety of cash awards, merchandise, instructions ("Go Back Two Spaces" or "Pick a Corner"), bonus spins, or the dreaded Whammy—a red goblin with a dollar sign on its chest, smiling evilly in every square where it appeared. Contestants pressed their buttons to stop a light that flashed from square to square, earning whatever was in the square where the light stopped. A Whammy took away everything the contestant had accumulated; to add insult to injury, each Whammy was accompanied by a brief animated cartoon, showing the Whammy celebrating the contestant's failure.

Contestants could keep spinning as long as they wanted, as long as they still had spins and so long as they didn't accumulate four Whammys, in which case they forfeited the remaining spins and had to stop playing. If contestants were getting fearful of the Whammy, they could also pass their remaining spins to an opponent and hope they got zapped by the maniacal little creature on their turn.

The game mesmerized viewers. Although the game was mostly luck, strategy was an important consideration; the possibility of losing everything on every single turn guaranteed a climactic finish every day; the bright, shiny game board with every color of the rainbow, flashing lights, a "boop-boop-boop" that emitted

A chance at thousands of dollars in cash and prizes looms in the background. The massive board had a secret. Only the most alert viewers figured it out. (Jason Hernandez Collection)

with every spin undoubtedly turned small children everywhere into game show fans for life. The animated Whammy cartoons—drawn by future film director Savage Steve Holland—gave the show a hook and an identity that couldn't be confused with any other show. The game's mantra—"Big Bucks! No Whammys!"—

shouted by contestants as they wished themselves luck at the beginning of each turn, endures as a part of pop culture to this day.

And there was just something about the game that brought out raw emotion from contestants as they got absorbed into the battle to accumulate more and dodge the Whammys. A contestant named Karen kept screaming "A pool table for Dan!" on every spin until she finally got it, then let out an anguished scream of "Ooohhhh noooooooo!" when she lost it to a Whammy moments later. One named Gene leapt from his chair after a big win and made it a point to look into each camera and let out a triumphant scream. There was Jim, whose foul mouth after hitting a Whammy somehow slipped past the CBS censors.

One of the earliest big winners on *Press Your Luck* was future game show announcer Randy West; not only did he clean up, but in the process, he discovered a quirk about that big board that caused big repercussions much later.

LET'S MEET OUR CHAMPION: RANDY WEST

An exclusive interview for This Day in Game Show History

I knew Rod Roddy through a mutual friend. *Press Your Luck* was a brand-new show, it hadn't been on the air yet. I was there for shows nine, ten, and eleven. I knew Rod was doing game shows, but I didn't know which one and I hadn't heard of *Press Your Luck*. I get to the studio, and I hear Rod's voice, and I think, "Oh my god, that's Rod, I know his voice."

So they bring the contestants onstage for the next taping, and Rod reads the name tags as we emerge, and he introduces us to the audience. I walk out with my opponents, and he says "Here are our contestants, Pam, and Maggie, and...*Randy*." And we looked at each other and I turned my head away. Rod was just the announcer, he didn't have access to any game material, but that might have been a standards and practices issue.

What I remember about being in that studio was how big the game board was and how noisy it was. The game board had a bunch of slide projectors in it, more than fifty, and they would switch back and forth constantly to change the squares, so fifty slide projectors changing; when you sat in the studio, all you could hear from the board was the ka-clunk, ka-clunk, ka-clunk of the shutters flipping back and forth. I remembered watching the show a few weeks later and being amazed that the sound didn't come through on TV.

I was the first contestant to win a car on the show. There was a guy on that episode who was an attorney, and he was very high-voiced and persnickety, and very important-acting. And every time he pulled ahead, he'd look down at me. And we're at a point late in the game where it looked like he was about to win. I was down $5,000 and he was pretty much counting his money right there, and I had one spin left and had to hit something worth $5,000 or more, and I land on a car and the car is worth enough for me to win the game, and he was dumbfounded.

After the game, I went up to him to be a good sport and shake his hand. He wouldn't shake my hand; he would not even look at me. And I thought to myself, "Dude, it's a game show, come on." So I thought if he won't shake my hand, I'll pat him on the back. He was wearing a suit, and I patted him on the back and got my hand wet. He had sweated completely through his suit.

I had a friend in the audience for the first two episodes I did… he was a film professor at UCLA. And he says, "Randy, there's a pattern to that board." I said, "You sure?" He said, "There's two or three," and he starts showing me with his finger, "There's one where the light goes here, and then down here, and then it goes to the big money space." But I couldn't grasp it sight-unseen without being able to see the game board, and I was afraid I'd rely on it and it wouldn't work.

So I come back for the taping of show #11, and I see what the light is doing, and I think to myself, "My god, that's what he was talking about." But the game was too nerve-racking and I didn't trust myself to always use it, and the board didn't always do what he described, just some of the time, so I didn't do it. But somebody else did, you know.

What Randy and his friend noticed, that most viewers wouldn't stumble upon once *Press Your Luck* went on the air, was that the flashing light that seemed to bounce aimlessly from square to square was not actually a random event. With limited technology at the time, the game board utilized a computer that had five patterns of flashing lights programmed into it. Before the series began, the staff voiced concerns that a low number of patterns could be memorized by attentive viewers and contestants. The staff asked CBS executives to consider purchasing a computer with more memory to accommodate more patterns or random patterns. CBS rejected the proposal, feeling it was an unnecessary expense.

The days before May 19, 1984 were very typical days for the offices of *Press Your Luck*. A number of people replying to newspaper ads and the "contestant call" inserted into each episode of the show had arrived to audition for a chance to become contestants. One scruffy-bearded man named Michael Larsen introduced himself and told a peculiar story; he lived in Ohio, drove an ice cream truck in the summer but spent the rest of the year unemployed, and that he had come straight to Los Angeles to try out for *Press Your Luck*.

The contestant coordinators were torn; he played the game well, but there was something odd about him that nobody could quite put their finger on. The other contestant-hopefuls in the room recalled later that they sensed something strange about him, too, and just couldn't figure out what. One contestant coordinator, Bobby Edwards, said he didn't trust Michael and didn't want him on the show. Producer Bill Mitchell overruled him and called him back to be on the show.

The taping happened on a Saturday and Michael's game, episode #188, taped late in the day. Michael had jitters in the first question round, answering "fifty-dollar bill" to a question about coins and wincing visibly when he realized he had blown it. He earned three spins and moved onto the big board.

He hit a Whammy on his first spin, cringed, but chuckled about it, seemingly shrugging off that laughter as he pressed twice more. $1,250 the second time, and $1,250 the third time, finishing the round with a respectable total of $2,500.

They moved onto the second question round and Michael gradually eased into things. Now more comfortable than he had been in the first half of the game, he accumulated seven spins. The game moved into one more run at the big board, and Michael was the first contestant to take his spins. And something astonishing began happening…

$4,000 + one spin…$5,000 + one spin…$1,000 + one spin…a trip to Kauai…$4,000 + one spin…$500 + one spin…$700 + one spin…$1,000 + one spin…$750 + one spin…$5,000 + one spin…$2,250…a new sailboat…$3,000 + one spin…$500 + one spin…$4,000 + one spin…

The staffers on stage and the control room immediately recognized what had happened. Their premonition from those days before the show premiered had turned into a reality. The taping couldn't be stopped. Everybody just had to brace themselves, sit back, and wait for this guy to finish playing…if he ever did.

Michael Larsen was a man obsessed with get rich quick schemes, and during his extended spell of unemployment, he had assembled a wall of TVs in his living room and would watch several shows at once, looking for the next big opportunity. He was fascinated with game shows and *Press Your Luck* caught his eye early on. After watching the show purposefully and intensely for several weeks, he had broken the game's "code." He had memorized the five patterns that the game board used, and immediately headed for Los Angeles to make his fortune.

$750 + one spin…$3,000 + one spin…$1,000 + one spin…$1,000 + one spin…$1,000 + one spin…$3,000 + one spin…$750 + one spin…$3,000 + one spin…

The audience was alive as it had never been before. There was a constant wave of cheers rolling toward Michael, who reveled in his success while simultaneously cracking under pressure for it. Watching the episode now, one can see his face constantly alternating between a broad smile and sweat-soaked panic with every spin. Even Peter Tomarken and the other contestants became concerned for him. But Michael kept his concentration and kept on spinning and winning.

$500 + one spin…$500 + one spin…$500 + one spin…$4,000 + one spin…$5,000 + one spin…$4,000 + one spin…$5,000 + one spin…$4,000 + one spin…$4,000 + one spin…$500 + one spin…$4,000 + one spin…$3,000 + one spin…$4,000 + one spin…$500 + one spin…$4,000 + one spin…$5,000 + one spin…$3,000 + one spin…

Michael had broken six figures by that point, with $102,851 in the till. He finally had enough. He passed the four spins he couldn't get rid of, and the audience gave him a standing ovation. The game wasn't over yet by a long shot though. Host Peter Tomarken was the first to recognize it. He ignored the standing ovation and moved right on to dealing with Michael's opponents and their spins, rushing through the game, under the impression that the game was now pressed for time and that it would have to be squeezed into a thirty-minute broadcast.

Remarkably, after Michael passed his spins, one of his opponents immediately hit a Whammy. Even more remarkably, that same opponent then immediately hit the $5,000 + one spin space twice in a row. It was as if Michael had rubbed off on him.

Michael's other opponent managed to collect $9,385 in cash and prizes and passed her three remaining spins to Michael, who immediately looked discouraged by that call.

$4,000 + one spin…$750 + one spin…a trip to the Bahamas. He passed two spins back to his opponent, and she couldn't even come close. The game ended, and Michael finished with the amazing sum of $110,237.

After the game was over, Peter interviewed Michael, who told the aw-shucks story of how he was wearing a shirt that he paid only sixty-five cents for, and that his daughter's birthday was the previous day, but he didn't have the money to buy her anything. He promised she would get a few gifts after this turn of events, though.

Peter asked him why he kept pressing his luck and Michael was evasive in his answers. "Number one, it felt right, and the second was, I still had seven spins and if I passed them, somebody could have done what I did. That was a lot of spins to pass."

The taping concluded, and the staff's job was just beginning, it turned out. CBS was convinced they had a cheater on their hands and the network was determined to deny payment. They began checking the paperwork that Michael had filled out, looking for any loophole that would render him ineligible. They couldn't find one. It was clear that he had memorized the patterns on the board, but CBS and the production company quickly realized that there was no rule on the record that stopped a contestant from doing that.

There was also a debate about whether or not to air the games. Whereas today, a prime time game show touts the fact that a million-dollar will happen on next week's show, CBS was embarrassed by the fact that they had a system that could be beaten, and that somebody had done exactly that. Michael's game—divided into two episodes in post-production because it had taken so long—eventually did air.

The shows were treated just like any others, with no promotion or press releases. The network didn't want them shown at all, in fact, but they lost that battle. The games aired only once; when reruns of the show were sold into syndication and to USA Network later in the decade, Michael Larsen's episodes were not included.

$110,000, sadly turned out to be not-quite-enough for a man driven by a desire for more. A few months after his big score, Michael Larsen saw an opportunity to cash in with a contest on another game show. *Sale of the Century* presented a home viewer contest in which the contestants' final scores were combined to form a six-digit number. Viewers were encouraged to mail in any one-dollar bill that had those six digits in the correct order; any viewer who did would win a share of a $40,000 cash jackpot. Michael went straight to the bank and withdrew everything he had won, in the form of one-dollar bills, spending every day sorting through the money to find a winning bill. The money disappeared late one night while Michael was out of the house.

Michael was also susceptible to assorted schemes and scams and his money gradually dwindled. Michael disappeared a short time later, and his brother got a strange visit from FBI agents, asking where Michael was. Nobody in the family knew. Michael stayed largely in hiding, emerging to give interviews to *TV Guide* and *Good Morning America* after the film *Quiz Show* was released in 1994.

Michael died in 1999, largely penniless and in hiding. Most of his family didn't even know where he lived until they were notified of his death; he had been living in Florida. His penchant for scams had alienated him from his loved ones. His wife left him after he accused her of stealing money. His son refused to speak to him in his final days. It was a sad ending to a rags-to-riches-to-rags story.

Whatever type of man Michael was away from his fifteen minutes of game show fame, he earned the respect of CBS executives, *Press Your Luck* staff, and his opponents. When Game Show Network produced a documentary about the scandal, host Peter Tomarken said, "He was guilty of nothing more than being enterprising. For what he did, I actually think he was underpaid."

May 20

1973 - *Sports Challenge* Premieres on CBS

Dick Enberg asks questions to legendary baseball players Waite Hoyt, John Vander Meer, Wally Post, Ray Fosse, Alvin Dark, and Ken Harrelson on *Sports Challenge*. (Fred Wostbrock Collection)

"This is a country that loves sports. It also loves nostalgia and trivia. *Sports Challenge* combines them in a package that includes the best of then and now." –Associated Press review

For what it was, *Sports Challenge* was as well-crafted as it could be. Legends of the sports world came together and, no longer able to put up the strong games they were capable of as active competitors, competed on a more even playing field: a trivia contest. And yet, producer Gerry Gross, the mind behind *Sports Challenge*, didn't merely toss sports legends and trivia in front of the viewers and hope that was sufficient. The game was a very engaging half-hour.

The weekly program premiered in syndication during 1971 and stayed for eight seasons. In 1973, a second episode aired each weekend on CBS. The host was Dick Enberg, already a celebrated play-by-play man for the Angels, Rams and Bruins. During his run on *Sports Challenge*, he joined NBC Sports, where he remained for twenty-five years before jumping to CBS.

Two teams, each comprising three renowned players from a specific franchise, would watch a series of film clips. For each clip, host Dick Enberg asked a question about the game or the players. Ringing in with a correct answer scored ten points and an opportunity to score more points with two bonus "free-throw" questions. The final film clip of the day, the Classic Round, was worth thirty points.

The climax of each game was the Bonus Biography. With the silhouette of a famous athlete as the backdrop, the teams listened to a series of clues from announcer Johnny Gilbert. Ringing in with a correct answer awarded one point for every second left on the clock. The team in the lead at the end of the game received $1,000 worth of sports equipment for the team's favorite charity and returned the following week to face new opponents.

An amazing lineup of legends appeared each week; over eight years, Joe Louis, Ted Williams, Joe DiMaggio, Red Auerbach, Dizzy Dean, Satchel Paige, Deacon Jones, Merlin Olsen, Gaylord Perry, Mickey Mantle, Joe Namath, Johnny Bench and Billy Martin were part of the all-star roster that did battle with their buzzers. The spark of competition lived on in all the players. One article about the show described contestants chatting in the green room as they waited. When Satchel Paige walked in the room, one of his opponents that day, Dizzy Dean, looked at him and asked, "Was Abraham Lincoln a crouch hitter?"

Trash talking was alive and well on the set of *Sports Challenge*, yet so were strong feelings of mutual respect. Gerry Gross marveled at the frequent sight of contestants asking each other for autographs at the end of each game. As it turned out, the reason the show worked so well, with such competitive games, was that in addition to being great stars of sports, these legends were great fans of sports.

May 21

1924 – Peggy Cass' Birth

Peggy Cass joined host Bud Collyer and fellow regular Kitty Carlisle in 1960, beginning a nearly two-decade run on *To Tell the Truth*.

Longtime Goodson-Todman director Franklin Heller once said that casting a panel for a game show was a bit like casting a play. Yes, it's important to assemble people who can play the game well, but it's also important for the personalities to complement each other. Every panelist must contribute something unique and create a yin/yang dynamic. On the surface, Peggy Cass' distinguished career in Broadway and films seems to put her in the same realm as fellow *To Tell the Truth* panelist Kitty Carlisle. In reality, the two women couldn't be more different. Kitty brought worldly elegance and grace to the panel. Peggy Cass was pure brass and sass.

Peggy spent years waiting for a break in acting. She attended the Cambridge Latin School, where she was a member of the drama club for three years without a single speaking part. She joined a USO troupe but didn't appear in any shows. She finally got her break as an understudy for the musical *Born Yesterday* and as a member of the main cast in *Touch and Go*. Her defining role was that of Agnes Gooch in *Auntie Mame*, for which she won a Tony; when the musical became a film, she was nominated for an Oscar.

Having found her defining role in film and on Broadway, she didn't search very long before landing her defining role in television, playing the part of, well, Peggy Cass. After a hilarious spot on Jack Paar's *Tonight Show*, America discovered what a naturally spunky, witty woman she was underneath the characters she portrayed. She joined the panel of *To Tell the Truth* for the first time in 1960 and became a regular.

As a panelist, she shone by revealing that beneath that accomplished exterior were the heart and mind of a pop culture junkie. When lyricist Tim Rice was a contestant, Peggy was the first member of the panel to recognize the cut from *Jesus Christ*

Superstar that Garry Moore played at the start of the game. After a game involving William Hanna, she told Hanna to ignore advocacy groups' criticism and continue making Tom & Jerry cartoons "good and violent, the way I like 'em."

Peggy had a bluntness about her that made her stand out. When Alex Haley was a guest, Peggy casually mentioned having ancestors who wound up in bogs. One contestant advocated for heavy people by noting that many foreign countries celebrate the overweight; Peggy fired back, "That's because it's an economic accomplishment! They don't have enough to eat!" She argued with a stuntman when she didn't believe he had achieved a thirty-foot jump.

After all of the effort she had put into launching an acting career, her legacy was playing a game as herself. Looking back at that change in direction, in 1993 she told a newspaper reporter, "I loved doing it."

Peggy was welcomed back to the show year after year after year, serving as a regular panelist from 1960-1978, returning for frequent appearances during the 1980-81 season and taking a few final turns at playing the game in 1990. She died in 1999. *People* magazine called upon her panel mates to eulogize her. Kitty Carlisle recalled Peggy playfully calling her "Madame Butterfly" on a day when Kitty showed up for a taping in a chiffon gown while Peggy wore a sweater. Orson Bean remembered, "She was always laughing. She was just a joy to be around."

May 22

1910 – Johnny Olson's Birth

Johnny Olson, every audience's best friend.
(Author's Collection)

"Come on down!"
"Get ready to match the stars!"
"Number one, what is your name please?"
"Let's all play *What's...My...Line?*"

One voice was responsible for all of those distinctive greetings. Johnny Olson didn't have the typical rich baritone announcer's voice, but he had an enthusiasm and a down-to-earth sincerity that connected with viewers unlike anybody else.

Johnny Olson was the tenth child born into a family of dairy farmers in Windom, Minnesota. As a teenager, he worked a part-time job at a jewelry store; one day, he wandered over to an electrician's repair shop and saw that the electrician had pieced together a crude radio transmitter. Johnny sang a song into the microphone and enjoyed it so much that he returned again and again to perform on pirate broadcasts, thinking of it as an amusing way to pass the time. To his amazement, he began receiving fan mail.

Johnny's father didn't think much of his son's skills as a singer and urged him to pursue a more practical career. His older sister Pearl, a self-taught pianist, encouraged Johnny to ignore such a request and pursue his newfound ambitions for show business. Finding himself more and more fascinated by radio, Johnny built a crude device of his own called a "crystal set," the same means by which many future broadcasters of his generation discovered radio. It was a homemade device fashioned from an oatmeal canister, a pebble-sized chunk of a natural mineral, a small wire and a set of headphones. From his family's farm in Minnesota, Johnny managed to pick up broadcasts from all across America and even a few from Mexico and Cuba.

Johnny spent the remainder of his teenage years honing his performing skills, singing and acting at local theaters and talent shows. By the time he finished high school, he had an unpaid, but regular, gig singing under the name "The Buttermilk Kid" for a station in Poynette, Wisconsin. Before he turned eighteen, he was working paid jobs in much larger Madison, Wisconsin, singing and acting as "Uncle Johnny" for a children's program. By the time he reached adulthood, he was the manager of a new AM station; at age eighteen, he was the youngest radio station manager in America.

Johnny did a little bit of everything on the station. He played the piano, sang, delivered farm reports, spun records, delivered sermons, wrote and performed sketch comedy, provided play-by-play commentary for sports and even stepped up as repairman, often fixing glitches in the equipment while he was on the air delivering the news.

Johnny briefly veered into professional singing, performing with two big brass bands, but he found he missed radio. He moved to South Dakota to go back to work in radio and just as he had before, did a little bit of everything. He moved on to Milwaukee; during this, *Radio Guide* held a poll asking readers to vote for the best radio announcer in America. Johnny placed number thirty-seven in the poll, which was quite remarkable, because he was heard on only one station and wasn't known nationally yet.

In 1941, Johnny set his sights on bigger things and moved to Hollywood, where he hosted several programs for station KMPC, later the radio home of Gary Owens, Wink Martindale and Geoff Edwards. This marked the first significant struggle of his broadcasting career. He had so much trouble finding consistent work that, to hedge his bets, he recorded broadcasts on discs and sent them to Milwaukee so that his large and loyal audience could continue tuning in.

Johnny finally hit paydirt with *Johnny Olson's Rumpus Room*, an early form of *American Bandstand*. Each week from 10:30 p.m. to midnight, three hundred teenagers would come to the studio, chat with Johnny and dance while Johnny played tunes for them and for the audience at home. The show was so successful that NBC took it national, and it stayed on the air until 1948. In 1949, a TV version became the first daytime network entertainment series to emanate from New York. In addition to the TV version of *Johnny Olson's Rumpus Room*, Johnny's weekly itinerary in 1949 included more than twenty half-hour radio broadcasts.

Johnny had initially gone to New York to act as a substitute host on a late night broadcast, but he impressed the bosses so much that he kept getting new assignments, including a weekly talent contest, his own regular late night series, a daytime music program and a quiz show. His breakout success was an audience participation show, *Ladies Be Seated* (see June 26).

Increasingly, game shows were among Johnny's assignments in radio and early television. For radio, he hosted *Movie Quiz*, *Second Chance*, *Get Rich Quick*, *What's My Name* and *Whiz Quiz*. For television, he hosted *Fun for the Money*, *TV Auction Club* and *Homemakers' Jamboree*. In addition to all the fun and games, Johnny was hosting variety, interview and kids' shows at this time, making him one of the busiest and most versatile broadcasters in the country.

Johnny gradually began easing his way into the job for which he'd be most identified: game show announcer. *Break the Bank* and *Stop the Music* were among Johnny's earliest credits in that field. He would occasionally step in as guest host for many of the shows

Johnny whips the audience into a frenzy for a taping of *Snap Judgment*. (Author's Collection)

for which he announced but, increasingly, he stayed behind the camera as game shows began taking over television.

Johnny Olson served as the announcer of more than thirty game shows, but arguably his greatest work was never seen on camera. A game show wouldn't feel like a game show without an electrified studio audience laughing and cheering at all the fun breaking out on stage, and as a warm-up man Johnny Olson generated more electricity than a nuclear turbine.

One night on *What's My Line?*, Johnny pulled double duty, acting as both announcer and contestant. The blindfolded panel tried to figure out that Mister X's line was "Announcer for *What's My Line?*" After the game, moderator John Daly summarized for the home audience Johnny's role as announcer and warm-up man:

"Johnny is not only extraordinarily good in his field as an announcer but, for instance, on *What's My Line?* he talks to the audience before our program begins, and I don't think anybody in television has a better running start than we do because he does it. He's such a friendly and engaging and sincere and nice guy that audiences respond to him and it makes it much easier for us when our time comes."

"Talking" to the audience was a mild way of putting it. Johnny would appear accompanied by blaring Top 40 songs—he later became fond of disco—and danced in the aisles, climbed into audience members' laps, planted big kisses on the women, engaged the audience in brief games with dollar bills as prizes, turned cartwheels, ran on and off the stage and worked up a sweat, often panting as he subsequently went through the instructions about when and how to applaud. Mark Evanier, a fan who attended many tapings involving Johnny Olson, recalled many years later on his blog, "By the time Johnny was through with you, you'd give a standing ovation to a potato race."

He became revered as a warm-up man beyond game shows, too. Jackie Gleason would not walk in front of an audience without Johnny Olson stepping out before him. When Gleason's show, *The American Scene Magazine*, began taping in Miami, Florida, Gleason used his considerable clout with CBS to make a special arrangement. Every week, CBS would have Johnny fly from New York to Florida so he could walk on stage for fifteen minutes, warm up the audience for Gleason's show and hop right back on the airplane to go home.

In 1972, Johnny was preparing for retirement, purchasing several acres in Lewisburg, West Virginia, where he and his wife Penny hoped to spend their golden years. But to Johnny's surprise, he was only just beginning, and the final decade of Johnny's life proved to be one of the busiest and most productive periods of his life.

Johnny was asked to serve as announcer for *The New Price is Right* on CBS and immediately gained friends in high places. Host Bob Barker was surprised to learn that his mother Tilly was a big fan of Johnny's, dating back to his radio days. Bob himself became so fond of Johnny's work that he personally lobbied to make Johnny a more visible part of *Price.* He and Bob would banter on camera and, when the show began making sketch comedy a regular feature of the daily Showcase at the end of the show, Johnny was a regular player, showing up in outlandish outfits and playing eccentric, goofy characters in parodies of *Rocky, Star Wars, The Exorcist,* and *Jaws.*

Goodson-Todman appreciated Johnny's role on *Price* and his talents as an announcer and warm-up man in general. The man who planned on winding down and relaxing on his West Virginia ranch was rarely there during the '70s, instead constantly commuting to Los Angeles to announce *Price*, *I've Got a Secret*, *Concentration*, *Match Game*, *Tattletales*, *Now You See It* and *Double Dare*.

Johnny didn't like working alone, though. He frequently called on co-workers and audience members to be his co-stars for those delightful fifteen minutes before the cameras started rolling.

Randy West, who later became a game show announcer himself, remembers a Johnny Olson warm-up from *Snap Judgment*:

"He comes out on stage and shouts, 'Ho ho, how's everybody doing!' And before long, you had a party in that audience; it was incredible. He was lively and energetic, and he had all these strangers who were bored and had to stand in line for an hour and had that New York attitude, 'Come on, entertain me,' and now they were all giggling and laughing and he was dancing, doing a burlesque bump and grind.

"During his warm-up, he says, 'Who wants to get me a drink of water?' And a few hands go up...he picks me. And he pulls me on stage and he says, 'Now, there's a water fountain on the eighth floor. Go to the hallway, make a left, go down the stairs, make a right, then make a U-turn and go all the way to the end of the hall, then follow the hallway to the end on the right, come back to the steps, but you can't take those steps, so you'll take the elevator.' And I scratched my head and rolled my eyes and I got giggles. I walked offstage and just stood there and waited because I knew I obviously wasn't getting him a glass of water. I came back and stood in the wings. Johnny looks at me and I figured that was my cue to walk back onstage, and Johnny says, 'Be careful, don't step over the cable!' And I did a pratfall. And Johnny looks at me irritated and says, 'You spilled the water when you tripped! Go sit down!'"

The bit got so many laughs that when Randy kept coming back to tapings of *Snap Judgment*, and later, *What's My Line?*, Johnny did that bit with him every time Randy was in the studio. Randy would later write the definitive biography of the legendary announcer, *Johnny Olson: A Voice in Time*.

Another co-star was Roger Dobkowitz, a young production assistant at the time that *The Price is Right* re-launched in 1972. For about ten years, he was prominently featured in Johnny's warm-up. Johnny would give detailed instructions to audience members about how to conduct themselves as contestants if they were called to "come on down." He told them: come down quickly, don't clam up, show energy, speak up, don't hesitate, be confident.

To illustrate the points he was making, he would call, "Roger Dobkowitz, come on down!" and Roger would run from the back of the studio, screaming and waving his arms. Johnny developed a crazy camaraderie with Roger, gradually adding to the routine and expanding it. Roger would later tell stories of sitting in the audience forty-seven times, writing in for tickets under his dog's name and seeing his dog win a car. He would catch the audience off-guard by excitedly kissing Johnny like a female contestant would kiss Bob and, when Johnny complained about being slobbered on, Roger would reach into his back pocket and pull out some underwear to help Johnny wipe his face.

Funny as he was, it's easy to forget how truly good Johnny was at announcing. Roger Dobkowitz estimated that in all the years he did *Price*, he flubbed his lines three times. Nothing could faze him. As a prank one day, several staffers snuck up behind him and unbuckled his pants. Johnny smoothly continued with the program with no trouble, without the home audience aware that he was being disrobed.

At one taping, Johnny took questions from the audience, as he often did, and called on an eighteen-year-old who wanted to know how to break into the announcing business. Johnny offered him a chance to "audition" on the spot, telling him to perform his very best "Come on down!" The young kid complied, and Johnny got a laugh by feigning discomfort at how good the youngster was at his job. The kid was future *Price is Right* announcer Rich Fields.

Into the 1980s, Johnny continued being a regular presence on what had become one of television's longest-running games. The show only got better with age; in its eighth season it became the number-one-rated show on daytime TV, a position it would retain for decades. Johnny was as synonymous with the program as Bob Barker. He had perfect attendance, never missing a taping of *The Price is Right* until 1985. What made that streak particularly notable was, years later, the discovery of a note from Goodson-

Todman Productions urging Johnny to put something in writing because the company had no formal agreement with him. For all those years of announcing dozens of shows, Johnny only had to give his word that he would be there.

Early that September, the Daytime Emmy Awards ceremony included a salute to Johnny, commending him for his forty-year career in television. Johnny eagerly ran to the stage to accept his special award from Bob Barker and said he was looking forward to spending forty more years as the announcer of *The Price is Right*.

Late on Sunday, October 6, 1985, Johnny's body was found in his car, slumped over the steering wheel. The scheduled tapings of *The Price is Right* were canceled that week while Johnny lingered in the hospital, clinging to life. On Saturday, October 12, he died.

Roger Dobkowitz remembers, "Johnny Olson was the nicest, happiest, most positive person who ever lived. Nothing was ever wrong with him. Always smiling, always happy, always full of energy, extremely kind…never got mad. Just a joy to be around."

(Author's Collection)

May 23

1980 – *The Gong Show Movie* is Released

Chuck Barris runs into trouble from a pair of performers—played by Phillip Simms and Vincent Schiavelli—who are annoyed at getting gonged in *The Gong Show Movie.* (Author's Collection)

Chuck Barris did an admirable job milking *The Gong Show* as much as he could from its premiere in 1976 throughout its run and beyond. There was an official *Gong Show* book, *Gong Show* bubble gum cards, prime time specials, a *Gong Show* board game and even an official Chuck Barris Halloween costume for children. In 1980, Chuck unleashed perhaps the ultimate tie-in to his masterpiece: *The Gong Show Movie.*

Starring, directed, produced and co-written—with Robert Downey—by Chucky Baby himself, the film seems to exist for the sole purpose of being Chuck's personal therapy couch. He felt overwhelmed by the popularity of the show, and this is essentially a fictionalized version of his real-life problems, with the line between reality and the big screen blurred as thoroughly as can be. His girlfriend is played by his actual girlfriend. His daughter plays his daughter. The film splices documentary footage of contestant auditions and clips of the show's most memorable acts, including a few segments that got censored in the initial broadcasts.

The film's Chuck Barris is recognized at every corner by aspiring contestants. A homeless man tries to impress him with the ol' soft-shoe, and singers and musicians follow him from the elevator to his office. He's badgered by network Vice President Larry Didlo for ratings slippage, even when Didlo admits that the ratings are up; he just *senses* they're about to go down. Didlo follows him to restaurants and shows up in Chuck's bedroom one morning to pester him about *Gong*'s brewing troubles. Chuck picks fights with rude people on the street, losing miserably.

Problems mount for the movie's Chuck in unlikely ways. He goes into a deep depression after an elderly contestant has a heart attack during a taping; the contestant had been gonged by the panel, but his act so delighted Chuck that he kept getting pulled back onstage for encores until he collapsed. The distressed host visits the victim in the hospital and is shocked when the man jumps out of bed and stages an audition for the next act he hopes to do on the show. Film Chuck is held at gunpoint by the children of a losing contestant and avoids an early demise by letting them be contestants.

After consulting a psychiatrist and getting into a heated argument with his girlfriend, our star leaves the country (don't blink or you'll miss Phil Hartman in an airport scene) and makes his way to a Moroccan desert, where he simply sits in the sand, isolating himself from the world and seemingly happy—until the film's show-stopping climax. Didlo finds him in the desert and imports a massive support group in the form of *Gong Show* judges, acts and Chuck's personal friends to perform a lavish musical number called "Don't Get Up." The surprisingly catchy tune turns around Chuck's attitude. He returns to life at *The Gong Show*, and the film ends with a content-looking Chuck introducing another bizarre collection of performers.

It received negative reviews almost across the board, although a few critics tried to be generous. Jim Moorhead marveled, "The film has a high energy levels and a furious pace...parts of it are outrageously funny...If you're a fan of the TV show, and you've a bawdy streak, I can't imagine your not liking *The Gong Show Movie*."

The film was in and out of theaters "in a weekend," as Barris later remarked. Although it bombed, it provided an uncanny glimpse into the future. Barris actually did wind up fleeing the country after it left theaters, heading to Europe, where he eventually settled into premature retirement on a private island in France. He shut down his entire television empire during the summer, with *The $1.98 Beauty Pageant*, *The Dating Game*, *The Newlywed Game*, *Camouflage*, *3's a Crowd* and *The Gong Show* all ceasing production, and that adds a notable footnote to the film for fans of the show. *The Gong Show Movie* was the last hurrah of the one-of-a-kind series.

May 24

1975 – The Pilot for *Showoffs*

In 1975, Mark Goodson-Bill Todman Productions could do no wrong. *Match Game '75*, *The Price is Right*, *To Tell the Truth*, *Concentration* and *Tattletales* were chugging along nicely. Two shows were fading away that year, *Password* and *What's My Line?*, but it looked like the company was about to turn that into a positive.

Line host Larry Blyden agreed to host another show that Goodson-Todman persuaded ABC to use to replace *Password*. Plans were made to shoot a pilot for the project, titled *Showoffs*. And here's how valued Goodson-Todman was by that point. On May 22, two days before taping the pilot, ABC sent out a press release announcing the new series, scheduled to premiere on June 30.

The game was charades. Two teams competed; each consisted of a contestant and two celebrity partners. One team went into an isolation booth while the other team played. For sixty seconds, two members of the team would try to convey as many words as possible to their partner. After that, the other team would be brought out, play the same list of words and try to beat that score. Whoever guessed more words won the round; two out of three rounds won the game.

In the bonus round, all four celebrity guests would perform for sixty seconds while the contestant tried to guess as many words as possible for a dollar apiece. After that, another thirty seconds would go on the clock, and up to three more words would be played. Guessing one word paid ten times the money, guessing two paid one hundred times and guessing all three paid one thousand times.

The actual pilot taping proved to be a mild disaster, due mostly to a personality clash between Larry Blyden and Mark Goodson. Goodson scheduled a week of rehearsals for the impending pilot, but Blyden, a noted quick study, felt he had the game down pat after about thirty minutes of preparation on the first day and got annoyed that Goodson insisted on continuing with rehearsals. Goodson was a stickler for details and held up the taping while he nitpicked about scorekeeping, sound effects and anything else that bugged him. Larry, on the other hand, hated wasting time. He got so frustrated that he left the studio and told Mark to call him at his hotel when the taping was finally ready, which shocked the staff. When Larry returned, a technical problem delayed taping so long that he wound up missing his young daughter's play, which made him furious because he was promised the taping would end in time for him to see it.

Finally, they worked out the bugs, the pilot was taped and they all went their separate ways, eagerly awaiting the big premiere on June 30. And then…tragedy.

Larry took a vacation to Morocco and went on a drive to look at some native jewelry. His rental car turned over and he was rushed to a local hospital, where doctors were unable to contact his family for some time because Larry was traveling without identification. On June 6, 1975, Larry Blyden died.

Understandably, this blindsided just about everybody even remotely connected with the new project. Press releases for the show were already sent out and were still circulating after Larry died. As late as June 16, articles about the upcoming show were still reporting that Larry Blyden would be the host. Goodson-Todman was suddenly in search of a new host with only twenty-five days to prepare and train one—even less than that since, like any game show, *Showoffs* was pre-recorded.

Nine days before the premiere, the job was formally given to Bobby Van, a singer/actor who had frequently appeared on *Match Game* and *Tattletales* as a guest, but this was his rookie hosting assignment. Whether he was a good host on such short notice is a matter of taste; Goodson-Todman producer Gil Fates thought he was sub-par but, in his memoirs, added "excusably" to that assessment. Meanwhile, backstage the staff was still coping with the shock of losing a colleague and friend. Announcer Gene Wood years later described the sad mood that permeated the entire show.

The show, which had ABC so excited that they bought it sight-unseen, now seemed virtually cursed. It suffered low ratings against *The Young and Restless* on CBS, it had an inexperienced host who enjoyed the job but could seem overwhelmed by it sometimes, and it had unprecedented morale problems among the staff. With that many elements working against it, failure was inevitable. *Showoffs* came to an end on December 26, 1975.

May 25

1963 – The Pilot for *Let's Make a Deal*

How will this deal turn out? (Author's Collection)

Monty Hall and his business partner, Stefan Hatos, had an idea for a straightforward game: present an audience member with a gift along with a chance to exchange it for an unknown quantity. Sometimes the replacement would be an improvement, and sometimes it would be worthless. As easy as the game was to explain, getting it on the air proved rather difficult.

As Hatos and Hall pitched their new game, they kept hearing the same concern from the representatives of the major networks: "What do you do the second time?" There was no challenge, it was all pure luck and the networks couldn't imagine the audience sitting through a game with no skill or knowledge required. Shouldn't the contestants have to do *something*?

Hatos and Hall were convinced that the networks were wrong and, to prove it, they took the game wherever they could. They would go to small functions like Weight Watchers meetings, fundraisers and women's clubs, and just have the people in attendance pretend they were playing for the marvelous prizes as Monty walked them through the game as host.

"We wondered if there would be any bugs in the idea," Monty admitted to a reporter. "So we tested the show under audience fire. We didn't know for sure how people would react to trading something valuable for a pig in a poke. We discovered the idea played beautifully."

Even in the mockup, with nothing actually at risk, the contestants just had to know what was behind that curtain. The suspense filled the gap left by the lack of skill and knowledge contests.

NBC finally agreed to a pilot. Monty offered prizes concealed all over the studio—behind doors, behind curtains, in boxes and even in his pockets. The dilemma for the contestants was that their hunches were in constant conflict, and they had to decide which

These contestants could win a trip to Switzerland, a Swiss watch, or a hunk of Swiss cheese. (Author's Collection)

hunch was right. NBC picked up the show, putting it on the air on December 30, even though many in the network were still headstrong that a luck-based game show was destined for failure.

Producer Mark Goodson admitted years later to being one of the doubters, likening the show to flipping a coin over and over again. Essentially, that's what *Let's Make a Deal* was. The reason it worked was twofold: Monty Hall's undeniable effectiveness as host, and the complexity of the deals that often far exceeded flipping a coin.

One of the first deals featured on the series featured a cow with a bell tethered around his neck. Monty offered a female contestant an option: The cow or a diamond ring. The contestant went with the diamond ring. Monty then reached into the cow's bell and pulled out $500 in cash. He then offered the contestant a chance to trade the diamond ring for whatever he had in his pocket. The woman kept the ring. Monty revealed that the "diamond" was actually bottle glass and he had $500 in cash. Another contestant bartered his way from one ton of peanuts to $900 in cash to a pile of mud from the Mississippi River. Yet another traded away her $400 and came away with a mink coat. The pleasant surprise in all of this was that no matter what happened to the contestants, they came away smiling and happy, even the ones saddled with bottle glass and mud.

Monty could make these contestants feel pretty ragged if they wind up with a Zonk. (Author's Collection)

Monty explained in 1964, "Something irrational happens to people when they start trading things and they are all good sports, win or lose. I never tell them what to do. It's like Las Vegas without wheels."

The show was an immediate hit, staying competitive with CBS's *Password*, which had previously steamrolled four other shows right into cancellation. Audiences couldn't wait to see what Monty offered next; that peanut shell might be covering a set of earrings or the garbage can may be hiding a mink coat—or, it could just as easily be filled with garbage.

The garbage, the broken down car, the moth-eaten fur coat, the bicycle with the flat tire and all those other duds that contestants got stuck with were known collectively as "Zonks." As the show went on, the Zonks became more elaborate and silly. *Let's Make a Deal* found ways to make losing as much fun as winning. There were donkeys, a rusty fighter plane husk with a stuffed Snoopy perched atop it, a Zonkmobile that looked more dilapidated with every appearance or unusable furniture like a ten-foot-tall rocking chair.

Every day, Monty finished the half-hour by offering the contestants a chance to trade everything they had already won for a chance at the Big Deal of the Day. Each of the Big Deal's three doors always hid an array of prizes, but one door was far more valuable than the others. It was a climactic way to conclude the show, although Monty still wasn't done dealing. As the theme music played and the credits rolled, he wandered through the audience offering small cash prizes for odd items like a hard-boiled egg, a credit card, a rubber band or anything else that popped into Monty's head. He once got into hot water by approaching a female contestant dressed as a baby and offering her money for a baby bottle. When she successfully produced one, Monty offered a bonus: "For $200, show me another nipple!" The audience laughed

Monty's bucks or Jay's box—which will this contestant take? (Author's Collection)

for several seconds before the blushing host realized what he had just said.

Monty didn't work alone on *Let's Make a Deal.* He had two assistants joining him for the dealing. One was announcer Jay Stewart, usually appearing with a big box on a tray as the contestants furrowed their brows and wondered what might be in that box. Sometimes he was "Baby Jay," dressed in jammies or a Buster Brown suit and hyperactively popping balloons or steering a wagon around for the Zonks. There was also the lovely Carol Merrill, who earned her pay more than any other game show model as she bounded from curtain to box and back again, stopping frequently backstage for a costume change.

Those crazy costumes! *Let's Make a Deal* didn't look like any other show on TV. (Author's Collection)

The real stars of the show, as with any game show, were the contestants. Little did Monty or anybody else at *Let's Make a Deal* realize how famous they would become and how much more exposure they would give the show. *Let's Make a Deal* was already an emerging hit when one contestant, eager for Monty to select her to play, had an idea for grabbing his attention that would permanently alter the future of the series.

She came into the studio with a sign around her neck reading "Roses are red/Violets are blue/I came here/To deal with you." Monty was so taken by the sign that he naturally picked her. Before long, everybody seeking to be a contestant was showing up for tapings with a sign. After so many weeks of signs, it became hard to make one that really stood out, so another contestant came up with a solution; she showed up holding a sign and wearing an odd-looking hat. Monty couldn't ignore the odd-looking hat, so he chose her. People began arriving with signs and hats and, before long, the audience of *Let's Make a Deal* was packed with hobos, beauty queens, vampires, ghosts, wrestlers, girl scouts and Groucho Marx impersonators. Anybody planning a trip to the studio to deal with Monty first went up to the attic and slapped together whatever could be assembled from the contents of the trunks. With no prompting or promotion at all, *Let's Make a Deal* turned into the world's biggest costume party, five days a week.

At first, Stefan Hatos was irked by the development and called a meeting to instruct the staff to stop the contestants from doing this. One staffer stood up and asked, "Why?"

Hatos didn't have a ready answer for that. The staffer kept protesting. "Don't you realize there's never been a show like this before? People are dressing up…and it makes the screen come alive."

Stefan Hatos backed down, and the costumes became the show's identity. Any channel surfer could immediately recognize *Let's Make a Deal.*

As the show's popularity grew, it became a target for critics, and Monty came to feel that he was constantly defending his show.

- *"Let's Make a Deal promotes greed!* "If gamblers can be called greedy, then each and every one of us is greedy. I can't imagine a game show becoming successful by parading greedy, avaricious contestants before the cameras. The viewing audience would quickly be turned off, and would turn the programs off."
- *Those audience members and contestants are wearing bizarre costumes—this is a freak show!* "Researchers who have studied our audiences say that they represent a true cross-section of America...We get doctors, teachers, social workers, psychologists, all sorts of professionals."
- *This show represents the worst qualities of America and Americans!* "It can't be, because...they have a version of *Let's Make a Deal* [in] Japan, Spain, Sweden, everywhere."
- *Why such extravagant prizes instead of useful things, like scholarships?* "...[T]hey'd probably want the cash anyway."
- *Let's Make a Deal and all the other game shows are taking valuable time away from shows with more substance!* "Nobody can force stations to try new shows. Game shows are popular and cheap, so they get made and sold."

Thankfully, Monty didn't have to fight with audiences. They loved the show so much that NBC gave it a prime time slot for the summer of 1967. NBC refused to extend it beyond that, though. Monty said years later that an executive told him, "We don't put that kind of show in prime time."

The relationship between Hatos-Hall Productions and NBC became rather frosty after that; in 1968, Monty negotiated a new contract with the network. Former NBC executive Dan Fox recalls what happened as a result of those negotiations.

"Monty wanted more money and threatened to take the show to another network. NBC ignored that because they figured he was bluffing. So they didn't give him the money and next thing you knew, the show was on ABC."

Monty signed off from NBC's *Let's Make a Deal* on Friday, December 27, 1968 and welcomed viewers to ABC's *Let's Make a Deal* on Monday, December 30, 1968. ABC gave Monty the prime time slot he wanted so badly, airing the show for more than two years before Monty took the prime time version into syndication, where he stood to make more money. The syndicated version thrived for six seasons while the daytime version kept chugging along.

The lovely Carol Merrill with the quintessential game show prize, and *Let's Make a Deal* had plenty of them to offer. (Author's Collection)

As time went by, the show offered more gimmicks to keep the show interesting. Bigger prizes and cash were up for grabs. A weekly celebrity guest, like Nipsey Russell or Milton Berle, would make deals on behalf of a home viewer. A new bonus added to the end of the show, the Super Deal, gave the contestant who won the Big Deal of the Day an opportunity to trade it for a chance at three more doors, each hiding either $1,000, $2,000 or $20,000 in cash. A contestant who picked the $20,000 door won that cash and also was permitted to keep the Big Deal.

The "all good things" cliché held true for *Let's Make a Deal*, and the daytime version ended on July 9, 1976. The prime time show lasted for one more season, with Monty moving production to the lavish Hilton Hotel & Casino in Las Vegas for its last hurrah. The ratings were still there, but on December 23, 1976, Monty taped the final episode of the prime time version, voluntarily pulling the plug on his creation. Final tally of the original run of *Let's Make a Deal*: thirteen years, 3,800 episodes and $36 million in cash and prizes given away. Monty admitted to being tired of the grind, later saying he wished he had ended the show a year earlier.

In 1980, Monty brought the show back for a one-season run. The show taped in Canada with a new staff and a lower budget, troubled by a syndication distributor that was quickly running out of resources. With game shows experiencing a renaissance in 1984, the show resurfaced in syndication as *The All-New Let's Make a Deal*. It enjoyed only moderate success, airing two seasons and narrowly missing out on the renewal for a third year, but this version enjoyed a surprisingly long life in reruns starting in 1987, airing for many years on USA Network, The Family Channel and Game Show Network.

Deal in the 1980s...Monty returned, and so did those wild costumes. (Author's Collection)

Deal in the 1990s...Monty Hall, joined by Dick Clark and Bob Hilton, plus some eager contestant hopefuls, at Walt Disney World in Florida. (Author's Collection)

In the summer of 1990, Monty Hall returned to NBC, teaming up with Dick Clark and Ron Greenberg to launch a new incarnation of *Let's Make a Deal* taped at the Disney-MGM Studios at Walt Disney World in Orlando. Monty actually made an effort to pass the torch; he was initially just the producer of the show, with Bob Hilton taking over at host. Bob proved awkward and uncomfortable as host, and ratings suffered. NBC demanded that Monty take over as host to save the show, but the damage had already been done and this version of *Let's Make a Deal* was gone after January 1991.

In 2003, *Let's Make a Deal* returned to prime time, ironically on NBC, the network that decades earlier didn't want it there. Monty co-produced this version as a summer replacement series hosted by Billy Bush of *Access Hollywood*. Despite being fully involved, Monty hated this version of the show. The network wanted sexually suggestive deals, under the assumption that people watch game shows for sex. Monty compromised by allowing one "naughty" deal per show but otherwise vetoed every off-color idea thrown at him. The show didn't last.

In 2009, *Let's Make a Deal* ended a sixteen-year drought, hitting the airwaves on CBS with host Wayne Brady and becoming the first new game show introduced on network daytime TV since *Caesar's Challenge* in 1993. Once again, the show that nobody saw a future in back in 1963 was a hit.

What's remarkable about *Let's Make a Deal* is that it never completely disappeared. On top of the reruns, Monty Hall promoted a *Let's Make a Deal* 900-number in the early 1990s, an electronic table top version later in the decade and a DVD video game a few years later. There's even a *Let's Make a Deal* stage show. The game's place in pop culture is secure. Monty Hall and *Let's Make a Deal* are frequently invoked by ESPN anchors reporting on the latest free agent negotiations. "The Monty Hall Problem" has stymied math students everywhere. It goes to show, if a producer can come up with a game that everybody can play, everybody will watch.

May 26

1911 – Ben Alexander's Birthday

Ben Alexander is best remembered as Officer Frank Smith, the laid-back counterpart to by-the-book Joe Friday on *Dragnet*. After the nighttime drama's original television run came to an end in 1959, Ben made the jump to daytime TV with an audience participation show, *About Faces*, produced by Ralph Edwards.

Each episode included a variety of small games, many involving faces. An audience member might be shown a baby picture and have to guess which celebrity that baby grew up to be. Celebrities were brought out to play a game similar to *Place the Face* (see July 3). Sometimes guests were shown photos from their own lives and had to describe the people in the pictures. Being a Ralph Edwards Production, the show also did its best to feature the often-emotional surprise reunions that had made *This is Your Life* and *Truth or Consequences* so delightful.

The show was relatively short-lived, but it did last long enough to produce one truly great story, courtesy of the show's announcer, Tom Kennedy. Here's Tom's story about one taping, transcribed from a speech he gave at Game Show Congress 3 in 2004.

> Ralph loved to surprise people and sometimes people surprised him...They had saved up...from their budgets over the last thirteen or twenty-six weeks and they were going to put on a lollapalooza: Four-generation Czechoslovakian reunion. I don't know all the story about why and how it was that particular family, but you can rest assured it was an exotic story.
>
> But can you imagine the logistics of getting these people? The great-grandmother was there in Czechoslovakia, the grandmother was in New York, the daughter was in—I think—Denver, and her daughter and her family were in Los Angeles. And to bring all these people together...motels, rooms, get 'em into the studio, and none of these family groups could see each other. None of them knew the others were going to be on that lot.
>
> And they brought them in...they would bring family group number one, the great-grandmother and her group, and bring them behind curtain number one with a big partition, family group number two was the grandmother, and then curtain number three and then curtain number four...Shh! (Whispering) Very quiet. It's like Churchill Downs getting them in there. Shh, shh, get in there, don't sneeze.

Now they're taping this because it's going in either as a wild piece or splice it up and go through sweeps week, I don't know what they were going to do with it…But anyway, they were going to tape it. So here we go…We have a live audience, we have five cameras, Ben Alexander is center stage, the lights are ready, the sound is ready. The director says, "Slate it."

A little guy came out, who hadn't been a stage manager too long, as you can instantly fathom…Ben called him Fat Freddy. I won't give you his name because he's probably a network executive today. He came out with this chalkboard and he went center stage, and he says, "Great Grandmother Czechoslovakian Reunion, take one!"

OUT THEY CAME! They came from here, they came from there! "Mama, mama, where is she?!" He was completely swarmed by the bouncing Czechs.

May 27

1911 – Vincent Price's Birth

Vincent Price was anything but terrifying for viewers of *The Hollywood Squares*. Here he hobnobs backstage with host Peter Marshall, Rose Marie, Douglas Fairbanks, Jr., and Linda Day George. (Author's Collection)

On the big screen, Vincent Price meant terror beyond your imagination. He had an imposing build, a steel gaze and a chiseled face that could contort itself into scowls and glares that spoke volumes.

On the small screen, it turned out that Vincent Price was pretty darn funny. He was a semi-regular throughout the original run of *The Hollywood Squares*, cracking up Peter Marshall and the audience with pitch-perfect comedic delivery of his zingers, as well as brilliantly slinging out both correct answers and sly bluffs. From 1966-80, he made audiences scream more than ever...but for different reasons. Affectionately called "Vinnie" by Peter Marshall, Price often played off his own creepy public image for laughs and traded barbs with Rose Marie during each game.

PETER: Research shows that about ten percent of people do something with their blankets at night that is actually unhealthy. What do they do?
VINCENT: Sneeze in them.

PETER: Has a bull ever sired more than 15,000 offspring in three years?
VINCENT: That kind of question gives us all hope...I don't think so, but they had a good try.

PETER: True or false? In the Middle Ages, a person accused of a crime was tortured in a variety of ways, and if the wounds healed within three days, the person was found innocent of the crime.
VINCENT: Oooooohh, I long for those good old days.

PETER: According to a recent survey...what was named the most boring job on earth?
VINCENT: Rose Marie's social secretary.

PETER: Who wrote the immortal work "Air on the G-String"?
VINCENT: Whose G-string?

PETER: In what event are you most likely to be confronted by a dog leg?
VINCENT: Sleeping under a tree.

PETER: If you surprised your wife, who is in the audience this evening...Oh, no, she isn't in the audience this evening...
VINCENT: Well, it doesn't matter, it's a surprise.

PETER: If you surprised your wife with aluminum foil, what anniversary would you be celebrating?
VINCENT: It would be my last anniversary!

PETER: True or False? In a true Finish sauna, you are to beat yourself with twigs.
VINCENT: And if it's a true German sauna, you beat a stranger.

PETER: What do you call that mental state in which a person sees, hears, tastes, smells or even feels something that isn't there?
VINCENT: An obscene phone call.

PETER: Jupiter, Saturn and Uranus have them and now scientists believe our sun might have them. What does our sun have?

VINCENT: Our son has Peter Marshall's eyes.

PETER: Chicago. October 8, 1871. What's all the excitement about?

VINCENT: That was the professional debut of Rose Marie.

ROSE MARIE: Oh shut up!

May 28

1975 – The End of the Line

ABC's counter to Johnny Carson in the '70s was an anthology series called *Wide World of Entertainment*, which consisted of absolutely anything ABC was able to plug into the ninety-minute slot starting at 11:30 p.m. Investigative reports by Geraldo Rivera, "unauthorized biographies" profiling top stars, and even reruns of *Monty Python's Flying Circus* were among the entries. In 1975, Mark Goodson-Bill Todman Productions approached ABC about featuring a silver anniversary tribute to *What's My Line?* and the network cheerfully accepted, even though ABC had never aired *What's My Line?* Behind the scenes, the staff poured heart and soul into the project, led by executive producer Gil Fates.

There were a few reasons for that. The first was to say goodbye to the revered game show in proper fashion. Due to the nature of the show's taping schedule, *What's My Line?* had taped its final episode three months before the staff knew the show had been canceled. The final entry was a very typical one, interchangeable with countless other episodes, and even somewhat subpar. Fates, who took detailed notes about each taping, included a note instructing the staff not to air this show as part of a rerun package. With twenty-five years under its belt, the feeling was that *What's My Line?* deserved a better send-off.

The second reason was that even though a TV show isn't a living thing, the longtime staffers felt a sense of gratitude toward *What's My Line?* The program had established Goodson-Todman's reputation in the television business and ensured a strong future for the firm. With game shows on the decline in 1968, the syndicated version of *What's My Line?* kept the company afloat and kept everyone from having to look for a new job. This single program had meant a lifetime of job security and comfort for a number of people. Those staffers didn't just want the show to fade away.

Given a budget of $60,000 to put together the ninety-minute special, Fates and his staff got to work on the eye-blurring task of poring through all surviving films and tapes of *What's My Line?* and collecting the clips. According to Fates' memoirs, it was a task full of surprises. Segments that nobody remembered proved to be a goldmine, while segments that were remembered fondly turned out to be incredibly dull upon second viewing.

Getting permission from dozens of celebrities to use clips of their appearances threatened to put the show $50,000 over budget if every celebrity got paid for every clip used. The show came up with a compromise, sending a letter to all the stars asking permission and promising to pay a royalty if the celebrity's face was onscreen longer than two minutes.

Frank Sinatra sent his lawyers after the show, so his clip was dropped from the final cut. Casey Stengel and Leo Durocher both called to personally say "Drop dead!" Kirk Douglas had no issue with the pay haggling; he declined merely because he hated how his appearance on the show had turned out. Johnny Carson called Goodson-Todman to explain that he'd love to be a part of the show but, since the special was airing in direct competition with *The Tonight Show*, he was concerned that his bosses at NBC would be furious with their top star airing against himself.

Thankfully, many stars were enthusiastic about being a part of the retrospective, payday or not. Danny Kaye came to the Goodson-Todman offices to personally watch the clip they wanted to use and, determining it satisfactory, signed a paper for the legal department and walked out smiling. Greer Garson was so excited that she called the office and described, from memory, the exact dress she had worn on the specific clip they wanted to use.

In its finished state, the special consisted of Mark Goodson, Arlene Francis and John Daly chatting it up around a coffee table to introduce each montage of clips. There was no grandeur, no musical numbers, no mawkish sentimentality. The special turned out very much like the show it was celebrating: simplistic and charming.

May 29

1958 – *Music Bingo* Premieres

Music Bingo seemed like a can't-miss prospect. A few game shows, such as *Name That Tune*, had already proven that viewers liked to test their knowledge of song titles, and fundraisers and socials had sufficiently proven that people like playing Bingo. So host Johnny Gilbert was onto something when he opened each program by proclaiming, "Everybody plays *Music Bingo*!"

Name That Tune creator Harry Salter was the mind behind this game. Two contestants competed, one represented by a sharp symbol and one by a flat symbol. Johnny would draw a card representing a space on the massive twenty-five-square Bingo card onstage. The players would hear a tune and ring in to answer; as on *Tune*, they had to run across the stage to get to the buzzer. A correct answer put their symbol on the proper square. There was also a designated square on the board in which a correct answer awarded a contestant all of the opponent's captured squares. The first player to score Bingo earned $500 and faced a new opponent.

The game originally premiered in prime time and ran through the summer on NBC. It returned in December 1958 as a daytime offering on ABC, airing for just a little more than a year.

Music Bingo was the first game show hosted by singer Johnny Gilbert, and newspaper critics were quick to point out that he had some of the showings of a rookie in his early weeks. One remarked that he was visibly nervous on the premiere broadcast and another noted that he winked at the camera quite often. Surviving footage of the show, from later in the run, reveals a host more in his element by that point, amiably chatting with the camera and smoothly, confidently singing a few tunes with the show's live band backing him up. The moderate success of the program was sufficient to establish him as a viable star in the game show galaxy, and he stuck with the genre for decades after *Music Bingo*.

May 30

1951 – *Down You Go* Premieres

In the beginning, there was a game called Hangman, played with pencil and paper. Then Merv Griffin came up with a lavish game show called *Wheel of Fortune*. And in between, there was *Down You Go*.

Fans of the bright and cheery *Wheel of Fortune* would be amazed to see the earthy, humble form that a similar game took in the 1950s. The unlikely host of *Down You Go* was Dr. Bergen Evans, an erudite English professor from Northwestern University who would line up numerous TV jobs over the years but continue teaching at Northwestern through all of it—he continued teaching right up to his death in 1978. Originating from Chicago for the Dumont Network, Dr. Evans was joined each week by four panelists, including, at various points, Prof. Robert Breen, Fran Allison, Phil Rizzuto and Boris Karloff.

The puzzles featured on the show were submitted by home viewers, who received $5 if their puzzle was used on the show and $25 plus a dictionary if they stumped the panel. Dr. Evans would start the game by reading a witty or punny clue. For example:

"A place where many Americans first came to their senses."
– MATERNITY WARD

"A famous female who, though the motherly type, in her lifetime set many men aflame."
– MRS. O'LEARY'S COW

Dr. Evans had an unusual work ethic for a television host. He didn't stop at just hosting the show, in addition to his duties as a college professor. In interviews, Dr. Evans took great pride in noting that the show received 60,000 entries from viewers every week, and he personally selected each episode's batch from that pile of mail. And yet, none of it felt like work to him.

He once remarked, "I never cease to marvel that I am paid money for this at all."

To play, the panelists called out letters and, as long as the letters were in the puzzle, they stayed in the game. If they guessed a wrong letter, they were eliminated. The game appealed to viewers who stood to make a few easy bucks by contributing whatever wit they had to offer and to critics who were delighted to see such a high-brow game on the airwaves. Raved one critic, "At long last! A quiz is droll and literate!"

In the following five years, the show underwent a number of changes. Dumont uprooted it from Chicago to New York, although

Evans remained host and commuted by air to accommodate his teaching schedule. Over the years, the show made its way from Dumont to CBS to ABC to NBC.

In its final three months, the show made a drastic switch in presentation. Bill Cullen became the host, and a new panel—Arthur Treacher, Hildy Parks, Jayne Mansfield and Jimmy Nelson—played the game for laughs. The show disappeared quietly on September 8, 1956. Bill moved onto *The Price is Right*, and Dr. Evans cut back his television appearances to one per week as the supervisory "authority" who sat onstage and judged the answers for *The $64,000 Question*.

May 31

2006 – *Gameshow Marathon* Premieres

The Price is Right, *Match Game*, *Family Feud*, *Press Your Luck*, *Beat the Clock*, *Let's Make a Deal*, and *Card Sharks* have all left the airwaves and returned with new rules, new sets, new hosts, new prizes…but it seems like no matter what facelift a vintage game show gets, many fans feel like they got it right the first time.

That was the thinking behind *Gameshow Marathon*, a seven-episode summer replacement series based on a British series. Six celebrities—Leslie Nielsen, Paige Davis, Tim Meadows, Kathy Najimy, Lance Bass, and Brandy Roderick—competed in a series of one-night-only revivals of classic game shows. Each episode began with a loving tribute to the game being played that night, complete with classic clips narrated by Rich Fields. To give the show a vintage feel, the look and sound of the shows weren't updated. Each episode featured a faithful duplication of the original set, as well as the original theme music. The only new thing about it was host Ricki Lake.

Viewers at home had a chance to get in on the winning. They'd be shown a clip of the classic game of the night and asked a question about how that game turned out. A lucky viewer chosen from the ones who called in with the correct answer won some of the loot awarded that night.

Night one featured *The Price is Right*, with the stars bidding their way to the stage for a chance to play classic pricing games like Hole in One, Race Game, and Plinko, plus a spin of the big wheel and a crack at the showcases.

For night two, the stars donned their craziest costumes for *Let's Make a Deal* and dealt with some of the show's best known recurring deals, like the Money Machine. *Gameshow Marathon* even included a special guest Zonker. Among the duds that the stars wound up with were Gilbert Gottfried in a bathtub and Gilbert Gottfried dressed as a giant baby.

Night three brought *Beat the Clock*, with the contestants playing in an elimination tournament involving stunts featured on the original Bud Collyer series. The stars had to put caps on milk bottles filled with dry ice before pressure caused the caps to blow off. Helium balloons had to be caught with nets before they flew to the ceiling, and Paige Davis won a car for a lucky viewer by maneuvering her way under a hat attached to a string and putting it on without using her hands.

In night four, Leslie Nielsen, Kathy Najimy, and Tim Meadows squared off in *Press Your Luck*, using a magnificent reincarnation of the original game board designed by game show fanatic Dan Berger. Original Whammy animations were used in the game, and the program concluded with a special tribute to host Peter Tomarken, who was killed in a plane crash earlier in the year.

Night five began the semi-finals with *Card Sharks.* Paige Davis and Brandy Roderick went head-to-head, trying to decide how many waiters had spit in a customer's food, and how many newlyweds re-gift a wedding presents.

Rounding out the semi-finals on night six was *Match Game.* Ricki Lake was bestowed with her very own ECM-51 (see May 7) to make sure the game had the right look. Lance Bass and Kathy Najimy dueled. Popping in to act as panelists were George Foreman, Kathy Griffin, Bruce Vilanch, Adrianne Curry, Adam Corolla, and Betty White, sitting in the same chair that she always found herself in for the '70s version. Dumb Dora even returned for a question.

The grand finale was *Family Feud,* with Kathy Najimy squaring off against Brandy Roderick. What many viewers may not have realized was that Kathy came into the game with an advantage. Her family had actually appeared on *Family Feud* with Richard Dawson over twenty years earlier. Maybe that gave her an edge, because Kathy won the tournament and $100,000 for charity.

Gameshow Marathon achieved only middling ratings. Ricki Lake, in a tough spot of having to master six games in three weeks of rehearsal, was criticized by some for an awkward hosting style. Stretching games designed for thirty-minute timeslots for an hour show also had a detrimental effect. Fast-paced games like *Card Sharks* sometimes seemed to screech to a halt out of necessity. The experiment was abandoned by CBS after only one Marathon.

June 1

2008 – *Million Dollar Password* Premieres

The prime time game show renaissance that began with *Who Wants to be a Millionaire?* spawned numerous short-lived million-dollar games, but none made game show purists rejoice like the news that *Password* was coming back.

Fans immediately sensed from the title that this wouldn't be the *Password* they knew and loved. There were obviously changes afoot, but hopefully buried somewhere under the fresh coats of paint was that classic word association game.

Fans didn't have to worry. FremantleMedia, the production company backing the series, brought original *Password* creator Bob Stewart's son Sande on board to serve as a creative consultant to guide the format along. The host was Regis Philbin, an old-school broadcaster with modern-day sensibilities. The celebrities featured included a mix of established game players and game show lovers, including Neil Patrick Harris, William Shatner, Rosie O'Donnell, and Mrs. Password herself, Betty White. Nineteen years earlier, on the final episode of *Super Password*, she had joked, "This is the fifth final *Password* I've been on...we'll be back in a minute." It may have taken longer than a minute to get there, but Betty was clearly glad to see she was right.

Executive producer Vincent Rubino called the original *Password* a "parlor game," which was a fair assessment. He said his goal was to make it the type of "prime time spectacle" that modern audiences expected. The result was a fast-paced game, played entirely against the clock. Teams competed against each other in a series of thirty-second rounds, trying to convey as many passwords as possible. The highest score after four rounds played a bonus round for a potential one million dollars.

Now the teams played up to six ninety-second rounds. The clue-giver could only give a maximum of three clues per password before being forced to try another password. The goal each time was to convey five passwords, with the cash payout getting bigger and the room for error getting a little tighter each time. For the first round, teams had to convey five out of ten passwords. For the second, five out of nine, then five out of eight, and so on until the million-dollar step, where they had to convey five out of five.

Although markedly different from its predecessors, purists and critics were impressed. Washington Post TV critic Tom Shales was critical of the constantly fast tempo of the show, but had kind words for the host and the contestants: "(Allen) Ludden, it turns out, is not precisely irreplaceable, at least in this role: Regis Philbin, one of TV's most entertaining talkers, has been recruited to host the latest incarnation of the game show...makes himself comfortable quickly and injects as much of his disarming personality as the drum-tight format will allow…[T]he contestants are considerably less demonstratively demented than those on NBC's hellish *Deal or No Deal…*"

Another critic, Joel Keller, spoke for quite a few *Password* purists after seeing the first episode. "[E]ven an objective observer can see that the gameplay has some flaws that are going to need to be worked out for the show to succeed. I know (the producers) want to build tension, but there was nothing wrong with the old method...Maybe they just thought it was too slow and 'think-y' for them…*Million Dollar Password* needs to be tweaked, no doubt about it. And I wish the format of the play-in game was more akin to the old version than what they have now. But the show has the potential to grow on me."

Alas, the show never got that chance. CBS pulled the plug after thirteen broadcasts divided over two seasons. During its initial summer run, the show consistently placed in the top twenty every week—finishing as high as number three overall for two episodes—but up against new episodes of hit shows during the following winter, the show withered.

LET'S MEET OUR CHAMPION: CHAD MOSHER

An exclusive account for This Day in Game Show History

I had originally learned about the show from news sites that were covering the production of the first season for June 2008. I had no intentions of auditioning until I was contacted by a casting coordinator on behalf of the producers in July 2008 when I auditioned in Chicago. I had made PowerPoint presentation software based on the program, for people to play it at home, and posted the link at the Game Show Forum (a message board for game show fans). She said that her producers were impressed and wanted to invite me to audition for the program.

I was certainly a fan of the old versions, after seeing reruns of GSN for years. The original *Password* moved fairly slowly but it was indicative of its times, whereas *Password Plus* and *Super Password* added a unique spin that extended the franchise's longevity. I certainly enjoy the pre-2000s versions of the show but I thought *Million Dollar Password*'s speedier format brought the show into a modernized version very well. It took classic elements of *Password*, splashed a bit of *Pyramid* and *Millionaire* in there and created what I thought was an enjoyable show.

For the audition, we first took a five-password test; three clues given by the contestant coordinators for each word. I'm nearly certain you had to get four out of five or five out of five to pass. We were then randomly paired up with other people who passed to play sample games in front of coordinators. We were interviewed, but it was a very casual atmosphere. The players that they liked the most were invited to callbacks the next day where they did the same thing, but this time with producers watching as well as a video camera recording. I believe it was about two weeks after my audition that I got the call to let me know I'd been selected to play.

My partners were Phil Keoghan and Julie Chen. Julie was very intelligent and very fun. I chatted and joked a bit with her regarding me being a fan of *Big Brother*, the show she hosts. I told her that we could give "inside" clues since I was familiar with the show, but that never happened. It was cool to meet someone I'd watched regularly for a few seasons.

I was really surprised that I didn't have to play the fourth round since I won mathematically, although it did hurt me since I had to play with the weaker celebrity in the money round, in my opinion. Now and again I kick myself for not walking with the $50,000 knowing Phil was a bit weaker at the game, but it's not often you have a reasonable chance at $100,000.

I won $25,000. I bought myself a new mattress, HDTV and PS3, used it for a couple of trips, used most of it to pay for some of my college, invested a bit of it in the stock market and kept some of it for general spending money. A bit of it actually still remains.

My advice for anybody who wants to be a contestant: I always suggest that in audition, you should be yourself but only bigger. Turn your really personality up, speak a bit louder and be more energized. But never, ever, ever be fake. The people in charge are trained to spot fakes and they will.

June 2

1997 – *Make Me Laugh* Returns

BY 1997, NO ONE EXPECTED TO SEE A GAME SHOW resurrected from the dustbin of ideas rejected by Mark Goodson & Bill Todman. In a 1951 *Time* interview, Bill Todman described a project titled *Don't Make Me Laugh*, which the company had shot down. The game challenged contestants to listen to a comedian for three minutes and, if they didn't laugh at all during the performance, they would receive $100. The idea was rejected because, in practice games, there were very few losers.

Todman said, "We found that, for $100, a guy could stay grim no matter what happened."

But Goodson-Todman's trash was another production company's treasure. Under the guidance of Mort Green, George Foster, and Sylvester "Pat" Weaver, the retitled *Make Me Laugh* first arrived on television on March 20, 1958. Robert Q. Lewis hosted as contestants faced comics Sid Gould, Buddy Lester and Henny Youngman. Contestants earned a dollar per second for up to three minutes' worth of jokes.

TV critics felt the same way that Goodson-Todman had, with one critic calling it "the easiest way to earn $180 yet." Opening night contestants were uniformly successful, save for the "special guest contestant," Tony Bennett, who broke up after hearing a single joke.

The game disappeared in only three months. In 1979, though, *The Tonight Show Starring Johnny Carson* and Los Angeles nightclubs like The Comedy Store and The Laugh Factory had turned stand-up comedy into big business, and the time was right to try again.

This time around, *Make Me Laugh* appeared as a daily game show hosted by Bobby Van. A galaxy of rising stars took their turns at trying to crack up contestants. Among the performers on this incarnation were Garry Shandling, Bob Saget, Howie Mandel, future *Just the 10 of Us* star Bill Kirchenbauer, future *Late Show with David Letterman* regular Johnny Dark, and even The Unknown Comic. This run of the show was considerably more successful, surviving for a year and a half in syndication. Even with all the star power, though, the 1979 version of *Make Me Laugh* is probably best remembered for its dynamic disco-powered theme music, which was released as a single after the show was canceled.

Then in 1997, *Make Me Laugh* returned once more, quite appropriately on Comedy Central. Hosted originally by Ken Ober and later by Mark Cohen, the game was played the same right down to the bargain basement payday of one dollar per second. Again, it still proved to be a formidable showcase for rising stars. George Lopez, Jimmy Pardo, Wendy Leibman, and Bill Dwyer all made some of their earliest TV appearances on Comedy Central's *Make Me Laugh*.

June 3

1929 – Chuck Barris' Birth

Chuck Barris kicks back in his office. (Author's Collection)

He's a polarizing figure in game shows. He created some of the greatest hits of all time but, by his own admission, he actually hated game shows. He became one of the most visible performers on television, despite the fact that he was awful at performing. His legacy may be that his game shows arguably opened the door for an entirely new genre: reality TV.

Chuck Barris grew up in the suburbs of Philadelphia to parents who didn't really seem to care how he did in school, or anywhere else for that matter. With no parental guidance to speak of, he eventually attended Drexel University and wrote for the student newspaper. After college, he worked in a clothing factory and settled down early, marrying his girlfriend, Lynn Levy, the daughter of a CBS co-founder. Her family strenuously disapproved of the union, disinheriting her for a time.

Deciding that television was where he wanted to be, Chuck left his factory job to become a page at NBC. He slowly climbed the industry ladder, becoming a standards-and-practices representative for ABC in charge of *American Bandstand*. Chuck wrote a song for singer Freddie "Boom-Boom" Cannon, "Palisades Park," which hit number three on the Billboard charts but landed him in hot water with his ABC bosses who, in the wake of the Payola scandals, felt it looked unbecoming for a network employee to write songs for the guests on a musical program.

Nevertheless, Chuck was eventually promoted to the daytime programming department and placed in charge of selecting new game shows for the line-up. He felt so little confidence in the new ideas he was hearing that he quit ABC to become a producer and create his own shows.

Chuck launched his own production company with a motley crew of staffers in sandals and blue jeans who didn't look like they belonged in television. The boss would pour beer over his own head to mark a formal announcement that a new series was sold. He kept his guitar at work and encouraged employees to bring instruments for jam sessions. One employee recalled that to make a good impression, he showed up for his first day wearing a suit and tie, which gave the staff a laugh as they destroyed the tie with scissors.

In 1965, Chuck pulled it off, successfully launching *The Dating Game* at his old stomping grounds, ABC. Hosted by Jim Lange, the show featured a woman asking questions to three hidden suitors and using only their voices and responses as the basis for selecting the contestant who would accompany her on a date. Typically, the contestants were young and sexy, and the questions were sexually charged in a way that was unheard-of not just for game shows, but for any television show. Critics derided the tasteless nature of the game, but audiences soaked it up. ABC eventually introduced a prime time version to capitalize on the program's popularity.

Barris followed that success in 1966 with *The Newlywed Game* (see July 11), another naughty show that shocked viewers and critics as host Bob Eubanks asked the contestants questions about "whoopee" in the shower, on an airplane and, most outrageously by 1966 standards, before marriage.

Outrageous as he was, Chuck was just hitting his stride, branching out with a prime time variety show titled *Operation: Entertainment*, and a novel, *You and Me, Babe*, which became a bestseller. His game show attempts were met with mixed success. Although *Dating* and *Newlywed* thrived, even ardent fans might have trouble remembering *How's Your Mother-in-Law?* and *The Game Game*.

In 1975, Chuck had an idea for a talent show and, after quickly discovering how few good acts were showing up for the auditions, he took the idea to the opposite extreme. Even though

A casual Chuck enjoys nature in the 1970s. (Author's Collection)

only one NBC executive liked the pilot, the network picked up *The Gong Show*. Originally at the helm was John Barbour, but Chuck was so unhappy with his performance in the role that after taping five episodes, he fired Barbour, refused to air those episodes and stepped up to host the show himself.

Chuck proved to be awkward and stiff. He grinned emotionlessly, clapped his hands, read cue cards in a monotone, giggled, looked at his feet, stared at the ceiling—nervous habits that would get any other host fired. Yet, for such a tacky and silly show, an awkward host proved to be a perfect fit. Chuck could never convincingly host any other game show, but he was perfect on *The Gong Show.*

"Chucky Baby" on *The Gong Show*. (Fred Wostbrock Collection)

NBC capitalized on the success of the twisted show with a prime time special and a short-lived prime time variety show, *The Chuck Barris Rah-Rah Show*, where Chuck showcased established celebrity performers like Ray Charles and Alice Cooper as well as performers from *The Gong Show* who had turned out to be decent.

By 1980, things were becoming difficult for Chuck. Fifteen years of critics' barbs were taking their toll, and selling shows in syndication was becoming difficult and stressful. His daughter, Della, a regular on *The Gong Show*, was dealing with serious emotional problems and turned to drugs; at his suggestion, which he later regretted, she left home for a while so she could do whatever she wanted and get it "out of her system." Chuck's film, *The Gong Show Movie*, bombed. With stress overwhelming him, Chuck walked away. He shut down his production company, moved to France and, for a while, Chuck Barris relaxed.

During the 1980s, he dusted off some of his biggest hits for new versions of *The Dating Game*, *The Newlywed Game*, *Treasure Hunt* and *The Gong Show*. Other than *The Newlywed Game*, the revivals were duds. Chuck largely kept himself away from hands-on production, trusting his staff to run things while he pursued writing. In 1984, he released *Confessions of a Dangerous Mind: An Unauthorized Autobiography*, in which he claimed to have been a CIA assassin. It was followed by a sequel, *Bad Grass Never Dies*. He maintained that the dream vacations for winners on *The Dating Game* were a ruse to give him a reason to fly to the exotic locations and carry out a series of murders. Chuck consistently has insisted that this account of his life is true, although the CIA issued a formal statement denying that Chuck was ever employed there. *Confessions of a Dangerous Mind* became a film, directed by and co-starring George Clooney (see November 5). In the early 1990s, Chuck sold his production company to Sony for $200 million, and he left television behind.

In the late 1990s, Chuck had a bittersweet reunion with his daughter Della. She was still a drug addict and still dealing with psychological problems, but the bond between father and daughter was undeniably strong and they continued to have contact. In 1998, Chuck flew into California to pay her a visit and learned that she had died earlier that morning from a massive overdose. The death was ruled a suicide, although Chuck maintains in his 2010 book, *Della: A Memoir of My Daughter*, that it was an accident.

After that, Chuck seemed to spend his golden years trying to find himself. He reconciled himself to the *The Gong Show* being considered as the high point of his career but once stated that, if he wrote enough books, he hoped people would remember him as a writer. He released an album, *Confessions of a Dangerous Singer* and, when asked, continued to play coy about that CIA story.

June 4

1984 – *Body Language* Premieres

Tom Kennedy returned in 1984 with *Body Language*.
(Fred Wostbrock Collection)

Mark Goodson loved the idea of charades as a game show. *Showoffs* (see May 24) was arguably doomed in 1975 by circumstances beyond its control, but the following decade, Mark Goodson asked his staff to rework the idea, and in 1984, another game of charades burst onto the scene.

Replacing another Goodson offering, *Tattletales*, on the CBS daytime schedule, *Body Language* was hosted by Tom Kennedy. Tom's previous hosting job had been Goodson-Todman's *Password Plus*, a format from which *Body Language* cribbed a few rules.

Two celebrity-contestant teams competed. One player conveyed clues via charades and the designated guesser had sixty seconds to guess up to five words. Afterwards, the guesser saw a brief paragraph with seven blanks. The words guessed were plugged into the appropriate blanks, and the guesser tried to figure out the subject that the paragraph was describing. The teams played a series of puzzles worth $100 and $250, with $500 winning the game and a chance to play Sweepstakes, another series of words that could pay up to $10,000.

Body Language enjoyed more success than its predecessor, lasting eighteen months in a weak time slot (4:00 p.m., meaning it was subject to preemptions for local and syndicated programming in many cities). The game came to an end shortly after the new year in 1986.

LET'S MEET OUR CHAMPION: MICHAEL BRUNO

An exclusive account for This Day in Game Show History

I had never been on a game show before, never even tried out for one. I had just moved to Hollywood in 1983. I didn't try out for *Body Language* initially; the show wasn't even on the air yet. I had actually auditioned for *The $25,000 Pyramid*, another CBS show, and got rejected. The contestant coordinator called me back and said, "We can't use you because you're funnier than the celebrities."

I felt bad, but I laughed it off after I heard that. Then the coordinator said the network had a new game show in development and asked me, "Do you like charades?" I said "Absolutely." I love party games, I had a theater background, and I was delivering singing telegrams. I was very outgoing, so charades was going to be a lot of fun.

I did the audition, which consisted of playing charades and doing some word puzzles like they had on the show. I think I got on the show because I had a handle on those word puzzles. The people auditioning were all very good at charades but those word puzzles tripped up a lot of them. After the first two of them, I got into the writers' heads and I was able to figure it out, even with only one or two words showing. The writers had a sick sense of humor, and I could read the puzzles and think, "Oh, I know where they're going with this."

So I got on the show, and I really got into the rhythm of the game quickly. I was the first really big winner on the show, I was a three-day champion early in the series, and I won $16,100, which paid off a few credit cards, and the rest I used to buy a convertible.

I remember the stars I was with; Soupy Sales was very nice but I didn't get to play with him very much. Abby Dalton was *very* sweet to me, and I loved-loved-*loved* Didi Conn; she and I were like kindred spirits. During commercial breaks, she would turn to me and say such kind things: "You're really great...you're really sweet...I feel sorry for you because you're stuck with Dick Shawn as a partner and he's obviously on drugs..." We bonded, and actually after that we became close friends. We still are.

Tom Kennedy was a very nice man on and off the air. He was flattering and complimentary toward me. Very gentlemanly, very encouraging, not just to me but to all the players, and I remember that he actually seemed sad when I lost. He talked to me for a few minutes afterward and said some extremely kind things to me and congratulated me for being the first big money champion on the show.

I actually got into the game show business after that. I was a contestant coordinator for a lot of shows, like *High Rollers* and *Love Connection. High Rollers* was wonderful. *Love Connection* was hell on earth and you can quote me on that. And I was a contestant for dozens of run-throughs and pilots. I did one based on the Mister Game Show toy, they had this giant robot in the middle of the stage that looked like Wink Martindale, with Shadoe Stevens doing the voice. That was bizarre.

But the game show business was good to me for a lot of years. I moved to Wisconsin in 2001, and I have a theater company called WhoopDeDoo Productions. We do a play called *The Game Show Show*, where the premise is that the audience is seeing a game show taping, and we have local celebrities come in and be the celebrity guests, we bring audience members onstage to be contestants, and we actually have a game show being played on the stage, and the plot of the show is about what happens behind the scenes. So the audience will see things unfold backstage, and then see a round of the game. All the backstage stories in the plot of the show are true stories from my experiences, by the way.

June 5

1943 – Jim Peck's Birth

Jim Peck shares a smile with contestants on *You Don't Say!*
(Fred Wostbrock Collection)

Jim Peck was a broadcaster's broadcaster; like Bill Cullen before him and Tom Bergeron after him, he has fans who remember him strictly as "the game show host" even though he was more accurately a jack-of-all-microphones.

Born in Milwaukee, Jim grew up obsessed with radio. As a child, he'd sit in the audience of the local NBC radio affiliate, which conducted broadcasts from a large auditorium. He knew early that he wanted to be a broadcaster, although when he reached college he veered away from this goal somewhat to pursue acting. He performed in several plays and, after finishing a stint in the Army Reserves, he acted in summer stock productions of *Brigadoon* and *West Side Story*.

By the time he was twenty-five, Jim was pursuing his broadcasting dreams, hosting two local talk shows in his hometown. He eventually made his way to a larger market, Washington, DC, to host another talk show. In 1973, after five years of talk shows, Jim wanted to try something different, and it turned out all he had to do was ask. He watched NBC's *The Who, What or Where Game*, read the credits carefully and made a phone call to creator/producer Ron Greenberg asking to audition for a future game show project.

He made a good impression and his timing turned out to be perfect because, at the moment he called, Ron Greenberg was developing a new game for ABC. Greenberg offered an audition, Jim delivered an impressive one and Greenberg eagerly showed the tape to ABC, which approved of the unknown newcomer for the upcoming pilot.

ABC picked up the pilot, and *The Big Showdown* premiered on December 23, 1975. Each day, three contestants competed in six categories, with each category worth a value of one to six points. A predetermined "payoff point" was established and the contestants would answer questions from the categories, attempting to hit the payoff point exactly for a cash bonus; the wrinkle was that if a point value would put one contestant over the payoff point, that player wasn't allowed to answer the question. The contestants played as many payoff points as time allowed, with the winner rolling special pairs of dice for possible bonuses of $5,000 or $10,000.

Jim's entrance each day on *The Big Showdown* involved descending a large staircase and bounding to his podium. On one episode, he lost his footing, tripped and fell on the stairs. The audience howled with laughter. Jim humbly refused an offer from the director to re-tape the opening, calling his blooper "a human moment" and playing it up through the episode, kicking the staircase at one point in the game. The blooper strangely became something of a legacy for Jim. Decades later, he described periodically receiving residual checks from remote corners of the world because his tumble had been used in blooper specials everywhere.

The Big Showdown was gone in six months, but Jim had made such a strong impression on ABC that the network signed him to a one-year contract. He guest-hosted a week of *Good Morning America* and a series of game show pilots. He returned to ABC in 1976 with *Hot Seat*, a spin on *The Newlywed Game* in which contestants had to predict how their spouses would answer personal questions when hooked up to a lie detector. It was on and off in thirteen weeks, but the host stayed optimistic.

After *Hot Seat* was canceled, he assured a reporter, "Each new failure takes me higher on the ladder."

ABC kept trying, airing two prime time specials starring Jim and putting together a pilot for a talk-variety show for him. Meanwhile, he went back to work with another game show, *Second*

Chance (see March 7). More short-lived games followed, including a revival of *You Don't Say!* and *3's a Crowd*.

3's a Crowd was a game that Jim described to a reporter as "*The Newlywed Game* with fangs." It was a rather shocking game from producer Chuck Barris in which a husband appeared onstage with his wife and his secretary, who competed to see which of them knew him best. Suspicious behavior, sometimes even an affair, was acknowledged in some of the answers and, on at least one occasion, a fight broke out during the game.

Jim was philosophical about the reaction of viewers and critics who called the show tasteless. "I'm not aware of any game show that has been called tasteful," he told a reporter. "Basically, game shows don't receive critical acclaim. There are no redeeming values. The only thing they are supposed to do is entertain, and I think that's redeeming enough. We don't make any social points; we are there to titillate and have fun."

It's curious to imagine what may have become had *3's a Crowd* stayed on the air, but Chuck Barris shut down all of his programming in 1980 and *3's a Crowd* vanished.

In 1983, Jim became the regular guest host of *The Joker's Wild*. Jack Barry was dealing with health problems and found the taping schedule of five episodes per day too much for him, so he began alternating weeks with Jim, with the long-term plan being for Jack to announce his retirement at the beginning of the 1984-85 season and pass the torch to Jim. When Jack died suddenly, those plans changed. Bill Cullen, who Barry & Enright Productions deemed to have "bigger marquee value," was given the job, although Jim would still guest-host the game occasionally.

After five seasons at the helm of *Divorce Court*, Jim returned to his roots in Milwaukee, hosting local radio and TV shows once again and holding down a day job in the PR and Fund Raising

Department at his alma mater, Marquette University. Working a full-time job with a TV gig on the side proved more alluring to him than a retirement of rest and relaxation. He told author David Baber, "The trick is to retire *to* something and not *from* something."

June 6

1949 – *It Pays to be Ignorant* Arrives on TV

The Golden Age of Radio was crawling with experts, the "Answer Man" and his ilk, who claimed to have the answer to any question that a listener wanted to pose. As the gimmick grew more ubiquitous, a spoof became inevitable. Little could anyone guess that the spoof would be strong enough to merit its own series.

It Pays to be Ignorant, premiering in 1942, turned the premise on its ear. Creator/host Tom Howard would reach into a dunce cap and pull out questions with obvious answers. The panelists—George Shelton, Lulu McConnell and Harry McNaughton—would argue, rant, deliver monologues, sling insults and get sidetracked to the point that they would even forget what the question was.

"What river is shown in the famous picture of Washington crossing the Delaware?"

George Shelton: "Who painted the picture?"
Lulu McConnell: "Can you show us the picture?"
Tom Howard: "You don't need to see the picture! What river is shown in the famous picture of Washington crossing the Delaware?"
Lulu: "Was it done in oil? I was done in oil once."
Tom: "So are sardines."
Lulu: "Did you know it only took Washington ten minutes to cross the Delaware?"
Tom: "How do you know that?"
Harry McNaughton: "She was rowing."

The show proved to be as popular as the programs they were spoofing. For a period, Warner Brothers even considering adapting *It Pays to be Ignorant* as a series of short subjects to be played in theaters before the feature presentation. That plan fell through, but the idea of adding a visual to the popular radio game was a solid one, and in 1949, *It Pays to be Ignorant* arrived on CBS as a summer replacement for *Arthur Godfrey's Talent Scouts*. In 1951, it returned as a summer replacement for another comedy quizzer, *You Bet Your Life*.

The show vanished for two decades before returning for a one-season run in syndication in 1973. Produced by Stefan Hatos and Monty Hall, this version was hosted by Joe Flynn (*McHale's Navy*) and featured panelists Charles Nelson Reilly, Jo Anne Worley and Billy Baxter. But the Golden Age of Radio wasn't suited for television in the 1970s, and *It Pays to be Ignorant* was soundly ignored.

June 7

1955 – *The $64,000 Question* Premieres

Hal March in front of the famous isolation booth on *The $64,000 Question*. (Author's Collection)

In September 1955, a convention of wholesale druggists was held at the Greenbrier Hotel in White Sulphur Springs, WV. On the evening of the 13th, the convention was interrupted for a major announcement. Was there some sort of emergency? Did somebody need to move his car? No. The announcement was bigger than that.

"The Marine has answered the question!" The druggists erupted with cheering and applause before resuming the scheduled events of the evening.

In New York City that night, Captain Richard S. McCutchen, a self-proclaimed expert in the field of cooking, had stood beneath the searing lights of a television studio, trapped inside a tiny booth, as master of ceremonies Hal March posed a question: "Name five dishes and two wines from the menu of a royal banquet given in 1939 for French President Albert Lebrun by King George VI of England." Captain McCutchen calmly and surely answered, "Consommé, quenelles, filet de truite saumonée, petit pois a la française, sauce maltaise, corbeille; the two wines were Chateau d'Yquem and Madeira Special."

And just like that, the Marine coasted into television history as the person to win the most money at that point—$64,000—on a quiz show.

The $64,000 Question was rooted in a popular radio quiz, *Take It or Leave It*, hosted by Garry Moore. The top prize had originally been sixty-four dollars. Louis G. Cowan, whose *Stop the Music* had been one of the most successful radio game shows, decided to ramp up the money by adding three zeroes to that sixty-four dollar question and making it a prime time TV quiz.

To Cowan's surprise, though, not everybody shared his enthusiasm. Garry Moore, who had been closely identified with *Take It Or Leave It*, wanted no part of the big money version, because the amount of money made him squeamish. With

$64,000—a lot of money today, but an absolute fortune at that point—up for grabs, Garry suspected that "hanky-panky" would inevitably take place backstage.

Cowan went to his old business partner, Mark Goodson, who co-produced *Stop the Music*, and found that Mark was just as unenthusiastic, telling him point-blank, "This is only going to work if you fix it."

Cowan insisted that Mark Goodson was wrong. Mark's argument was that, with contestants required to risk whatever they had already won in order to go for the next level of money, the stakes were too high to work. Nobody would throw $32,000 in the trash for a possible $64,000 without knowing that it was pretty much a sure thing, Mark reasoned.

Cowan kept pushing. CBS finally picked up the show, with cosmetics maker Revlon signing on as the sponsor, and television's first big-money quiz show, *The $64,000 Question* premiered in the summer of 1955. And it didn't just premiere, it exploded.

Edward R. Murrow, whose *See It Now* had attracted acclaim and controversy for CBS, sat in a control room with his producer, Fred Friendly, and watched the premiere of *The $64,000 Question*. When the program concluded, Murrow somberly asked Friendly, "Any bets on how much longer we'll keep this time period now?" Both men sensed that quiz shows were about to take over TV.

Sonny Fox, later the host of spinoff game *The $64,000 Challenge*, described on a PBS report a hot summer night when he walked through a neighborhood where all the windows were open. Out of every window for the entire block, he heard *The $64,000 Question*.

On the same program, Jack Narz described it this way: "You could shoot a cannon down the street, because nobody was out on the street. Everybody was at home watching that show."

Question was the number-one rated show in America for the 1955-56 season; at its peak, better than eighty percent of TV viewers on Tuesday nights had their dials tuned to CBS. It inspired board games, a magazine, books and even a record, *$64,000 Jazz.* Revlon sales improved so drastically that shortages were caused and the show's host, Hal March, had to use the designated commercial time to ask the audience's patience while new supplies were manufactured.

Behind the scenes, *The $64,000 Question* was a bizarre blend of real people and manufactured drama, true knowledge and intelligence offset by meticulously planned outcomes.

The audience at home saw a contestant stroll onstage, introduced by host Hal March, who would reveal a large board with the names of many categories. The contestant would select one category as a field of expertise, and Hal would press a button that set an IBM sorting machine into action. Cards each containing a question from that category would pop up in the slots at the bottom of the board. While viewers were told that a computer had selected the questions to be used, this was pure show; in reality, the same pile of cards would appear no matter which button was pressed.

The questions did result from an involved process. Dr. Bergen Evans (see May 30), a professor and quite legitimately a brilliant man, wrote many of the questions himself; for his weaker areas such as sports, another writer was hired. After the show's staff verified and edited them, the questions were locked in a Manufacturers-Hanover Trust Company vault until show day when Evans, sitting onstage surrounded by armed guards, would personally hand the questions to Hal March. As rumors about the credibility of the show mounted, the unsuspecting Evans argued for the legitimacy of the game. He admitted he was being paid a tidy sum to write and research the questions, not to mention being flown from Illinois to New York at the show's expense every week, and it was inconceivable to him that a show would spend so much money for something that wasn't on the up-and-up.

Hal would ask the contestant a series of questions; as long as correct answers were given, the contestant could keep playing, but a wrong answer forfeited all the money. In an initial appearance, the contestant heard questions worth $64, $128, $256, $512, $1,000, $2,000 and $4,000. At that critical juncture, Hal would send the contestant home, to give some thought to risking $4,000 for a shot at $8,000.

The contestant would return the following week with the decision. A contestant who went for $8,000 was moved into a "soundproof booth" about the size of a telephone booth. The reason given on the show was to prevent the contestant from possibly hearing an audience member shouting out an answer. The real reason was to confine the contestant in a tight space to create extra tension and drama. Winning contestants would repeat this process for up to five weeks, doubling their money as long as they were correct, until they finally topped out at $64,000.

As the show grew in popularity, so too did Revlon's involvement. Although Revlon co-founder Charles Revson would maintain that he had no idea the show was rigged, and producer Steve Carlin insisted as late as 1995 that his staff ignored any orders given by Revson, director Joseph Cates and co-producer Merton Koplin recalled that Revson led weekly meetings to discuss the contestants, the following show's contestants and the ratings. According to Cates and Koplin, the orders were clear: the contestants whom Revson and the audience seemed to like were allowed to keep winning.

The rigging was kept as subtle as possible. Whereas other big-money quiz shows prepared and scripted players point-by-point and question-by-question, as if the show were a movie or a play, *The $64,000 Question* took an approach so low-key that some contestants didn't even realize their games were rigged; they didn't know what had happened to them.

If a potential contestant seemed like an interesting prospect—an unlikely expert such as a little old lady who knew baseball or that Marine captain with impressive cooking expertise—the person was given a two-hundred-question test on the identified field of expertise. If the applicant was chosen to be a contestant, that test was used as a reference for the person's extent of knowledge about the topic.

For example, Gino Prato was a shoemaker who claimed to be an expert in opera. The test revealed him to know only about Italian operas; he was largely clueless about operas from other countries. When Prato proved to be a popular contestant, he was consistently given questions only about Italian operas. Had he proven unlikable, the show might have thrown him a curveball by asking about a French opera. Prato went on to win $32,000 before voluntarily retiring, disappointing fans who eagerly wanted to see him win the top prize.

For producers to keep constant tabs on the contestant's level of knowledge, each episode was preceded by a "warm-up" session, during which a staff member would barrage the contestant with questions. Typically, among those questions would be the actual question, or a very similar one, that would be asked on the show that night. And if it was a popular contestant, and that contestant gave a wrong answer in their warm-up, the correct answer was supplied. That's how the outcomes were rigged without explicitly letting contestants in on the ruse.

Some players were clueless; others caught on but kept their mouths shut. In his memoir about the quiz show scandals, former New York District Attorney Joseph Stone recalled McCutchen angrily describing how embarrassed he felt as he stood in the isolation booth, heard one of the questions and realized exactly what was happening. He was able to so calmly rattle off his $64,000 answer about the royal banquet menu only because it was one of the questions in the warm-up session that night (although one could argue that he earned the money by remembering that lengthy answer). Another savvy contestant, Rev. Charles "Stoney" Jackson, won $16,000 but noticed that the staff treated him in a rather distant, icy fashion afterward so, when he returned the following week, he played it safe and announced he was quitting instead of going for $32,000.

Perhaps the most famous contestant to emerge from *The $64,000 Question* was Dr. Joyce Brothers, who parlayed her victory into stardom for decades to come. The story of her triumph is a fascinating tale of dishonest people being outwitted by somebody who—possibly—had been just a little bit sneakier.

"Dr. Joyce" had written to the show explaining that she was a psychologist and wanted to play in the category of psychology. She was rejected, with a letter of explanation that, first, psychology was a nebulous field, based on theory rather than fact and, therefore, did not generate compelling subject matter for a quiz show and, second, that a psychologist who knew a lot about psychology just wasn't that interesting. Merton Koplin suggested that Dr. Joyce could be fascinating as an expert in, for example, football or boxing.

Dr. Joyce replied that she could play the game as an expert in boxing. She took the test and passed. She went on the show and began a five-week run, amazing the staff with the depth of her knowledge.

"She knew the heavyweights!" Koplin marveled on the PBS chronicle. "She knew the welterweights! She knew it all!" Koplin recalled that Dr. Joyce was a popular contestant with everyone except the sponsor, who urged the show to get rid of her because she didn't fit Revlon's concept "of what cosmetics were all about."

The show tried to please the sponsor by tripping up Dr. Brothers with a $16,000 question about referees, but it turned out she knew about referees, too. Despite furious protests from Charles Revson, Dr. Joyce Brothers couldn't be stopped. She won $64,000.

As far as the producers could tell, Dr. Brothers had been studying boxing constantly from the moment she first claimed to be an expert and, with a religious dedication to cramming, she was able to retain everything she had read in only a few short weeks.

When New York prosecutor Joseph Stone investigated *The $64,000 Question*, he learned another side to the story. Since question authority Dr. Bergen Evans was weak in the field of sports, *The $64,000 Question* hired another writer to prepare the questions for Dr. Joyce Brothers. The writer was Nat Fleischer, owner & publisher of *Ring* magazine and author of a book called *Ring Facts*. When investigators first began grilling Brothers about her appearances on the show, she told them that one of the books she had studied was *Ring Facts*. Stone learned of a deeper and likely less-coincidental connection: Nat Fleischer was a personal friend of the Brothers family. In fact, after the producers of *Question* learned this, they took no action because of the potential egg on their face from revealing they had been duped, but when Dr. Brothers returned for a stint on the spinoff, *The $64,000 Challenge*, the producers made it a point to hire a different writer.

Dr. Joyce Brothers wasn't the only contestant to revel in stardom after winning the big money. Gino Prato, the opera expert, received an audience with the Pope during a trip to Italy. An eleven-year-old spelling expert, Gloria Lockerman, spoke at the Democratic National Convention. Baseball expert Myrtle Power was hired by CBS to do sports commentary. Stock market expert Lenny Ross rang the bell to open the New York Stock Exchange one morning. Still others enjoyed privileges like publicity tours, awards and endorsement deals.

In 1956, *TV Guide* reported that "nasty whispers" were already circulating about what really went on at *The $64,000 Question*. The show attempted damage control with a publication called *Inside Story of The $64,000 Question* to refute the rumors but, as the truth trickled out about other shows, like *Twenty One* and *Dotto*, it was hard for America to accept the notion that the original big-money quiz was on the level. When the New York State District Attorney, Frank Hogan, ordered an investigation of all quiz shows, the number-one show only two years later plummeted to seventy-third place in the ratings. The show ended on November 2, 1958, unwept and unsung by the outraged former viewers.

June 8

1933 – Joan Rivers' Birth

Joan Rivers already had a solid career as a stand-up comedienne and writer for Johnny Carson by the time *The Hollywood Squares* came knocking and offered her a spot on the panel. She was one of numerous semi-regulars throughout the golden years of the show with Peter Marshall at the helm.

In 1987, Joan returned to the show, at that time hosted by John Davidson, as a full-fledged regular, gamely occupying the Center Square for two seasons with a sharp tongue and perfect timing that rivaled those of the legendary Paul Lynde.

PETER: In the Bible, King Balshazar saw the handwriting on the wall, and later that night something unfortunate happened. What?

JOAN: Yeah, well, he found out that Shirley's number had been disconnected.

PETER: *Time Life Books* calls it the most complex lump of matter known to man. What is it?

JOAN: My eggs benedict!

PETER: *Reader's Digest* recently carried a cover story listing three things entitled "Don't Let Them Wreck Your Marriage." Two were money and sex. What was the third?

JOAN: ...Little 18-year-old tramp!

PETER: According to Ann Landers, your husband, Edgar, is talking in his sleep. Should you be upset if he talks about his secretary?

JOAN: And how...his secretary is a guy!

JOHN: According to psychologist John Solomon, it is wise to avoid sex after what?

JOAN: After you become a TV evangelist.

JOHN: To an Englishman, what is a pasty?

JOAN: His mother's complexion.

JOHN: According to *Focus on Fashion*, today's most popular fashions include ice-blasted, bashed and destroyed. Fashions of what?

JOAN: Luggage.

JOHN: How long should you expect a vacuum cleaner to last?

JOAN: Forever, because I never use it.

June 9

1981 – Allen Ludden Dies

"Mr. Password," Allen Ludden. (Author's Collection)

When Allen Ludden appeared as a judge on *The Gong Show*, Chuck Barris introduced him by explaining he was there because "we decided the show could use a little class for a change."

Nobody could argue with that. There was something about Allen that was different from other hosts. The broad, confident stride as he walked across stage, his perfect elocution, his unmanufactured intellect, his sharp fashion sense, even the way he gestured with his hands—everything about Allen Ludden suggested a high-quality, rare breed of human being.

And yet, for all that, he was accessible. Audiences liked him and trusted him. He opened every show with a sincere smile and preferred to use the word "friends" whenever he looked into the camera. From any other broadcaster, that might have come across as phony and cliché. When Allen Ludden said it, though, a viewer knew it to be from the heart.

He was born Allen Ellsworth on October 5, 1917, in Mineral Point, Wisconsin. His hometown held a place in his heart through his entire life. During that week on *The Gong Show*, Allen decorated his portion of the judges' dais with a small handmade sign reading "Mineral Point—Hi!" He returned to the city for its sesquicentennial celebration in 1977 and remarked, "In this lovely garden spot of the world you have a sense of culture, sense of beauty and a great sense of fun. So I'm proud to be a part of it—to have my roots here. And I urge you all to hold it dear."

His father died in the 1919 influenza epidemic and, when his mother remarried, Allen took his stepfather's last name and became Allen Ludden. The family moved to Corpus Christi, Texas, in 1926 and spent the remainder of his childhood there. He enrolled at the University of Texas in 1937, where he became interested in theater, performing in and directing several plays while also concentrating on his studies. He earned his bachelor's degree in English and stayed a little longer to bump it up to a Master's degree.

Allen took his degree to Austin High School in Texas and taught English for a time before becoming an announcer for a local radio station. In 1942, he joined the Army. Because of his theater background, he was placed in the Special Services group and produced and directed forty shows for troops in the Pacific. The head of his group was Shakespearean actor Maurice Evans, who took a liking to Allen. After he was honorably discharged with a Bronze Star to his credit in 1946, Allen became Evans' personal business manager.

Allen Ludden, early in his broadcasting career.
(Author's Collection)

Evans was in demand as a lecturer, and occasionally he would call on Allen to fill in for him in that capacity. After a particularly impressive lecture in Hartford, Connecticut, local radio station WTIC offered Allen a job on the spot. Allen resigned from his managerial duties and returned to broadcasting.

On WTIC, he hosted a program called *Mind Your Manners*, in which teenagers would discuss current events, as well as giving advice on the appropriate way to react in a variety of situations that teens encountered. The program was so popular that NBC introduced a national television version in 1951.

After the show ended, Allen was commissioned by the New York Board of Education to host two educational shows. The elements were coming together for Allen's next career move, although he couldn't have realized it at the time. He had devoted so much time to education, and to broadcasting for the purpose of education, that he was the perfect candidate for the job offer he received in 1953.

Grant Tinker of NBC tapped Ludden to host a new radio show developed by producer Don Reid. It would be a quiz show pitting against each other teams of players from colleges across the country. Allen eagerly joined the venture, titled *College Bowl*, and hosted for two years. The program faded away as radio transitioned to continuous music.

In the ensuing years, Ludden hosted a number of local shows, including *Good Morning*, a *Today* imitation seen only in New York City on the ABC affiliate. He also hosted *Dance Time*, New York's local version of *American Bandstand.*

In 1959, *College Bowl* arrived on television, with Allen Ludden hosting the program every Sunday afternoon on CBS for three years. Behind the scenes, he was highly valued in various roles by the network. Allen was the program director for WCBS radio in

The varsity sport of the mind, *College Bowl.* (Author's Collection)

New York, eventually getting promoted to program director for all of the network's owned and operated stations. He was also a Creative Services consultant for CBS News, serving as a voice coach for Harry Reasoner and Charles Kuralt.

As Allen's professional life thrived, his family was experiencing a major crisis. His wife, Margaret, was seriously ill. She was diagnosed with lung cancer in 1957 and spent the next four years fighting it. By 1961, things weren't getting better, and the illness was taking its toll financially. Even with all of his responsibilities and success at CBS, four years of fighting lung cancer while continuing to raise three children almost completely depleted the Ludden family's finances.

Allen had the most expressive hands on television.
(Author's Collection)

Mark Goodson-Bill Todman Productions approached Allen with an offer to host a new game show with a paycheck that doubled what he was making at *College Bowl* and CBS combined. Seeing an opportunity to keep his family above water, Allen agreed to host *Password*.

The end of 1961 was a bittersweet time for Allen and his family. Margaret succumbed to lung cancer a month after *Password* premiered, but the show was a success, giving Allen job security and a large income that would allow him to rebuild his life.

About one week before Margaret died, Betty White appeared as a guest on *Password* but, given his personal circumstances, Allen took little notice of her. Early the following year, Betty returned to the show and, even though they had previously met, Allen felt the need to introduce himself. He spoke to her backstage and, after she walked away, Allen confidently leaned over to producer Bob Stewart and mumbled, "I'm going to marry that woman."

That summer, Allen returned to acting, appearing in a summer stock production in Massachusetts. He took the role because he knew it would be his children's first summer without their mother and taking a job in Massachusetts provided a good reason for them to be away from the house. To his complete surprise, Betty White was cast in the female lead.

Allen and Betty shared their first kiss onstage on opening night, since that was how the play ended. Allen admitted to holding the kiss longer than he was supposed to and, by the end of the summer, the cast mates had become lovers. Allen proposed almost immediately, but Betty refused. He proposed a few more times, and Betty still refused. Allen bought a ring, and she still refused. Allen stopped proposing but kept the ring, put it on a chain and wore it around his neck until Betty finally gave in. They were married on June 14, 1963.

As a family, the Luddens got off to a rocky start. Betty was a strict mother, because that was the kind of upbringing she had. To her exasperation, Allen was much more lax and prone to caving in when his children wanted something. Aside from those early clashes, though, they had an extremely happy home life. Allen took up gardening and, for family togetherness, Allen, Betty, and the kids would—what else?—play games. Chess, checkers, bridge, cribbage and gin rummy were all popular in the Ludden household. Betty liked to keep a cumulative score of all the gin rummy games played over the years in the house and, after two years of marriage, Allen told a reporter that he was trailing by a little more than six thousand points.

When asked why their marriage worked, Betty and Allen said they had struck on a unique secret to success: they didn't have very much in common. Betty explained in a newspaper article, "Although we have our work in common, there are marked differences in our tastes and interests...Despite our differences—or maybe because of them—we have wonderful communication. A successful marriage needs two people who are willing to bounce off each other in ideas, interests, competition, anger and love."

In the same article, Allen elaborated, "We thrive on our individual pursuits. I like the idea of Betty wanting a life of her own, of making it on her own terms. Although this does separate us, it nourishes the relationship. When we get together, there's so much to talk about! Our marriage works because it's a constant discovery."

In 1962, Allen had a difficult decision to make in his professional life. CBS decided to introduce a prime time version of *Password* and scheduled it so that it would go on the air only thirty minutes after *College Bowl*. General Electric, sponsor of *College Bowl*, didn't want Allen appearing on two shows in a single night, thinking it to be overkill. Allen was given an ultimatum: *College Bowl* or *Password*.

Allen explained his decision to the press: "*Password* offers scope, and a challenge...It has turned me into a fulltime performer.

Besides I'd done the other show for a long time, so it wouldn't prove anything much to me if I did another season of it."

Allen stuck with *Password* and was replaced on *College Bowl* by another bespectacled intellectual, Robert Earle.

Password ended production in 1967 but Allen wasn't gone long. Reruns of *Password* were sold into syndication and proved to be a surprise hit. Allen also hosted a new game show during the 1968-69 season. Called *Win with the Stars*, the game required celebrity-contestant teams to recite lines from popular songs, winning points for each word they correctly delivered in their performances.

The game lasted only that one season, and Allen decided it was time to branch out a little. Inspired by a fascinating interview Johnny Carson had conducted with Truman Capote, he tried being a talk show host for a time with an ambitious show titled *Allen Ludden's Gallery*. Each day's program was called a "Portrait" and focused on a noteworthy person like Wilt Chamberlain, Albert Schweitzer or Eldridge Cleaver. Allen would assemble a panel of reporters and authors who had previously written about that day's subject; they would compare notes, debate controversial points in the subject's

life and assemble something of a biography in that single program based on the talking points. Against a flood of competition, including Merv Griffin, Joey Bishop, David Frost, Mike Douglas, Steve Allen, Dinah Shore, fellow game show host Tom Kennedy and a newcomer from Dayton, OH, named Phil Donahue, survival was tough, and *Allen Ludden's Gallery* closed after one season.

The following year, Betty tried an ambitious talk show of her own, *The Pet Set*, with Allen serving as producer and announcer.

Password returned in 1971 on ABC, with stars like Elizabeth Montgomery and Burt Reynolds popping in to play. (Author's Collection)

Betty had as much trouble with competition as Allen had, and the show folded after another one-season run.

In 1971, Allen was back with *Password*. Syndicated reruns of the original show proved so popular in the preceding four years that Goodson-Todman convinced ABC to put a new version on the air. The version lasted four years, and Allen even got a chance to show his stuff as a player. Monty Hall acted as guest host for one week, with Allen playing so well against Elizabeth Montgomery that Elizabeth demanded a second week. On another occasion, Allen played while Betty guest-hosted.

The show came to an end in 1975. On the final day, Allen held back tears while he hosted a final game played by staff members instead of celebrities. Mark Goodson made his way onstage and presented Allen with a gold watch—a duplicate of one that Mark himself owned that Allen had envied. Mark dubbed his star host "Mister Password" at the conclusion of the show.

In 1976, Allen returned to game shows with *Stumpers!* Similar to *Password*, the game was cancelled after only thirteen weeks, but its final episode was arguably Allen Ludden's defining moment as a television host. He could have been flippant or nonchalant at the conclusion of a three-month assignment. Instead, clad in a tuxedo, Allen delivered an extended speech commending the staff for all of their hard work and expressing how honored he was to hear from teachers that the game had been used as a learning tool. He told the viewers that he appreciated the fan mail and assured them, as well as the staff, that he felt privileged to be host of that game. He assured the viewers not to be sad that the show was cancelled. "This is New Year's Eve," he told them. "This is going to be a great new year. We have a very exciting future in this country ahead of us! We have 1977 ahead of us!"

Allen moved onto *Liars Club*, which he used to help bolster the career of a young up-and-comer. While *Password* was on the air, Allen had done a series of publicity appearances. During one stop, in 1974 at an Indianapolis AM station, Allen was dazzled by the funny and skillful broadcaster interviewing him for a talk radio segment. The interviewer mentioned to Allen that he had considered moving to Los Angeles, and Allen happily gave him some contact information and told him to call if he ever made the move. When the youngster finally relocated and contacted his new mentor, Allen called in some favors to help him find work. He also convinced his bosses at *Liars Club* to give a spot on the panel to the unknown, and that's how Allen Ludden helped launch the career of David Letterman.

In 1979, Ludden excitedly bounded down the steps of a newly built set, ran toward the camera and proclaimed, "*Password*'s back!" The new version was *Password Plus*. Allen eagerly returned to his greatest role with vigor—and a secret. Allen had been ill shortly before production started but kept it to himself in fear of being asked to step aside from the show if he disclosed it. It took some time before doctors were able to diagnose the problem. Allen secretly went through a variety of tests and examinations until March 1980, when he was finally diagnosed with stomach cancer.

For the next month, Bill Cullen guest-hosted *Password Plus* while Allen underwent major surgery and recuperated from the effects. Doctors were unable to remove the cancer completely and told Allen that he had only a few months to live. Faced with that diagnosis, Allen made the amazing decision to go back to work. With the public told only that Allen had been ill and had gone through surgery, Allen returned to *Password Plus* and continued hosting as long as he could.

In October 1980, his weakened body gave out. He suffered a massive stroke and spent several days in a coma. Tom Kennedy took over as host of *Password Plus*—once Allen awakened from the coma, he personally recommended Tom for the job—and that was the end of the reign of "Mister Password."

(Author's Collection)

Allen recorded radio commercials for a local gas company but never returned to TV, spending his final months at home with Betty. He granted newspaper interviews, in which he discussed the "friends" at home one final time.

"I've been on television for about twenty years, and I just did my job," he said. "But the mail that I have had, the prayers I've had said—I start to cry every time I talk about it...You just don't realize how many people can really relate to you and care about you."

Allen Ludden died with Betty by his side just five days shy of their eighteenth anniversary. Tom Kennedy eulogized him for the Associated Press obituary, saying, "He was a very dear friend to me and my wife, both off and on the tube...No one will ever fill his shoes. We're just thankful for having had a friend like him during our lives."

Television lovers were thankful, too. In a special 2001 issue, *TV Guide* declared him the number-one game show host of all time. In 2009, his fans honored him with the Bill Cullen Lifetime Achievement Award at Game Show Congress 7.

June 10

1957 – Michael Burger's Birth

Michael Burger has gone here, there and everywhere in modern game shows, remaining involved even as games were disappearing from the airwaves. Burger began as the warm-up man for *Wordplay*, where he made such a positive impression that host Tom Kennedy made it a point to offer a few nice words about him for the viewers at home, even though Michael was never seen on camera.

Eventually he made it in front of the camera, hosting a syndicated game, *Straight to the Heart*, in 1989. Three men and three women would face each other and secretly answer a variety of questions. Each player would select the answers they liked best, without knowing which players gave them. The two players who liked each other's responses the most during the game then played a bonus round for a chance at a vacation. The game lasted only six months, but it gave Mike a bona fide hosting credential.

In 1991 he moved onto another dating game show, a CBS offering titled *Personals*. This show was unusual for two reasons: it was taped at Los Angeles International Airport, and CBS placed it in a late-night time slot to see whether a game show could compete with NBC's *The Tonight Show*. Given the circumstances, *Personals* actually had a fairly respectable run of fifteen months, and Michael established himself as a promising host. CBS hung onto Michael and gave him another crack at hosting a game show, a one-time special titled *Storm the Castle* on June 16, 1993.

In 1996, Michael replaced Ray Combs as the host of the *Double Dare* knockoff, *Family Challenge*. This put Michael at the helm of a show that attracted a great deal of undeserved negative attention in the wake of Combs' suicide, and the show stayed afloat only for one year.

Over the next few years, Michael moved on to talk shows with *Home and Family* and *Mike & Maty*. Then in 1998, he landed a job hosting what he called "the crown jewel of game shows" with a revival of *Match Game*. The new version was panned by critics and viewers and expired after one season.

Although his TV games experienced minimal acceptance, Michael has found a great deal of success in the newest form of the game show genre: live, untelevised stage shows. In casinos and theaters across the country, Michael is in demand as host of live productions of *Wheel of Fortune*, *The Price is Right* and *Family Feud*, He's received critical acclaim in the role and, without the thirty-minute constraint, he has an enviable amount of freedom for a game show host. Every wacky contestant gets a few extra minutes, every zany answer is milked for all it's worth, and no quick-witted remarks are left on any cutting room floor. It may not have a national audience looking in, but for fans who attend Michael Burger's live games, it's a show they'll never forget.

June 11

1976 – *High Rollers* Ends…For Now

Alex Trebek and Ruta Lee were on a roll in the 1970s.
(Author's Collection)

Merrill Heatter and Bob Quigley had a magic touch with games. They took tic-tac-toe and made it *The Hollywood Squares*. They spun blackjack into *Gambit*. In 1974, they took an old dice game called Shut the Box and turned it into *High Rollers*.

Two contestants faced a board displaying digits one through nine. Each number represented a prize. The contestants would answer questions for the right to roll a pair of large dice. The object was to eliminate numbers from the board, and the player could eliminate either the sum of the dice roll or any combination of numbers that added up to the sum. For example, rolling a nine gave the player a choice of removing the nine; the seven and two; the five and four; or the two, three and four. The contestants kept going until one of them cleared the last number—and won—or rolled a number that couldn't be cleared, in which case the opponent won. The winner claimed all of the prizes behind the numbers that player had cleared.

Heatter-Quigley charged Art Alisi with producing the new series, and Art approached the task with zeal. He had been a fan of Bill Cullen's version of *The Price is Right* and sought to present the same type of lavish and unusual prizes for the new show, such as a trip to New York including breakfast at Tiffany's; African masks; a $10,000 fish bowl; a computer that automated all lights and appliances in the home; or dinner from Kentucky Fried Chicken every Sunday for one year.

Art explains why he went all out: "It was the Tiffany game show. We gave the usual cash, the car, or trip. But those other prizes made it a little more special, made it stand out."

Alex Trebek hosted the show, coming literally immediately off a run as the host of NBC's *The Wizard of Odds*. Alex signed off from the final episode of *Wizard* on June 28, 1974, and welcomed America to *High Rollers* on July 1. At the time it premiered, *High*

Rollers was part of an uninterrupted four and a half-hour block of game shows on the NBC daytime schedule. One critic called the era's abundance of game shows "not a trend; that's a glut."

Joining Alex each day was Ruta Lee, a film and TV star of the 1950s and '60s who surprised some observers by settling into a new career as a game show hostess. For each program, Ruta rolled the dice on behalf of the contestants. That was the reason presented to the viewers to explain her presence, but Art Alisi reveals that she was actually there to serve a more important purpose.

"In run-throughs, Alex was a little laid back...he was a little shy at the time...and so I said, 'I think Ruta Lee can really sparkle, and give him enthusiasm.'"

Ruta provided a comforting presence for Alex, as well as something of an onstage "buddy." They would kid each other and banter during the game, and Ruta got the job done. She brought Alex out of his shell and made him a better emcee.

The relationship proved symbiotic. Ruta's daily appearances on *High Rollers* helped revitalize her career. She was back in demand to the point that she had to take time off from the show on several occasions, during which special celebrity guests like Linda Kaye Henning, Nanette Fabray and Leslie Uggams would roll the dice in her place.

High Rollers enjoyed a successful two-year run on NBC and even managed to parlay it into a one-season stint in prime time, with Elaine Stewart (Merrill Heatter's wife) rolling the dice for the nighttime show.

It returned in 1978 with a tweaked game. The nine numbers were now shuffled and arranged into a three-by-three grid, with each column representing a jackpot of prizes. Clearing the last number from the column entitled the winning contestant to those prizes. Alex worked alone on this version; there were models

Alex Trebek, going solo for the 1978 revival.
(Fred Wostbrock Collection)

showing off the prizes, but no designated hostess and no one to roll the dice for the contestants. The players rolled those dice themselves.

"Really, that made for a better show, anyway," Art recalled. "The players were in charge of their own fate."

The game did slightly better in its revived incarnation, staying on the air for just over two years before getting dumped in June 1980 as part of an overhaul of NBC's daytime schedule to make way for the original *David Letterman Show*.

The game returned in 1987 with new host Wink Martindale. Airing in first-run syndication, the show was pitched to local stations with a strange pilot including a bonus game in which a contestant competed against a tuxedo-clad monkey. The monkey didn't make it to the series, but a myriad of other bonus games did. Instead of a prize, sometimes a column would contain a chance to win special prizes by playing small games like Love Letters, Wink's Garage Sale, It Takes Two and Around the World.

Wink Martindale handled the dice in 1987.
(Fred Wostbrock Collection)

Art Alisi was philosophical about the failure of the syndicated version, noting that *High Rollers* was one of the more complex games produced by Merrill Heatter. He recalls, "Merrill used to say that the reason our show *Gambit* worked well was because it was blackjack and anybody can count to twenty-one. But with *High Rollers*, you had to look at the number rolled, then look at the board, figure out every combination that added up to that number, figure out where they were in each column, figure out what numbers would be left after each one, decide which prizes you wanted…It was complicated."

Contestant coordinator Michael Bruno agrees. "We recruited contestants by placing ads in the Sunday newspapers and, during the week, you'd see about four hundred people. We had a written test, a lot of trivia questions, that narrowed it down to seventy-five to eighty people. And then we played a practice game where we had them roll the dice and decide what numbers to eliminate and just demonstrate that they could add the numbers and knock off everything correctly. Believe it or not, that usually whittled it down to ten."

The players who made it to the show did play it quite well, but one contestant stands out for Michael Bruno more than others. "His name is Dan Campbell. He won't mind my telling this story. When he came to the studio for his audition, he was living out of his car, which was wrecked by the way, because he just got evicted from his apartment. And he did a fantastic audition, played the game very well. We put him on the show, and he was the first person to win a car on that version of the show. And the taping ended and he burst into tears, and he walks up, hugs me, and says 'You just saved my life; thank you for putting me on the show.' I said, 'You put yourself on the show! You were a good player!' He became a friend after that and he tells that story himself all the time. But that was probably my favorite experience as a contestant coordinator."

Wink's version lasted only one year in syndication in a crowded field for game shows, but the show went on to enjoy three years of reruns on the USA Network.

June 12

1955 – *Monitor* Premieres on NBC Radio

The many broadcasters who became successful game show hosts typically became known exclusively for their game shows. It makes sense. The host is typically the only regular cast member on camera, and if the game turns out to be a hit, it means increased visibility, linked almost exclusively to that show. Because of this, it's easy to forget that many game show hosts were busy doing other things when they weren't doling out the cars, the cash, and the refrigerators.

Many game show hosts plied their trade in radio, often spinning records for local stations in New York and Los Angeles. One show in particular, though, stands out as one of the most common "other gigs" among game show hosts. It was the show that saved network radio at a time when the medium desperately needed help.

In 1955, television had altered the way people listened to radio and there was no longer an audience for thirty-minute sitcoms, forty-five-minute game shows, and one-hour variety shows that had once populated radio. If people wanted that stuff, they turned on the TV, not the radio. NBC President Sylvester Weaver, who had helped create some of the marvelous and innovative television programs that helped solidify that medium's takeover, proved the unlikely source of an idea that helped save NBC's floundering radio network.

The new program, *Monitor*, became arguably the last great radio program. It went on the air Saturday mornings at 8 a.m. and concluded at midnight on Sunday; yes, a forty-hour continuous radio broadcast, each week. Gradually, it would scale back to thirty-two hours, then thirty-four hours, then thirty-four hours plus two hours each weeknight, then down to sixteen hours. NBC affiliates loved carrying the program because weekend radio brought in the lowest audiences and, therefore, the least money. Stations were happy to carry such a lengthy broadcast that carried no additional costs for them.

The program was an innovative one at the time, the first with what became known as a "magazine" format, with Sylvester Weaver boasting that a forty-hour time slot would allow stories to get as much coverage as they merited, instead of having to cater to a five-minute slot. A typical *Monitor* broadcast line-up for 1956 shows exactly how ambitious the program was. In that forty hours, the program included features on housing for guests attending for the Melbourne Olympics, the Tivoli amusement grounds in Copenhagen, a children's rodeo in Denver, an Oklahoma City chess tournament, a famous tavern in London, pig auditions for an upcoming "L'il Abner" musical, a trolley museum, and a Belgian festival. In addition to all that, there would be comedy from Bob & Ray, plus Andy Griffith. Interviews with Elia Kazan, Milton Berle, Gordon McRae, Louis Armstrong, Hedda Hopper, and Bob Cummings were scheduled as well. Between all that, there would be regular world news updates, weather reports, sports coverage, and music. All that for a single broadcast.

Obviously the show would require air talent capable of handling such a wide range of elements. Numerous communicators—Weaver liked that term more than "host"—would appear each weekend, handling a few hours at a time. Among the many communicators were original *Today* anchor Dave Garroway, newsmen Frank Blair and David Brinkley, sportscaster Mel Allen, and later in the run of the show, established disc jockeys Don Imus, Wolfman Jack, and Robert W. Morgan. This book belongs to the game shows, though, and this entry belongs to the game show hosts.

HUGH DOWNS (1955-1959) Hugh Downs was already an established broadcaster after many years in Chicago. He had only been in New York a short time, primarily serving as Arlene Francis's announcer on *The Home Show* when *Monitor* went on the air. *Monitor* was yet another stop on Downs's road to proving himself as the most versatile broadcaster in the business.

CLIFTON FADIMAN (1955) With *Information Please*, *The Name's the Same*, *Quiz Kids*, and *What's in a Word* under his belt, Clifton was a familiar face to TV game shows when *Monitor* began.

MONTY HALL (1956-1958) Monty had a great deal of trouble finding work when he came to America from Canada. His work as a communicator was actually one of his early breaks.

A fan of *Let's Make a Deal* would be surprised to hear the humorless, serious tone with which he did his communicating

GENE RAYBURN (1961-1973) Gene would be the longest-tenured *Monitor* communicator. He was also arguably the most popular, bringing his expected freewheeling style to radio listeners each weekend. While delivering a commercial for a line of combs, he ad-libbed a remark about how the combs were unbreakable and pulled a comb out of his pocket. After revealing that the comb in his pocket wasn't the sponsor's brand, he vowed to break it in front of the microphone...only to find that he couldn't. He also conducted an interview with Walter Matthau in which Matthau dropped his pants to show off the custom underwear he had made while shooting his last film...just as a page guiding a tour group through Rockefeller Plaza happened by. Gene himself always had something on hand for the tour groups peering into the studio whenever he was on the air. Gene indulged in his hobby during the many pre-recorded segments that made up a *Monitor* broadcast, and when a tour group happened by, Gene would happily show them the needlepoint sample he had been working on that morning. He was up to the task, however, if an assignment actually did require him to be serious. He was at the helm of the program the day after President Eisenhower died and spent the broadcast solemnly covering the numerous memorial services held that day.

BERT PARKS (1961) The folksy host of many prime time quizzes, and the Miss America pageant, sat in for a time.

WAYNE HOWELL (1961) He was the announcer for more than a dozen game shows from the 1950s through the 1970s.

HAL MARCH (1961) The former host of *The $64,000 Question* was so burned out from the high profile of that show that he spent years after its cancellation searching for any other kind of work to do, be it television acting, Broadway shows, or communicating on *Monitor*.

ED MCMAHON (1965-1968) Though primarily known as Johnny Carson's sidekick, he had quite a formidable set of jobs to keep him occupied away from *The Tonight Show* in the late 1960s. While communicating on *Monitor*, he was also hosting *Snap Judgment* on daytime TV.

HENRY MORGAN (1966-1969) The grouchy humorist never really had much of a television career outside of his run on *I've Got a Secret*, so when that show was in its dying days, he went back to his old stomping grounds in radio. Henry was somewhat better-behaved and more mellow on *Monitor*, though the old Henry occasionally shone through, such as one broadcast where he delivered a rant about the undependable early computers of that time that were starting to pop up in businesses across the country.

GARRY MOORE (late 1960s) – Garry, having "retired" from prime time TV earlier in the decade, was on the comeback trail when he began communicating.

JOE GARAGIOLA (1969) His post-baseball career flourished in the late 1960s. He started communicating in the same year that he started hosting game shows.

BILL CULLEN (1971-1973) Bill had spent six years hosting a morning radio show for NBC's flagship station, WRCA in New York, before *Monitor* came along. He lasted two years on the show, which is impressive because in a 1972 interview he claimed it was only supposed to be a temporary assignment while the network looked for a new communicator.

Bill's signature on *Monitor* was a self-deprecating sense of humor. He greeted viewers by saying, "Welcome back to the Big M, where we have a lot going for you. This is Bill Cullen, an exception to the foregoing." He would introduce gardening segments by talking about his brown thumb or follow sex advice from Dr. Joyce Brothers by admitting that he probably should have paid closer attention.

ART FLEMING (1972) Art hadn't done radio in nearly twenty years when he arrived for *Monitor*. Funnily enough, after the original *Jeopardy!* ended its run, Fleming rarely worked in television again and worked almost continuously in radio for the last seventeen years of his life

DAN DANIEL (1973) – Daniel only had very limited work in the game show business, serving as announcer on *The Big Showdown* after *Monitor* came to an end.

JOHN BARTHOLOMEW TUCKER (1974-1975) The former host of *Treasure Isle* was among the final communicators and the last voice heard on the program.

Monitor was silenced after twenty years in 1975, bringing a close to the last great network radio show.

June 13

1913 – Ralph Edwards's Birth

Ralph Edwards smiles devilishly during a stunt on *Truth or Consequences*. (Author's Collection)

Ralph Edwards Productions proudly boasts the slogan, "We put people center stage," because that's what the founder did best. Sure, his radio and television productions often relied on star power, gimmicks, silly stunts and sight gags, but at the heart of each show was an affection for people, a curiosity about them and a sense of realism frequently missing from the hands of lesser broadcasters and producers.

Edwards was born on a Friday the 13th in '13 in Merino, Colorado. Just before he turned thirteen, the farm boy was uprooted when his family relocated to Oakland, California. There, Ralph discovered a creative streak that his mother nurtured. He performed in school plays and, by age fifteen, he was a paid broadcaster—writing, acting and announcing for radio station KROW. When he attended the University of California at Berkeley, he got a job at KTAB doing all that plus producing and creating sound effects.

Once Ralph graduated, he relocated to New York and immediately got a job as a staff announcer at CBS. By age twenty-seven, Ralph had created and hosted his own radio show, a fun-filled game show called *Truth or Consequences* (see July 1). Ralph would bring contestants from the audience onstage, ask them trick questions, have them compete in stunts and races or play pranks on them, often telling the listening audience at the start of the show what he was about to do and giggling maniacally as he asked, "Aren't we *devils*?"

The pranks and stunts may have been devilish, but in the ensuing years, Ralph Edwards would reveal himself to be more angel than devil. He organized elaborate surprises for audience members that involved reuniting them with long-lost loved ones. As World War II raged on, he took the show on the road for a special series of broadcasts with audiences consisting of troops in training. He encouraged listeners to buy war bonds by charging admission to *Truth or Consequences* shows in the form of war bonds were sold at the door, and the greater the value of the bond, the better the seat. Under this plan, a single broadcast of *Truth or Consequences* sold $325,480 worth of bonds.

As critics raged about the greed and selfishness on display in giveaway shows, Ralph Edwards thumbed his nose at them by turning his lavish prize giveaways into charity drives. Listeners at home had a chance to win tens of thousands of dollars in prizes, but a prerequisite of each contest was that the listener had to make a donation to a designated charity. Another fundraiser encouraged listeners to mail their extra cash to a twelve-year-old Boston cancer patient, referred to as "Jimmy," who wanted a TV so he could watch his favorite team play. Not only did enough cash pour in for the TV purchase, but an extra $200,000 established the non-profit Jimmy Fund.

Truth or Consequences was one of the most popular radio programs of any kind. Countless imitators would spring up in the coming years with varying degrees of success. It would be lampooned as "Truth or AHHHHH!" with host Daffy Duck and contestant Porky Pig in a *Looney Tunes* short. Perhaps the strangest tribute the show received in its heyday, though, was the day that Superman was a contestant; the cover of Action Comics #127 depicted Ralph Edwards squirting the Man of Steel with a seltzer bottle.

Ralph Edwards was tireless. With as much time and money as he invested into *Truth or Consequences*—he said in one interview that he spent $100 of his own money for the props used in each week's stunts—he wanted more. He accidentally stumbled upon his next great idea in 1946 while surprising a wounded soldier by bringing out his family and friends. Edwards wrapped up the segment by shouting, "This is your life!" The fan mail in response to the segment was so overwhelmingly positive that Edwards turned it into a new show.

This Is Your Life became a radio series presenting a weekly tribute to a single outstanding individual, who would be lured into the studio and surprised by the honor, Introducing pivotal people against a narration of the person's life story, the show was another smash for Ralph Edwards. It spawned fewer imitators than *Truth or Consequences*, perhaps because it took twenty people and $11,000 per week to produce the show—high numbers by the standards of the time.

The results were worth it. In addition to featuring celebrities, the show would frequently dedicate an episode to one of the "ordinary people" of the world. One night, an organ grinder wandered from table to table at a restaurant to entertain the customers until Ralph Edwards emerged, told him he was on the air and one by one, brought out his brother, son, wife, sister and relatives from Italy whom the organ grinder hadn't seen in thirty-four years.

As a promotional stunt, Edwards once went into the street, selected somebody at random, and asked her to help the staff assemble a tribute to the person of her choice. The random recruit selected her husband, a Russian immigrant who wanted to open his own fruit stand. The show got right to work, reuniting him with several relatives as well as a small child whose life had been saved by the immigrant a few years earlier. Edwards found a piece of property, helped the man open his own fruit stand and launched the new business with a lavish Hollywood premiere, complete with searchlights and celebrities coming to the stand on opening night.

Celebrities tapped for tributes included Dick Clark, Eddie Cantor and Betty White, but not all guests appreciated the gesture.

Lowell Thomas was furious at the surprise, Laurel and Hardy were irritated that their first and only television appearance turned out to be a surprise on an unrehearsed show and Angie Dickinson declined a request to rebroadcast her appearance.

One of the most popular episodes of the series was a profile of Lillian Roth, who could prepare because she knew in advance that she'd be the subject of the program. She openly discussed her recovery from alcoholism in graphic detail, describing her time in a mental institution and the collapse of her marriages as "a sixteen-year stupor." The episode drew a great deal of positive attention to the efforts of Alcoholics Anonymous, and NBC rebroadcast the show twice in response to popular demand.

Some questioned the show's taste. *The New York Times* accused the show of "exploiting the raw and private emotions of the unfortunate." *Time* called it "the most sickeningly sentimental show on the air" in an article detailing a 1960 broadcast paying tribute to housewife Elizabeth Hahn, who was working three jobs because, the show said, she was determined to keep her husband and children off the streets. Hahn's husband sued NBC for $50,000 for showing his image on the program without his consent, revealing to reporters that, in reality, he had sued her for divorce and she had turned in her own daughter as a delinquent.

As recently as 2011, some of the more outlandish radio broadcasts of *This is Your Life* were still being analyzed and critiqued. NPR's *This American Life* looked at episodes profiling a Holocaust survivor and a Hiroshima bombing survivor whom Edwards surprised with a visit from Capt. Robert Lewis, the pilot of the Enola Gay.

In all the years that *This is Your Life* was on the air, there was one person never surprised with a profile and a series of touching reunions: Ralph Edwards himself. It's not that the idea didn't come up, but Edwards told his staff in no uncertain terms that they would all be fired if it happened. He felt that the audience would lose faith in the show if it served as an ego trip for the man who created it. Respecting this logic, Ralph Edwards's staff never surprised him.

Ralph Edwards, *Truth or Consequences* and *This is Your Life* would all eventually make their way into television, and the new medium gave Edwards' fertile mind new ways to explore the everyday people who fascinated him so much. Shows like *End of the Rainbow*, *About Faces*, *Place the Face* and *It Could Be You* featured the same blend of games, ordinary people, fascinating stories and touching reunions that Ralph Edwards and his crack staff had down to a science.

In 1956, NBC launched a new daily version of *Truth or Consequences* on television. With his workload as producer of other shows and producer/host of *This is Your Life*, Edwards stepped aside from his first-born show and turned the reins over to a local radio star who had impressed him when he happened to tune in one day. On New Year's Eve 1956, Ralph Edwards introduced America to unknown new host Bob Barker.

Barker would never forget the role that Edwards played in launching him to stardom and saw to it that Edwards would never forget, either. Barker made a note of the exact date and time—December 21 at 12:05 p.m.—when Edwards called him on the telephone to notify him that he was the new host of *Truth or Consequences*. For the rest of Ralph Edwards' life, Barker would show up at Edwards's front door at 12:05 p.m. every December 21 to present him with a gift.

In the 1970s, Ralph Edwards turned more toward pure game shows. With *Truth or Consequences* still going strong in first-run syndication, Ralph added two more games: a new version of *Name*

Ralph Edwards prepares Bob Barker to take over *Truth or Consequences*. (Author's Collection)

That Tune (see September 9) and an original series titled *Cross-Wits* (see December 15). For NBC, there was a daytime version of *Name That Tune* and, later, a comedy game show titled *Knockout*.

In the 1980s, Edwards launched an entirely new genre when he created *The People's Court*, giving birth to the courtroom show. He spent the remainder of the decade tinkering with new ideas, all rooted in reality: *Superior Court*, featuring scripted dramatizations of real trials; *Love Stories*, recounting the how-we-met stories of numerous couples; *Family Medical Center*, depicting dramatizations of real-life emergencies, and Edwards' final game show, *Bzzz!* which aired for one season in 1996.

Ralph Edwards died on November 16, 2005, at age ninety-two. A short time later, during a taping of *The Price is Right*, Bob Barker turned to the audience during a taping break and offered to answer questions. An audience member asked him if he had any comment about Ralph Edwards. Barker answered, "In this business, you hear positive and negative things about everybody. The exception to that was Ralph Edwards. In all the years I've been in show business, I never heard anybody say one unkind word about him. He's the only one I can say that about."

(Author's Collection)

June 14

1993 – *Caesar's Challenge* Premieres

In 1975, game shows peaked. A whopping forty-four national game shows aired on the major networks and in first-run syndication, while a handful of local games dotted the schedules for stations in New York and Los Angeles. Nothing lasts forever.

In 1993, game shows were gone from ABC. CBS had *The Price is Right* but had stopped production on *Family Feud Challenge* in March, feeding reruns to any stations that still wanted them. Over at NBC, no game show seemed to have any luck. *Family Secrets*, *Scattegories*, and *Scrabble* had all gone off the air. The network stopped production on *Classic Concentration* in 1991 but kept the reruns going for two years.

In 1993, NBC introduced *Caesar's Challenge* and the program signaled the end of an era. When it ceased production early the following year, *Caesar's Challenge* went down in the books as the last original network daytime game show. *The Price is Right* was the sole survivor. When another game show showed up on daytime TV in 2009, it was a revival of *Let's Make a Deal.*

The game was a joint venture between Rick Rosner, whose *Just Men!* had been a part of a resurgence of game shows on NBC a decade earlier, and noted producer Stephen J. Cannell, breaking free from his forte of hour-long prime time adventures. The settling was Caesar's Palace hotel & casino complex in Las Vegas. The host was NBC sportscaster Ahmad Rashad. Assisting him was a male model, Dan Doherty, clad in gladiator garb.

Three contestants duked it out in a game of words and wisdom. The contestants saw a series of scrambled words. For each word, Ahmad would ask a question; the contestant who supplied a right answer chose a letter in the scramble and it would be repositioned correctly. The first contestant to solve the word won money for each letter left unscrambled.

In the bonus round, a massive bingo-style cage lowered from the ceiling and rolled out a series of lettered balls until a bellow of "Caesar says stop!" which meant that among the letters that had rolled out to that point, there were nine that could be unscrambled to spell a legitimate word. The contestant was shown the nine letters and had ten seconds to solve the word; doing so won a car. Later, the bonus round involved five scrambled words, and the contestant had thirty seconds to solve them all. To close out each show, Ahmad and Dan would wander the audience and give spectators a chance to solve five-letter words for casino tokens and chocolate coins.

The game had the elements to succeed but not a lot of luck. Many NBC affiliates pushed it aside in favor of local news or syndicated programming. Those that did carry the show pitted it against CBS' dominant soap opera *The Young and the Restless.* The peacock plucked its last game show on January 14, 1994.

BONUS ROUND

Caesar says "Solve!" Read the clue for each scrambled word and decipher all of these game show-related puzzles.

1. *Villain* – GARDON
2. *Square* – CHINAVL
3. *Word game* – LBRACESL
4. *Truth seeker* – YRCELLO
5. *Producer* – THREIGN
6. *Matchmaker* – ODAWNS
7. *Voice* - JCBOAS

June 15

2007- Barker Says Bye-Bye, Bidders Bid Adieu

Bob Barker was actually the second choice to host *The Price is Right* when it was developed in 1972, but once he set foot on Stage 33 at CBS Television City, *The Price is Right* was all his. Number one in the daytime ratings, a pile of Emmys, and record-breaking longevity cemented Bob Barker as an institution. Pricing games were named after him; remember Trader Bob and Barker's Markers? Nighttime versions of the show hosted by Tom Kennedy and Doug Davidson had fizzled. When scandals rocked the show in the 1990s, the fans stood by Bob. When he was sidelined by an artery blockage in 1999, production of *The Price is Right* stopped until he returned; a guest-host just wouldn't do, apparently. The hospital where he was recuperating was deluged by phone calls and mail in the meantime. CBS eventually re-named Stage 33 "The Bob Barker Studio" and renamed the area where audience members waited in line the Bob Barker Promenade. A mural of Bob adorns the exterior of another studio at Television City. *The Price is Right* without Bob Barker would be like a one-dollar bill without George Washington.

On Halloween, 2006, Bob disclosed to the press that the final episode of the thirty-fifth season would be his last. The milestone also coincided with his fiftieth year in network television and, at age eighty-two, he felt that the time was right.

"I've decided to retire while I'm still young," he cracked.

In the last episode taped before he made the announcement, Bob had made a handful of mistakes and appeared bothered by them. At one point he told the audience that he thought he needed to see a psychiatrist. Whether the episode accelerated his decision or not, Bob decided that still being mentally and physically capable of hosting a daily game show into his eighties had been a blessing, and that it was best not to push his luck.

He told the Associated Press, "I'm just reaching the age where the constant effort to be there and do the show physically is a lot for me…I might be able to do the show another year, but better a year too soon than a year too late."

The outpouring in the months that followed was tremendous. Demand for tickets for Bob's final weeks as host was so tremendous that CBS removed the daily segment of *Price* where Rich Fields told viewers how to get tickets for a taping; the network had just plain run out of tickets.

In May, CBS aired a prime time special, *A Celebration of Bob Barker's 50 Years in Television*, showing clips of Bob's work on *Price*,

Truth or Consequences, and even his guest appearance on *Bonanza*. Actor Adam Sandler read a special poem honoring Bob.

On June 15, CBS aired Bob's final day on the job, a milestone that merited airing the episode twice that day; the network showed it in the regular daytime slot and then again in prime time before the Daytime Emmys ceremony that night. Among the contestants for the final show was a woman who had been in the audience 120 times before finally getting called to "come on down" and a man who had waited in line for five days to make sure he had the best seat for the final show. In the audience were VIPs like Bob's half-brother and even a few ex-staffers and their families. One excited audience member smuggled in confetti and launched it across the stage during Bob's entrance for a special feel.

Bob Barker's final *Price is Right* proceeded much like the 6,730 that preceded it, though with a few small touches to acknowledge the milestone. The contestants bid on a television that was playing a clip of Bob's entrance from the first episode. The final three pricing games played were Double Prices, Bonus Game, and Any Number. In reverse order, they had been the first three pricing games played in 1972.

After a big win in the Showcase, Bob turned his attention to the cameras and told the home audience, "I want to thank you very, very much for inviting me into your homes for the last fifty years. I am deeply grateful. And please remember: Help control the pet population, have your pet spayed or neutered."

After taping, he expressed similar words of gratitude to the studio audience and then stayed for several minutes to talk to the press. He admitted, "The thing that surprises me most is that I got through the whole (show) without crying…I really had myself worked up into an emotional state…And I thought, 'I've really got to get over there and do this show. Straighten yourself out, Barker.'"

After the prime time rebroadcast, viewers saw Bob stroll onstage at the Daytime Emmy Awards to pocket his fourteenth trophy for Outstanding Game Show Host. He expressed gratitude that the Emmys showed "sympathy for an old man who's out of a job."

June 16

1990 – *Monopoly* Premieres

Mike Reilly emerged from out of nowhere to become a prime time game show star in the summer of 1990. (Fred Wostbrock Collection)]

One of the hit game shows of the 1980s was *Scrabble*, based on the popular board game of the same name. For the next several years, producers worked on turning other board games into TV fare, with minimal success. Jay Wolpert produced a pilot for *Trivial Pursuit* that didn't get picked up. Barry & Enright Productions got a single season out of *Pictionary*. And while all that was going on, Merv Griffin Productions was tinkering with a perennial favorite, *Monopoly*.

Griffin was optimistic about the prospects for his new project. He told the press, "This game translates into great television—it's a classic, and it works."

As early as 1987, Griffin produced a failed pilot hosted by Marc Summers. The extremely complicated format randomly assigned properties to the contestants, who played mini-games when landing on a railroad, placed bets for the Chance and Community Chest questions and could improve properties only when Rich Uncle Pennybags permitted it.

Griffin streamlined the format and tried again with another pilot in 1988, hosted by Peter Tomarken, who years later recalled how bizarre the pilot was. The game involved a life-sized Monopoly board, with a midget in a tuxedo running around the board. The midget was instructed not to talk, and Tomarken was instructed not to talk to the midget. Tomarken objected because he felt it was dehumanizing. This pilot, too, was rejected.

Griffin tried one more time in 1990 and, with no host in mind, he conducted the run-throughs for the new format himself. His production company brought in several former contestants from *Wheel of Fortune* and *Jeopardy!* Among them was a waiter originally from Florida named Mike Reilly, who had been a contestant on the unaired Peter Tomarken pilot. He came away from his appearance on *Jeopardy!* with only a camcorder and a

Nintendo Entertainment System, but he left the run-through for *Monopoly* with much more.

Merv asked Reilly to take a shot at hosting the run-through for a few minutes and was so delighted with what he saw that he hired Reilly virtually on the spot. Griffin was famous for selecting hosts from unlikely places and succeeding with them. Pat Sajak, Chuck Woolery and Art Fleming were previous finds, and Reilly had a golden opportunity. With a different game, things may have worked out, but after three years of tinkering, *Monopoly* still didn't quite succeed.

Three contestants competed. For the first round, the contestants went to each color property on the board and answered a series of crossword-style clues to capture the properties and create monopolies. At the end of the round, they used the money they earned with their correct answers to buy houses and hotels and improve properties.

In the second round, a model—Kathy Davis, Kathy Karges or Michelle Nicholas—rolled the dice, triggering a neon light that traveled around the board. When it landed on a property, the owner had a chance to claim the rent with a correct answer. Utilities gave all three players a chance to answer. Chance and Community Chest offered penalties and bonuses, Income Tax and Luxury Tax cost the players money, Jail cost each contestant $250, Free Parking awarded a jackpot of $500 plus the money lost in penalties that the contestants had incurred up to that point and landing on a railroad offered a chance for a contestant to make a "hostile takeover" of another contestant's monopoly. All of this was actually fairly engaging, but the first round took so long that the more interesting part of the game went by rather quickly.

The winner of the game had five rolls of the dice to go completely around the board; rolling doubles earned a bonus roll.

The board was modified to include five Go to Jail spaces instead of one. If the player passed Go without hitting a Go to Jail space, the reward was $25,000. Landing exactly on Go was worth $50,000.

The game was part of a rare-for-the-time block of game shows in network prime time. For twelve weeks on the ABC line-up, it aired on Saturday nights along with *Super Jeopardy!* But the prime time audience wasn't enamored by it, and the show never resurfaced.

Monopoly is probably best remembered for the unusual theme music Merv Griffin penned for the show, a '50s-style tune with lyrics. A pair of singers spelled the title—with the female vocalist giving a suggestive delivery of the letter "O" each time—and told viewers, "Roll the dice! It's paradise! But if you fail…you go to jail!" Despite the obscurity of the show, in 2000 the theme music was released on an album, *Best of TV Quiz and Game Show Themes*.

June 17

1944 – Bill Rafferty's Birth

The always laid-back Bill Rafferty. (Author's Collection)

Bill Rafferty never fit into the mold of a game show host. Instead of dulcet tones, he had a thick New Yawk accent. Rather than making each point and moving on, he would veer into tangents and flights of whimsy. Rather than promoting a new car by declaring that it was beautiful, fabulous and shiny, he would gesture toward the vehicle onstage and say, "I gotta teenager back home who'd give up his puberty for a car like this!"

Bill grew up in New York. After finishing a tour of duty in Vietnam, he returned to the states and, instead of going home, he moved to San Francisco, aspiring to become either a disc jockey for a comedian. In the meantime, he worked day jobs chopping meat, collecting bills, driving cabs and cleaning airplanes.

While plying his trade as a comic, Bill befriended another hopeful at the San Francisco nightclubs named Robin Williams. In 1979, Williams was cast in an extremely short-lived revival of *Laugh-In*, and producer George Schlatter asked him for ideas about where to find young up-and-coming talent. With Williams' guidance, Schlatter caught a comedy show featuring Rafferty and signed him.

The new *Laugh-In* was cancelled after only six broadcasts, but Rafferty dazzled Schlatter so much that he was the first person hired when Schlatter developed his next project, *Real People*, a magazine/variety show that proved a surprise hit when it premiered on NBC. Rafferty traveled the country to profile unique individuals, choosing such unlikely candidates as a wheelchair-bound girl who aspired to become an actress, a man who accused a local beer company of preventing him from writing a novel and an artist who used toothpicks to recreate Da Vinci's *The Last Supper*.

Bill stayed on the road almost constantly during the show's five seasons on the air. The popularity of the show put him in demand as a stand-up comic, and he was typically on stage any night of the week he had free. He told a reporter that he called his children twice a day so they wouldn't ask "Who's this?" when he finally came home.

He admitted that he traveled first-class whenever he flew, but he brushed aside the notion that, as a rich and famous TV comedian, he lived a glamorous lifestyle. He told John Davidson, "People think my life is fast cars and fast women but, actually, it's just fast food."

In 1984, Bill made his game show hosting debut with a syndicated quizzer, *Every Second Counts*. Teams would alternate tackling topics like, "Is each of these a Baskin-Robbins flavor or not?" They'd answer yes or no to a series of possibilities, winning two or four seconds for each correct answer. The winners used their accumulated time to answer a series of questions in the bonus round for a chance to win a car. The game moved quickly enough that Bill frequently filled time by milking reactions to some of the questions. When "Wild Turkey" was suggested as one of the possible ice cream flavors, he indulged in mimicking a drunk enjoying an ice cream cone.

The game fizzled in one season, but Rafferty had his foot in the door as a game show host. In 1986, he hosted the nighttime version of *Card Sharks* for one season. He coined a catch phrase during his tenure, warning contestants on the verge of losing the game that, if they couldn't make a comeback soon, they would depart for "the land of parting gifts."

In 1987, Mark Goodson added to his new host's workload with a revival of *Blockbusters* on NBC. When both *Card Sharks* and *Blockbusters* ended in 1987, so did Bill Rafferty's brief but impressive career as a game show host.

Bill worked on and off as an actor for many years afterward. In 2007, he began a successful run on *Retired and Wired*, a cable TV show in which he explained technological advances, like HDTV and social networking, for retired viewers. After a brief illness, Bill died on August 11, 2012 at age 68.

June 18

1908 – Bud Collyer's Birth

Bud Collyer always had plenty of time for a good game.
(Author's Collection)

On radio, he was "the strange visitor from another planet." On television, Bud Collyer was anything but; he was the familiar, warm, gentle and human presence for more than a dozen game shows, virtually all of them hits.

He was born Clayton John Heermance, Jr. He led a dance band while attending college and landed a job at CBS earning $85 a week but, for a time, it looked like he wouldn't go much farther than that in entertainment. He worked as a law clerk for two years before he was overcome by boredom and decided to try showbiz. His mother and sister were both actresses using the name Collyer. Clayton followed suit and, as Bud Collyer, began acting on Broadway in 1934.

Collyer had only a handful of roles on Broadway, finding far more success as an actor in radio. In the following six years, he would play numerous roles on soap operas and adventure shows. In 1940, he landed his career-defining role as an actor when he was cast to supply the voice of Superman.

The producers of the radio show initially considered casting two actors—one for Superman and one for alter-ego Clark Kent—but Collyer won both roles with an impressive audition, speaking Clark Kent's dialogue in a somewhat high voice and lowering his voice when he became Superman, yet delivering the lines in such a way that it was clear that they were the same person. As radio's Superman, Bud would singlehandedly coin two of the character's most enduring trademarks. "Up, up and *away*!" and "This looks like a job…for *Superman*!" were both Bud Collyer creations.

Bud Collyer was such a hit as Superman on radio that he became the voice of Superman cartoons released theatrically starting in 1941 and, eventually, the voice of Superman in television cartoons. Although other actors would become stars in live action portrayals of the Man of Steel, for three decades of radio, film and television, Bud Collyer *was* Superman.

Collyer didn't receive any credit on the air or on the screen for his performances. DC Comics wanted to create the illusion that "the real Superman" was the star of the show. When a 1942 article identified Collyer as the voice of Superman, Bud was working as a superintendent for a large Sunday school and had to explain to 1,250 ecstatic children the distinction between a real person and a fictional character and that, to their disappointment, Superman was not running their school.

In 1945, he made his debut as a game show host, for Mutual Radio's *Break the Bank* (see October 22). Years later, he recalled the advice a producer gave just before he began hosting the shows. "Remember, you're going to be here tomorrow. (The contestant) won't." Collyer remembered the advice and followed it well. Each program was the contestant's day in the spotlight.

As a host, he would earn the praise of audiences and peers alike. Actress Faye Emerson once said, "Bud is gentle with his contestants and seems genuinely concerned with whether they win money or not."

He would host several other games, including *By Popular Demand*, *Time's A-Wastin'*—the game that eventually became *Beat the Clock*—and *Winner Take All*. The latter proved popular enough that it would be adapted for television in 1948, and Bud made his first appearance on the medium as master of ceremonies for the video version.

Toward the end of the decade, Bud added two more TV games to his credit, *Talent Jackpot* and *This is the Missus*. He also became a television pitchman for a line of cigars. A coworker told author Jeff Kisseloff about Bud's knack for taking long, slow puffs of the cigar on the air and telling viewers that smoking those cigars was one of the joys of the world. But eventually, Bud revealed to both the coworker and a representative of the sponsor that he threw up after every commercial because he couldn't stand the taste of cigars.

In 1950, Bud began a long run as the host of *Beat the Clock* on television for CBS, adding equal parts civility and enthusiasm for the zany stunts featured each week. Producer Ira Skutch marveled years later that, to prepare, Bud would perform each stunt himself, just to make certain that he had a firm grasp on how to explain it to players.

Bud Collyer's career prospered in the early 1950s. In addition to continuing with *Beat the Clock*, he began hosting a new version of *Break the Bank* for NBC as well as another game show, *Quick as a Flash*, for ABC. On *Quick as a Flash*, contestants would watch films containing misleading clues to the identities of famous people or events. For example, a clip that appeared to be a war movie might contain clues about the birth of the Dionne quintuplets, or actors with thick Brooklyn accents might be used to represent Henry VIII and Anne Boleyn. For ABC, he also hosted a talent search, *Talent Patrol*, in which the performers were all soldiers and veterans.

Collyer's reputation and resume just kept growing. In addition to four prime time shows, the early 1950s saw him at the helm of *Say It with Acting* (see May 12) and *Masquerade Party* (see July 14). He also hosted *On Your Way*, where studio audience members who correctly answered questions received the prize of transportation to any destination they wished. In daytime, he had *Feather Your Nest*, where contestants competed to earn feathers that could lead to rooms of furniture or even a new house and car. In prime time, he had *Penny to a Million*, where contestants could supply a series of answers, with the first correct answer paying one cent and the reward doubling and doubling with each subsequent answer to a total of one million pennies, or $10,000.

Bud can't help smiling. He knows he's hosting another hit. (Author's Collection)

In eleven years, Bud hosted a total of fourteen game shows and, amazingly, his biggest success as a master of ceremonies was yet to come. In 1956, he became the host of *To Tell the Truth* (see December 18). It was a hit with critics and audiences alike, bringing in a 23.3 Nielsen rating at its peak and spawning a daytime version. The daytime and prime time version were both gone by 1968, giving Collyer a total of twelve years as host.

Collyer stayed busy with outside projects in addition to his *Beat the Clock* and *To Tell the Truth* duties. In 1957, he was elected president of AFTRA, the performers' union for television and radio. He served a controversial two-year tenure in which he supported anti-Communist organizations, long after Senator McCarthy had been censured for spearheading such movements. He was also deeply committed to religion. He wrote two religious books for teenagers and continued teaching Sunday school, even as his broadcasting career soared.

After the end of *To Tell the Truth* in 1968, Collyer retired, working at a local church in his ample free time. In 1969, he was hospitalized with a circulatory ailment. After three weeks of treatment, he died on September 8, 1969. In a strange coincidence, on the day that he died, new versions of *To Tell the Truth* and *Beat the Clock* premiered across the country in syndication. Such is the legacy for many hosts: Collyer was gone, but his games lived on. He probably would have liked it that way. Jack Narz, who hosted the revival of *Beat the Clock*, revealed many years later that Collyer sent congratulatory notes to him and many of the show's staffers when the new project began production.

(Fred Wostbrock Collection)

June 19

1952 – *I've Got a Secret* Premieres

Garry Moore blows out the candles for an *I've Got a Secret* anniversary celebration. Clockwise from noon position: Henry Morgan, executive producer Gil Fates, director Franklin Heller, producer Chester Feldman, Bill Cullen, Betsy Palmer, Bess Myerson. (Author's Collection)

By 1952, Mark Goodson & Bill Todman had two established hits in prime time for CBS, *What's My Line?* and *Beat the Clock*. Seeking an idea for a third twinkle to put in the CBS eye, they held a meeting with two young comedy writers, Allan Sherman and Howard Merrill, who laid out their brilliant new idea: a panel of four celebrities would face a contestant and ask yes-or-no questions to discern something about them.

Goodson rejected it immediately, laying out the problem: Sherman & Merrill had just pitched a show that sounded like *What's My Line?* Goodson said that the company had no interest in copying their own ideas.

Sherman had a quick response: "You might as well, because if you don't start copying your shows, somebody else will." The word of caution left an impression on Goodson, and *I've Got a Secret* hit the airwaves in the summer of 1952, with Sherman on board as a producer.

Rome wasn't built in a day, and neither was *I've Got a Secret*. CBS showed remarkable patience with it, however. In later years, host Garry Moore was fond of saying that the show was on the air for more than a year before they got it right. The Goodson-Todman people were so unhappy with the premiere broadcast that they burned down the set immediately afterward and built a new set for the following week. The set wasn't the only problem. Initially, the game was played in a very serious, straightforward manner, with panelists attempting to win by solving secrets such as "I shook hands with the president" or "I am the Orange Bowl Queen."

The first fix came with a panel that cared more about being fun and freewheeling than trying to get into the contestant's head. Cantankerous Henry Morgan arrived early in the run of the series and couldn't be more transparent about his apathy for the actual game. His attitude surprisingly made the show more enjoyable for viewers, and fellow regular panelist Bill Cullen soon followed his lead. If the game got too difficult, they just stopped caring, and the emphasis shifted to having fun. Providing balance on the panel were the glamorous Jayne Meadows and Faye Emerson, later replaced, respectively, by Betsy Palmer and Bess Myerson.

The regular panel, Bill Cullen, Jayne Meadows, Henry Morgan, and Faye Emerson. (Author's Collection)

The second fix provided wilder and wilder secrets, more along the lines of "I throw knives at my mother-in-law," "I have two horses inside this box," "I have ten live snakes concealed on me" and "I can tear the Los Angeles phone book in half," all of course followed by demonstrations. Even the way the panel had to approach the questioning wound up being a source of inspiration. One night, the panelists were not allowed to begin asking questions until each of them had made guest Ed Sullivan laugh out loud.

Where once existed a panel show, now existed a variety show with a panel show gimmick. Having the panel ask yes-no questions for a while merely proved to be an excuse to put talented, eccentric or otherwise noteworthy people in the spotlight for a few minutes each week.

Contributing to the fun was a weekly celebrity with a secret and, as the civilian contestants' secrets became more elaborate, the celebrities, too, contrived increasingly crazy situations. Paul Newman's secret was that he had disguised himself as a vendor at Yankee Stadium and sold Henry Morgan a hot dog. Johnny Carson successfully used a bow and arrow to shoot an apple atop Garry's head. David Niven squirmed as the panel tried to figure out that he was sitting on a block of ice. Ronald Reagan's secret was that he was staging his appearance like a movie and, every time a panelist would say "uh," Reagan would walk offstage, Moore would reintroduce him and they would begin a new "take."

Audiences couldn't get enough. In ten of its fifteen seasons, *Secret* ranked as one of the top thirty shows on the air, peaking at number five in the 1957-58 season with a steady 33.4 rating. For a time, the show concluded each week with Garry Moore reading letters that home viewers had sent for the panel. The panelists were frequently featured in magazine profiles, and even in those raucous secrets.

The panelists had unmatchable chemistry, each of them bringing a clear and unmistakable personality to the group. Bill Cullen was smart and goofy; Henry Morgan was grumpy and cynical; Betsy Palmer was naïve and cheerful; Bess Myerson was worldly and elegant. As the fans of the show got to know more and more about the panelists, the secrets delved deeper into the panelists' lives. Jack Narz appeared on the show with the secret, "I introduced Bill Cullen to his wife." When Mark Goodson realized that he had never met panelist Betsy Palmer face-to-face, he showed up with the secret, "I'm going to meet Betsy Palmer for the first time tonight." Henry Morgan was dispatched to an opera house to act as a spear carrier for a scene. The women on the panel were tasked with an impromptu job babysitting a contestant's children after the show.

The show searched for viable secrets wherever they could. As it turned out, finding a good secret for *I've Got a Secret* wasn't a particularly easy job. Hopeful contestants turned up at the Goodson-Todman office with secrets that weren't particularly useful. One woman showed up saying that her secret was that she had never been to the Chrysler Building. A child showed up, saying that he had just eaten candy and planned on eating candy again the following day. A few people were so eager for the spotlight that they tried to get on the show with shocking secrets; one woman wanted to reveal she was having an affair. Another hopeful wanted to brag about how he had used a snare drum to smuggle diamonds.

I've Got a Secret actually depended on a large research staff to scour newspapers from around the country looking for viable material to use for segments. Through newspapers, for example, they were able to find the little league teams involved in a bizarre game in which the pitcher threw a no-hitter, but the other team won. A newspaper article also prompted the show to feature a contestant who was the last surviving witness to Abraham Lincoln's assassination.

Other segments were bits that the staff whipped up themselves. They had a man claiming to be an electrician remove the works from Betsy Palmer's watch and "rebuild" it into a miniature radio. The panel stared in amazement as the murmuring and static noises emitted from the watch. And then the electrician revealed his secret:

He was actually a ventriloquist, making those noises himself. An improvisational singer came in and wrote a song about the panel on the spot, based on info they had revealed about themselves. A nightclub magician picked audience members' pockets before the show went on the air.

Behind the scenes, though, whipping up secrets could often be the source of contention. Producer Allan Sherman frustrated the staff with the way he ran the show, often changing his mind and rejecting segments he had previously approved, or asking to do segments he had previously professed to dislike. He was also known to stonewall attempts to replace segments that were his own ideas. At one particularly heated meeting when Mark Goodson had rejected one of Sherman's ideas, Sherman instructed the staff to remain silent when Goodson asked them for other ideas.

The behind-the-scenes drama came to a head following a particularly awful night when Sherman insisted on a segment in which Tony Curtis would teach the panelists how to make small toys out of household objects and play simple kids' games. Most of the toys didn't work and Curtis had never heard of the games he was supposed to teach the panelists. The segment was so boring that Goodson fired Allan Sherman the following day. It was probably the best thing that could have happened to Sherman. He launched a singing career following his dismissal, amassing a cult following with his zany parodies of popular tunes.

In 1964, Garry Moore left *I've Got a Secret* after twelve years as host, although, after negotiating an unusual deal with Goodson-Todman and CBS, Moore actually wound up with fifty-one percent ownership of the program (for a time, Moore also owned the rights to *What's My Line?*). *I've Got a Secret* found a new host in Steve Allen. To symbolically pass the torch, Moore and Allen co-hosted a single episode together in 1964; the following week, Allen took over as sole host.

I've Got a Secret and Steve Allen were never really a perfect match. Allen's strength was as a comedian and joke teller, and so much of hosting *I've Got a Secret* required him to take a backseat to other actions taking place onstage. Furthermore, game shows on prime time TV were in sharp decline during the 1960s. The ratings for *Secret* eroded, and in 1967, it was cancelled after fifteen years on CBS.

Steve Allen and the panel, during the sunset years of *I've Got a Secret.*

Various attempts to recapture the magic have been made over the years. In 1972, Steve Allen returned as host of *I've Got a Secret* as a weekly prime time syndicated game show. The new incarnation lasted only one season, but very nicely captured the era that it was in production. Bob Barker appeared as a special guest one week, purloining the panelists' belongings for a series of games with the studio audience to demonstrate how his new game show, *The New Price is Right* would work. Rod Serling went head-to-head with Steve Allen for a game of Pong, one of the first times that the game was demonstrated on television.

A summer replacement series hosted by Bill Cullen ran for four weeks in 1976, with the possibility of more episodes down the road had the show brought in strong ratings. Unfortunately, it was against *Happy Days* that summer, and even in reruns, *Happy Days* was unbeatable.

A daily version arrived on the Oxygen cable channel in 2000, with Stephanie Miller hosting and Jm J. Bullock sitting in as a regular panelist. The program garnered respectable ratings and stayed on the air for three years, proving that there was still life in the venerable format, even in the hands of a new production team.

Host Bill Dwyer, hiding something from panelists Jermaine Taylor, Suzanne Westenhoefer, Frank DeCaro, and Billy Bean on the retro set for the 2006 *I've Got a Secret*.
(Fred Wostbrock Collection)

A late night version arrived on GSN in 2006. In an unusual casting choice, the entire regular panel—Jermaine Taylor, Billy Bean, Frank DeCaro and Suzie Westenhoefer (who called herself a "gay Kitty Carlisle" in an interview)—was openly gay. Stunt casting for a panel show may have been a risky proposition, but as it turned out they had great chemistry and, most important of all, they played the game well. At the helm was Bill Dwyer, cheekily introduced as "the straight man to the panel."

The eighty dollars and carton of cigarettes awarded by the original series fell by the wayside in favor of one thousand dollars and dinner for two in Beverly Hills. As on the original show, the game was always followed by a demonstration or a cute story, and to that purpose the research staff came up with some great "secrets" for this run.

- "I have Richard Nixon's half-eaten sandwich."
- "I'm a hula hoop champion."
- "We've been dressing alike for twenty-eight years."
- "I'm a toilet seat artist."
- "I rip decks of cards with my teeth."

Every now and then, celebrities dropped by. Unlike on the game's original version, the stars' secrets were not generated by the producers but, rather, involved true trivia about the stars. Adam West's secret was that he had the Batman logo on one of his teeth, fashioned out of porcelain by his dentist. Tom Green demonstrated how he'd taught his pet bird to clean his teeth for him and George Wendt confessed that he was expelled from the University of Notre Dame.

Viewer reaction was largely positive and even critics were receptive to it—one said, "goofier than the original, but it's fun"—

but one season was enough for Game Show Network and *Secret* was gone after only forty episodes.

June 20

1958 – *Haggis Baggis* Premieres

The game looked ordinary, but the title certainly wasn't. Fred Robbins hosted *Haggis Baggis*. (Author's Collection)

Perhaps the oddest game show title ever seen on American TV screens, *Haggis Baggis* took its name from a Scottish dish made from the internal organs of a sheep combined with oatmeal and served similarly to a sausage. No clear explanation is readily available for why Joseph Cates, producer/director of *The $64,000 Question*, thought this was a suitable title for his next game show project.

The host was nineteen-year-old Jack Linkletter, who took the assignment because he was looking for a summer job following his Freshman year at USC. Most nineteen-year-old college students don't ease right into a steady gig hosting a TV game show, but not every college student is Art Linkletter's son.

Contestants faced a twenty-five-square grid. Each column on the grid was represented by a letter; each row was represented by a category. Two contestants alternated selecting column-row coordinates and giving items that fit the category, starting with the appropriate letter. Giving an acceptable answer lit up a portion of a celebrity's photo. At any point in the game, either contestant could sound a bell and guess the identity of the star. A correct guess won the game. The action moved remarkably quickly. In the one surviving film of the program available to collectors, four complete games are played in a single half-hour.

The winner was shown two prize packages, called "Haggis" and "Baggis." Told the contents of each package, the loser of the game tried to select the one that the winner would like to have. The winner then selected a prize package and won it without having to do anything more. If the loser correctly predicted which one would get picked, the loser then received the unclaimed prize package.

Haggis Baggis launched in prime time and ran through the summer, concluding on September 29, 1958. A daytime series following on June 30 was hosted by Fred Robbins, who left the show on February 6, 1959. Dennis James took over and remained with the program until the show came to an end on June 19 of that year.

June 21

1938 – Ron Ely's Birth

Ron Ely grew up in Texas and made his way to Hollywood to build a career out of wandering through the jungle. Although he appeared in character parts on dozens of TV shows from the 1950s into the 2000s, he was best-known for his two seasons playing Tarzan on NBC.

Ely established a reputation for immersing himself into the role more deeply than any actor who previously had portrayed Lord Greystoke. He refused to use a stunt double, insisting on doing all the vine-swinging and fighting with tigers himself. In the first season alone, he suffered seventeen injuries.

In 1979, Ely unintentionally found himself embroiled in controversy when he replaced Bert Parks as host of the Miss

America pageant, a change that Parks learned about only from reading the newspaper. Viewers were outraged by the switch, and Ely was replaced after only two pageants.

In 1980, he hosted his sole game show, *Face the Music*, which combined *Name That Tune* with a memory quiz. For the first round, contestants were shown a series of photos that they had to pair up with tunes. For example, they might be shown photos of Mac Davis, Jon Voight, Pope John Paul II and Scooby Doo along with hearing "I Believe," "I Believe in Music," "When Johnny Comes Marching Home" and "How Much is That Doggie in the Window?" They had to identify the tunes and match each to the appropriate photo.

For the second round, players heard a series of songs with titles that served as clues to correct answers. "Sing," "Three's Company" and "The Alphabet" might lead to the answer "The Bee Gees."

The high scorer at the end of the game faced the returning champion in a game that could pay up to $10,000. The contestants would see a series of photos of a celebrity. The first photo, worth $10,000, was a baby picture. Subsequent photos were worth $5,000, $4,000, $3,000, $2,000 and $1,000; as the payoffs decreased, the photos grew more and more recent. For each photo, the contestants had to ring in and identify a song that provided a clue; a correct guess allowed them a shot at identifying the famous person. The winner was declared and returned champion to face the last player standing on the next episode. Any contestant who survived for five days received a car; lasting ten days added a trip around the world to the haul.

The game lasted a year and a half in syndication, but it enjoyed a long life in reruns, being carried into the 1990s on Christian Broadcasting Network, USA Network and The Family Channel.

BONUS ROUND

Can you identify game show hosts from these clues actually used on *Face the Music*?

Host #1:
"Dreams of the Everyday Housewife"
"Spinning Wheel"
"Who Will Buy?"
"Come On Down"

Host #2:
"Young at Heart"
"Shall We Dance"
"Bandstand Boogie"
"The Beat Goes On"

Host #3:
"When You're Smiling"
"Long Tall Texan"
"Nature Boy"
"There She Is, Miss America"

Host #4:
"Games People Play"
"Behind Closed Doors"
"1-2-3"

June 22

2010 – *Downfall* Premieres

Oversized props and set pieces have been a staple of game shows for years. *Video Village* endeared itself to viewers by placing contestants on a giant board game. *The Magnificent Marble Machine* blew away audiences with its ostentatious giant pinball machine. For 2010, ABC hoped to win over prime time audiences with a game show that boasted "the largest conveyor belt ever seen on TV." For viewers who had ever stood at the checkout line of a supermarket and thought, "I wonder what one of these would look like if it were really *big*," the new game was truly a godsend.

Hosted by professional wrestler Chris Jericho, *Downfall* brought contestants to the roof of a ten-story building in downtown Los Angeles to play a series of up to seven rounds.

For each round, prizes were placed on a giant conveyer belt, and contestants would have to supply answers to a series of clues. The farther players got in the game, the more answers were required and the more time they spent completing all of the responses. The longer the round took, the more likely the prizes were to go to the end of the conveyor belt, over the edge of the roof and crashing to the ground below. Contestants had the option to pass on clues if they couldn't come up with the answer but, if they passed, the conveyer belt moved faster.

A cash bonus was awarded for every round in which at least one prize survived. If anything remained after seven rounds, the payoff was a cool million bucks.

Downfall was a flop on the air; with the popular *Wipeout* as a lead-in, the premiere of *Downfall* lost about one-third of the audience. By July, it was down to a 1.4 rating and a 4 share—and a logistical nightmare behind the scenes. Shortly before production began, it was decided that, following recent natural disasters, wantonly destroying prizes would outrage viewers and that the suppliers of the prizes wouldn't like it, either. Instead, the items destroyed were replicas of the prizes, a fact that Jericho emphasized over and over. Creating replicas added expense to the show, plus the machine operating TV's largest conveyor belt was noisy and disruptive, which caused numerous problems for audio production on the program. The city of Los Angeles denied the show permission to shoot the program during the day, so each game of *Downfall* was taped overnight which, due to union regulations and state laws, mandated extra pay for the staff and production crew. All these elements added up to one very expensive failure and, although the network had contracted the production company, FremantleMedia, for six shows, only five were completed.

Meanwhile, shows like *Family Feud*, *The Price is Right*, *Wheel of Fortune* and *Jeopardy!*, none of which involved TV's largest conveyor belt, remained in production.

June 23

1925 – Larry Blyden's Birth

"Hey, that's terrific!" Larry Blyden was all smiles on his game shows. (Author's Collection)

He approached game shows with the same gusto with which he had earlier pursued a career on the Broadway stage, only to have both careers tragically cut short, leaving his fans wondering what might have been.

Ivan Lawrence Bliedin (pronounced, "Bleed-in") was born in Houston. His father was a lawyer who had financial trouble during the Great Depression, and Larry recalled later that the sight of debt collectors at the door left a haunting impression; as an adult, he was terrified of the very idea of a debt.

By age fourteen, young Ivan decided he wanted to pursue an acting career and took a drama course in high school. He worked as a radio announcer to pay for his own education at the University at Houston, taking time out for a few years to serve in the Marines during the tail end of World War II. After receiving his honorable discharge, Ivan finished his schooling, briefly managed the Senate campaign of George Petty—who lost to Lyndon Johnson—and moved to New York to refocus on the acting bug that had bitten him as a teenager.

He studied under Stella Adler for eighteen months until the famed teacher told him that he had learned everything and that she had nothing left to teach him. Tweaking his name to Larry Blyden, he made his Broadway debut in *Mister Roberts* and went on to rack up a long and impressive list of credits, including *What Makes Sammy Run?*, *Flower Drum Song*, *The Apple Tree*, *Blues for Mr. Charles*, *Luv* and *You Know I Can't Hear You When the Water's Running*. His Broadway career peaked with a Tony Award win as a performer and co-producer for *A Funny Thing Happened on the Way to the Forum*.

Before long, Larry began pursuing television, appearing frequently on the many anthology series of the 1950s. He was the star of two sitcoms, *Joe & Mabel* and *Harry's Girls*, neither of which survived a full season. For all of his gifts as an actor, Larry Blyden soon found that his most popular role on television would be that of Larry Blyden.

Being a game show host fit Larry Blyden to a T. Here he is on *Personality*. (Author's Collection)

On July 3, 1967, Larry Blyden made his game show hosting debut with the NBC series *Personality* from Bob Stewart Productions. Three celebrities competed on behalf of home viewers who had mailed in postcards. The celebrities heard a series of questions asked to other celebrities in pre-recorded interviews and tried to predict how the other celebrities had answered, with the high-scoring player earning $100 plus a vacation for the corresponding home viewer. Blyden proved surprisingly adept and comfortable as master of ceremonies, a role in which many actors, accustomed to relying on scripts and assuming personas, had faltered in the past and often still do. Each episode of *Personality* saw Larry chatting amiably with the celebrities and prodding them for stories and quips throughout the game.

In the summer of 1969, he became a regular panelist on another NBC game from Bob Stewart, *You're Putting Me On*. With Bill Leyden at the helm, Larry was joined each day by Peggy Cass and Bill Cullen, and each was paired with a guest celebrity. One team member would assume the identity of a famous person and answer a series of off-the-wall questions, while the partner would have to figure out who the person was pretending to be. On September 26 of that year, *Personality* went off the air, and the following Monday Larry replaced Bill Leyden as host of *You're Putting Me On*. On December 26, 1969, *You're Putting Me On* left the airwaves.

Larry found a new job without too much trouble, replacing Sonny Fox as the host of *The Movie Game* in early 1970. Two teams, each comprising a contestant and two celebrity partners, competed in a game of movie trivia, questions about film clips and player reenactment of scenes from films. The impressive array of stars joined Larry on *The Movie Game* during the next two years, including John Wayne, Hugh O'Brian, Dyan Cannon, David Janssen, Joan Crawford, Henry Fonda, Bob Hope, Dorothy Lamour, Gene Kelly and Jimmy Stewart.

When *The Movie Game* ended in 1972, Larry moved right on to another game, the venerable *What's My Line?* Producer Gil Fates recalled in his memoirs that Blyden was initially scheduled to come in to the Goodson-Todman offices for two days of preparation leading up to each five-episode taping session, but he was such a quick study and such a capable emcee that in a matter of weeks, this was reduced to a single rehearsal on the day of taping.

Larry hosted the show with unbridled enthusiasm. He would frequently scour the lists of Mystery Guests for upcoming tapings and instruct the producer to set aside a few extra minutes if he saw one that he found particularly interesting, and executive producer Gil Fates in his memoirs marveled at how skillful an interviewer Larry proved to be in those extra minutes.

For the rest of the game, Larry would frequently respond with a sincere, "Hey, that's terrific!" after learning something new about the esoteric occupations involved on the show. By that point, *What's My Line?* had taken to featuring onstage demonstrations of the contestants' occupations, and the contestants would frequently bring along the products they manufactured or the tools of their trade. Larry was prone, on the slightest whim, to buying anything contestants brought that he found particularly delightful. By the time *Line* ended in 1975, his apartment was cluttered with paintings, sculptures, lamps, a pool table, neon signs and bean bag furniture. Gil Fates occasionally had to step in and save Larry from himself; had Gil not stopped him, Larry might have acquired a traffic light from one guest and a crepe machine designed to serve two hundred from another.

After *What's My Line?* ended, Larry continued his career pattern and was poised to move straight into another hosting job. Goodson-Todman was so delighted with his work on *Line* that the company cast Larry to host its new ABC game show, *Showoffs*. Larry hosted the pilot taped on May 25, then left for a vacation in Morocco.

While in Morocco, Larry's rental car went off the road and crashed—although his *What Makes Sammy Run?* Co-star Barbara Rush and *The Apple Tree* co-star Robert Klein would both speculate years later that he was carjacked and violently assaulted. Doctors made several attempts to save his life in the coming days, including a last-ditch effort with major surgery, but to no avail. Larry Blyden died on June 6, 1975.

In his memoirs, Gil Fates eulogized Larry succinctly: "He had lots more to give. Too bad he didn't have more time. He would have worked something out. He could do that."

(Author's Collection)

June 24

1958 – *Win with a Winner* Premieres

To SAY THE LEAST, TV QUIZ SHOWS WERE IN TROUBLE during the summer of 1958. But even as accusations gathered steam, NBC boldly added another game to the prime time line-up, with the added twist that home viewers could reap some of the rewards.

Five contestants competed on a game board that resembled a race track. Contestants could choose the difficulty level of their questions; the harder the question, the farther a player advanced with a correct answer. The first player to cross the finish line won the game.

Each week's program concluded with an introduction of the contestants competing on the following week's program. Viewers were encouraged to send postcards with the name of the contestant they expected to win. All viewers who selected the correct contestant shared a cash jackpot equivalent to what the contestant won.

The show was originally hosted by Sandy Becker, who was replaced by producer Win Elliott after one month. Elliott was better known for his work as a master of ceremonies than as a producer. He hosted *Tic Tac Dough*, *Make That Spare* and *On Your Account*. He was also an announcer for *Break the Bank* and a guest-host for *Beat the Clock*. Outside of game shows, Win was most famous as a sportscaster for CBS Radio, as well as the play-by-play man for the New York Rangers.

June 25

1951 – The Premiere and Finale of *Who's Whose*

Airing on CBS on June 25, 1951, a celebrity panel faced three men and three women and tried to figure out who was married to who. If this doesn't sound like a terribly engaging game show to you, you aren't alone. Sponsor General Mills pulled the plug, back when sponsors had that kind of power. The show was cancelled after a single broadcast, the first game show to bag that dubious distinctions. These one-shot wonders followed…

Fun and Fortune – Airing on June 6, 1949, Jack Lescoulie hosted this game show contestants tried to identify an object from a series of clues. Guessing on the first clue paid fifty dollars, with the cash diminishing after each wrong guess.

You're in the Picture – See January 20 for a description of this, probably the best-known game show bomb.

The Rich List – A Fox Network show from November 1, 2006. Contestants were given a category with specific correct answers (Top fifty longest-running Broadway shows, or Books by Steven King) and bid on how many correct answers they could give. The bonus round presented a list with fifteen correct answers. Giving all fifteen would have paid $250,000.

Secret Talents of the Stars – On April 8, 2008, CBS presented this all-star version of *The Gong Show*. Celebrities competed in a talent contest, with one all-important rule: their talent couldn't be related to what they were best-known for.

June 26

1944 – *Ladies Be Seated* Premieres

JOHNNY OLSON AND HIS WIFE PENNY HAD BEEN TOILING in New York for some time and were still searching for a big break. Johnny had been offered a chance at a full-time job in Milwaukee and briefly entertained it, but the Olsons decided to stick it a little bit longer in the Big Apple, and things finally worked out. On June 26, 1944, Johnny & Penny Olson became the stars of ABC Radio's *Ladies Be Seated.* Johnny and Penny wouldn't just co-host the show; they produced and wrote the show, and armed with a budget of $6,000 a week, they obtained their own prizes.

Ladies Be Seated was an audience participation show, much in the style of *Truth or Consequences.* There was no format set in stone; the listeners just knew for sure that the program would consist of Johnny & Penny choosing contestants from the studio audience and giving them stunts, games, or other tasks to complete for prizes. There were some recurring segments featured on the program, including "Penny Mystery," a lighthearted whodunit caper with clues for the contestants to solve; "Johnny One-Note," where contestants tried to guess the names of songs; "Kindly Heart," which offered prizes to audience members who had done good deeds, and "Johnny Crooner," where Johnny would serenade a small child from the audience and then have a lighthearted talk with them.

His interviews with small children briefly landed him in hot water with the sponsor of *Ladies Be Seated*, Phillip Morris. Johnny intentionally made it a point to talk to a girl that he knew to be the daughter of a Phillip Morris executive. The girl caught Johnny and Phillip Morris off-guard when she revealed that Daddy preferred Lucky Strikes.

At the height of the show's popularity, Johnny and Penny took *Ladies Be Seated* on the road, airing a special program from Chicago. They had originally intended to broadcast from one of the studios in Chicago, but *Ladies Be Seated* was hastily moved to the Civic Theater after the mail brought in requests for more than 100,000 tickets.

Ladies Be Seated kept going on the road after the tremendous success of that week, traveling to Virginia, New Jersey, North Dakota, and all points between. It was a special show from Orlando, Florida that stood out above the rest. One of the contestants was a woman eight months pregnant, and the excitement of the program and the thrill of winning a prize proved too much for her. She went into labor on stage. A doctor in the audience ran up to help her. Meanwhile, obeying the axiom that the show must go on, Johnny and Penny kept playing games with other audience members until they were interrupted by the sound of crying. The woman gave birth on the air to a baby boy.

Fittingly, she named the child Johnny.

June 27

1975 – *Split Second* Splits

Tom Kennedy has a question or three for players to deal with on *Split Second*. (Fred Wostbrock Collection)

Split Second was a quiz show assembled by people seeking to break free from their comfort zones. The show was created by Stefan Hatos-Monty Hall Productions, the company that unleashed the zany and colorful *Let's Make a Deal* on game show audiences the previous decade. The host was Tom Kennedy, who had made a career out of lighthearted games and celebrity fun with *You Don't Say!* and *It's Your Bet*.

On March 20, Tom and Hatos-Hall arrived on ABC and could excusably have borrowed a line from Monty Python if they wanted. For the host and the company, *Split Second* was "something completely different"—a fast-paced, heart-stopping quiz show.

The game pitted three contestants against each other, and Tom would present a question with three clues. For example, the clue could be: "L.A. Lakers Star, She Done Him Wrong, *The Day of the Locust*; each of these is a clue to the identity of a famous person with the last name 'West.'" The first contestant to press a buzzer would have the opportunity to provide any one of the answers—in this case, Jerry West, Mae West or Nathaniel West. The remaining contestants could answer any part that hadn't already been answered correctly. If all three contestants supplied a correct answer, they each received five dollars; if only two were correct, those two each received ten dollars, and if only one gave a correct answer it paid twenty-five dollars. Halfway through the game, the payoffs jumped to ten, twenty-five, and fifty dollars.

To finish off each game, the contestants played the Countdown Round. For this round, a contestant could supply one, two or all three answers to a question as long as the answers were correct. The money accumulated up to that point determined how well the contestants needed to do to win the game; the contestant who had won the most money needed to give only three correct answers and theoretically could win on a single question; the player in second place needed four correct answers; the player in third place needed five correct answers.

The winner then faced a row of five cars. Selecting one of five keys at random, the contestant would choose one car and insert the key into the ignition. If the car started, the contestant won that car plus a cash jackpot that started at $200 and grew in $200 increments every day until claimed. A contestant who was unlucky at this part of the show but kept defeating opponents day after day could retire undefeated after five days, automatically receive the cash jackpot and choose any car as a bonus.

The bonus round was the source of a memorable blooper. To safely cram five automobiles into the confined space on the stage, the *Split Second* crew would disconnect a coil in each car before the tapings. At one taping, a mechanic accidentally disconnected a spark plug instead of a coil. When the contestant tried his key in the ignition, the automobile began spewing smoke and continued smoking for a full minute. *Split Second* handled the crisis by apologizing and giving the contestant the car anyway.

Critics who had been so biting toward *Let's Make a Deal* now eagerly heaped praise on the new creation from the Hatos-Hall factory, and Tom Kennedy established himself as one of the finest and most versatile emcees in the field. Writer Daniel Blanco marveled, "In an era where the wit of television emcees so often fails to match their mercurial deliveries, Tom Kennedy proves the delightful exception… With the excitement of the show's high velocity, it remains a well-constructed, polished half-hour of intensified drama."

The drama unfolded each weekday for three years. Augmenting its success was the fact that it was part of one of the strongest blocks of game shows in the history of daytime TV. When it arrived on ABC in 1972, *Split Second* joined a lineup that already included *The Dating Game*, *The Newlywed Game*, *Password* and *Let's Make a Deal.*

The show came to an end in 1975, and it was a tough day for game show fans, because ABC also ended *Password* and *Blankety Blanks* that day. Tom concluded the series by bringing out various staff members for a round of applause and thanking them for the fine work they did. Executive producer Monty Hall then strolled onstage and returned the goodwill to his superb host:

"I just wanted to jump out here because this is the final *Split Second* show, and on behalf of my partner, Stef Hatos, and all of the gang back at the office, we wanted you to know how proud we were of the job that the entire *Split Second* gang did for the entire three years and a bit...and the wonderful job that you did too. You brought a lot of class to our organization and you did it just beautifully. Thank you so much for the wonderful job that you did."

The game was revived for a single season in 1986, with Monty himself taking the reins as host. Ubiquitous reruns on The Family Channel and USA Network possibly made this the better-known incarnation of *Split Second* even though its run was less successful than the original. A pilot for a revival hosted by Robb Weller was produced in 1990 but didn't sell.

June 28

1940 – *Quiz Kids* Premieres

In 1942, eleven-year-old Richard Williams received a fifty-cent-per-week allowance from his parents, and he owed the IRS $1,000. Claude Brenner, thirteen, had it a little easier. He made $3.50 per week as a delivery boy for a dry cleaning service, and he owed $160 in taxes. Poor fifteen-year-old Jack Lucal was laid off from his father's tire shop due to the World War II rubber shortage and still had to scrape together $135 for Uncle Sam. How did kids wind up with such hefty tax bills? They made a fortune by being smarter than millions of listeners.

Quiz Kids was one of the most popular shows of the golden age of radio and the early days of TV. Hosted by Joe Kelly, it featured a rotating panel of five "child geniuses." Each week, Joe would read trivia questions in various subjects, all submitted by listeners. The home listener won a prize for stumping the kids, but about eighty-five percent of the time during the show's first five years, the youngsters correctly answered the questions and won bonds. The three kids who did the best job came back the following week, while the other two went to the back of the line and waited for another turn. Kids kept coming back as long as they played reasonably well until age sixteen, when it was time to say goodbye.

Among the show's regulars were kids with clear areas of expertise. Joel Kupperman was a math whiz. Gerard Darrow studied nature. Barbara Scott was a literary lass. Richard Williams knew current events. Some of the show's young contestants went on to do great things. Nobel Prize winner James Watson, film director Robert Easton, actress Vanessa Brown, producer Harve Bennett, Mayo Clinic Chief of Staff Richard Sedlack and poet Marilyn Hacker all started out as *Quiz Kids*.

As the show grew more popular—regularly bringing in 15 million listeners each week—it was spun off into a series of film shorts. It would be unthinkable today to go to the multiplex and plop down a few dollars to watch *Jeopardy!* but during the 1940s film lovers were regularly entertained by the panel of bright-eyed, big-brained wunderkinds. The kids frequently visited Washington, DC, where they were entertained in the White House by Eleanor Roosevelt, and three Senators paid tribute to them on the floor of the Senate. Even W.C. Fields couldn't resist them; when they first arrived in Hollywood to work on their film shorts, he invited them to his mansion for a visit. Taking a page from Ralph Edwards's book (see June 13), *Quiz Kids* began requiring studio audience members to purchase bonds at the door before they could watch the show, and *Quiz Kid*s helped raise more than $100,000 for the war. Perhaps the ultimate indication of the show's popularity was that *Quiz Kids* became a part of the American vernacular to refer to experts or know-it-alls of any kind.

Quiz Kids featured a number of special theme shows. For Father's Day 1943, the kids took the night off and their dads fielded the listeners' questions. During one of the frequent excursions to Washington, DC, *Quiz Kids* aired a special broadcast in which the little geniuses battled a team of four senators. At one point, Supreme Court Justice William O. Douglas disqualified a senator from answering because he cheated, and the senators just barely edged out the kids with nine correct answers to seven.

A regular segment of the show invited a guest questioner to attempt to stump the kids, and then turn the tables and field questions from the kids at the end of the segment. Guests for this segment included Bob Hope, Jack Benny, and Fred Allen. One guest was noted scientist Dr. Glenn Seaborg, who was appearing the day before he was scheduled to make a major announcement to the press. One of the kids curiously asked if any new elements had been discovered recently, and Dr. Seaborg elected not to wait for the announcement to the press. He told the kids and the listening audience about Americium and Curium, elements 95 and 96.

In 1949, *Quiz Kids* quite naturally made the move to television, airing for more than four years in prime time on NBC and CBS, but ultimately the show's popularity faded and the quizzing came to an end. In the wake of big money quiz show mania, *Quiz Kids* made a brief return to CBS with new host Clifton Fadiman in the summer of 1956. The show didn't make it past the summer, but a nine-year-old physics expert named Robert Strom was such a smash with viewers that he returned to TV as a contestant on *The $64,000 Question* and *The $64,000 Challenge* after *Quiz Kids* was cancelled.

It should be noted that, like *Question* and *Challenge*, *Quiz Kids* was a creation of Louis G. Cowan, and when the quiz show scandals erupted, even after *Quiz Kids* was just a memory, the controversy brought the classic radio show back in the limelight, admittedly for an undesirable reason. During the investigations conducted by the state of New York, it came out that *Quiz Kids* used what were informally called "controls" to keep the show interesting. The kids genuinely were smart—many were geniuses by some standard measures—but it's no fun watching a team of kids lose to a batch of postcards week after week so, to preclude this from happening, the show kept close tabs on the kids' fields of knowledge. The postcards and questions featured each week were not selected at random but chosen to accommodate a simple rule: don't ask the kids anything that they won't have a good chance of knowing.

Quiz Kids has made several attempts at revivals, without much success. *The New Quiz Kids* showed up in first-run syndication in 1978. The host was Jim McKrell, and the executive producer was, appropriately, former Quiz Kid Harve Bennett. Geoffrey Cowan, the son of Louis, was a consultant. Despite an impressive staff behind the scenes, the show survived only a few months.

In 1981, the fledgling CBS Cable channel introduced another revival, which is largely remembered not for the kids, but for the unlikely host: renowned TV sitcom producer Norman Lear. Harve Bennett and Geoffrey Cowan were co-executive producers of this version, which made it through a full season before coming to an end.

In 1990, Geoffrey Cowan took one more crack at his father's creation with a significantly revamped version titled *The Quiz Kids Challenge*, hosted by Jonathan Prince and pitting a team of three kids against a team of three adults each day for cash prizes. The contestants faced a board displaying eight categories, and they could answer up to three questions in each category as long as they kept giving correct answers. The game concluded with a one hundred-second round that started questions at fifty dollars and doubled the value every twenty-five seconds. Again, it lasted only a single season.

In the literary world, in 1982 former Quiz Kid and author Ruth Feldman released a book, *Whatever Happened to the Quiz Kids?* The book examined the pressure on children who were not only famous, but famous for being smarter than they should have been. She came to find that some of the kids had gone on to live surprisingly normal lives once they grew up—one was a computer programmer, another played piano at a bar and one worked an office job by day and took small acting gigs in his free time. There were others who did the expected extraordinary things when they reached adulthood; among their ranks were a diplomat, an early software developer for Apple and Xerox, a philosophy professor at the University of Connecticut, and an admiral in the Navy who went on to work for the CIA.

June 29

1987 – *Bumper Stumpers* Premieres

No one can predict how where the next idea for a game show will come from. Wink Martindale might never have had an idea for a successful game show if he hadn't become bored during an airplane flight.

Wink and his wife Sandy were flying home from a vacation in Hawaii when he grabbed a copy of the airline magazine and began thumbing through it. He came to an ad for a rental car agency that included pictures of license plates from every state. It got Wink to thinking about crazy vanity license plates he had seen, and he reasoned that everybody, at one time or another, has seen a strange custom plate and has tried to decipher it. Maybe that should be a show.

A year later, he suggested the idea to Dan Enright. Dan had recently seen his two biggest hits, *Tic Tac Dough* and *The Joker's Wild*, come to an end and needed a new idea to revitalize Barry & Enright Productions. He was intrigued with Wink's idea, and together they tinkered and refined it, developing the concept into a game they called *License to Steal*. Producer Mark Maxwell-Smith suggested the title *Bumper Stumpers*, and it went on the air in 1987 as a joint venture between America's USA Network and Canada's Global Network.

Billed as "the show that turned a highway hobby into ready cash," the game pitted two teams of "road scholars" against each other. The contestants would face a pair of license plates and a question. For example, the plates "IIPI" and "10RTHZ" could accompany the question, "Which license plate might belong to Bill Cosby?" The teams would ring in with their guess and then decipher the plate they chose. In this case, the first license plate is correct because it translates to "I's Pi" or "I Spy," the name of Bill Cosby's first series.

A correct answer gave the contestants a chance to solve the Super Stumper, a harder license plate with seven blank spaces. One blank would be filled in, and the team had a chance to guess. The first team to solve two Super Stumpers won the game.

During the show's run, several bonus games were used. Initially, the contestants faced a series of monitors, each hiding a Stop Sign. The contestants had thirty seconds to solve a series of vanity license plates. Each one solved removed one of the Stops and replaced it with a money amount. After time expired, contestants would select monitors, trying to accumulate $500 or more without uncovering one of the remaining Stop Signs. Doing so doubled the money earned, and a contestant who solved all seven license plates automatically won $2,000.

Later, the bonus game changed and contestants had to solve at least four license plates in thirty seconds in order to win their first $200. Each plate after that was a double-or-nothing proposition, with a top payoff of $1,600. Still later, each of the plates served as a clue to the identity of a famous person, place or thing, and solving that identity was worth $1,500.

The series ended in 1990, although reruns aired in Canada for the following five years, and American viewers got treated to reruns on Game Show Network in 2000. The show was just successful enough to leave its mark on pop culture. A 2010 newspaper about customized license plates mentioned that many DMV employees colloquially refer to such plates as "bumper stumpers."

BONUS ROUND

Below, you'll see some apt clues and license plates for game show lovers. Can you solve them?

1.) A plate belonging to a Dick Clark fan **XK$PRMD**
2.) A plate belonging to a winner on *The Joker's Wild* **CNODVLS**
3.) A plate belonging to a contestant on *Hollywood Squares* **3*S2N**
4.) A plate belonging to Marc Summers **DARDAR**
5.) A plate belonging to a rebus lover **CN¢RHN**
6.) A plate belonging to The Banker **26KKS**
7.) A plate shared by Bill Cullen & Bob Stewart **IGS**
8.) A plate belonging to Betty White during her bachelorette days **D88ALN**

June 30

1989 – *Liars Club* Ends

IT WAS A CAREER MOVE THAT NOBODY COULD HAVE anticipated. Rod Serling was a television writer, producer, screenwriter and novelist who used science fiction and high tension to address difficult and sometimes controversial issues in society. His reputation as a master of his craft was sealed with his TV series *The Twilight Zone* and his film *Planet of the Apes*. And with those significant accomplishments to his credit, Rod Serling, in 1969, became a game show host.

The syndicated show, *Liars Club*, brought two contestants together to face four celebrities. A strange-looking, esoteric object was brought out for all to see, and each panelist would give a different explanation for what it was. Only one was truthful, of course. The contestants selected the story they thought was correct.

At the end of the show, the contestant who had most often chosen correctly received one hundred dollars.

In its original incarnation, *Liars Club* lasted only a single season. Serling walked away from game shows altogether and picked up where he left off, creating and hosting *Night Gallery* for NBC.

When *Liars Club* returned in 1976, announcer Bill Armstrong stepped in front of the camera to act as host. There were now four contestants staked one hundred dollars to start, and odds were posted for each item—1:1, 2:1, 5:1, 10:1 or even 20:1 early in the series' run—and the players placed bets on which star had the correct explanation.

Armstrong departed from the show and was replaced by Allen Ludden for the following two seasons. Among the frequent panelists were Fannie Flagg, Joey Bishop, Dody Goodman and Larry Hovis. Behind the scenes, Hovis was also producing the show and, before each taping, he briefed his fellow panelists on how to tell convincing stories.

In all incarnations of the show, the host was never a part of that briefing. The hosts were kept in the dark, the show's staff fearful that a knowing smile or tone of voice might give away a correct answer. In a 2009 article, production assistant Shelley Herman recalled that the staff even went to the trouble of hiding the objects for upcoming tapings whenever Allen Ludden came by the office.

Keeping the host in the dark had a way of adding to the fun, though. One day, Allen was particularly amused by a length of cord and played with it, twirling it and winding it around his hands and fingers as the celebrities gave their explanations. He smiled and continued entertaining himself with his new plaything until the end of the round, when the announcer revealed that the cord was inserted into hospital patients to detect colon polyps.

Liars Club returned one more time in the fall of 1988, with host Eric Boardman and a new array of strange items to stump the panel. The new version flopped, though, and *The New Liars Club* closed its doors after only a single season.

Answers

Page 385 – *You Don't Say!*

1.Tot + Nude + Done = TODD NEWTON
2.Marks + Hum + Hearse = MARC SUMMERS
3.Gym + Pair + He = JIM PERRY
4.Bat + Say + Jack = PAT SAJAK
5.Bop + You + Bangs = BOB EUBANKS
6.Chick + Bear + Hiss = CHUCK BARRIS
7.Meter + Tomorrow + Kin = PETER TOMARKEN
8.Heart + Leak + Litter = ART LINKLETTER

Page 477 – *Double Dare*

1. Dolls
2. Swimming
3. Pipe
4. Bathtub
5. Gambling

6. Winston Churchill
7. Frisbee
8. Yo-yo
9. Glasses
10. Boomerang

Page 663 – *Caesar's Challenge*
8.*Villain* – **DRAGON**
9.*Square* – **VILANCH**
10.*Word game* – **SCRABBLE**
11.*Truth seeker* – **COLLYER**
12.*Producer* – **ENRIGHT**
13.*Matchmaker* – **DAWSON**
14.*Voice* – **JACOBS**

Page 691 – *Face the Music*
1.Bob Barker
2.Dick Clark
3.Ron Ely
4.Monty Hall

Page 714 – *Bumper Stumpers*
1.) A plate belonging to a Dick Clark fan
"THE $10,000 PYRAMID"
2.) A plate belonging to a winner on *The Joker's Wild*
"SEE NO DEVILS"
3.) A plate belonging to a contestant on *Hollywood Squares*
"THREE STARS TO WIN"
4.) A plate belonging to Marc Summers
"DOUBLE DARE"

5.) A plate belonging to a rebus lover
"CONCENTRATION"
6.) A plate belonging to The Banker
"TWENTY-SIX CASES"
7.) A plate shared by Bill Cullen & Bob Stewart
"EYE GUESS"
8.) A plate belonging to Betty White during her bachelorette days
"DATES ALLEN"

Bibliography

"1988/1982 College Bowl Co. Regionals." *Buzzer: Official Journal of Academic Buzzer Competitions.* Volume 1, Issue 3. Spring 1988.

Aitchison, Marion. "Plenty of Chuckles Mark Florida Theater Program." *St. Petersburg Times.* 18 Aug. 1940.

Akers, Marshall. *To Tell the Truth on the Web.* Web. 17 May 2011. <http://www.ttttontheweb.com/>.

Alexander, Ron. "Friends Sign In Please at Tribute to Arlene Francis." *The New York Times.* 19 May 1987.

Allen, Fred. *Treadmill to Oblivion.* Wildside Press. 2007. Print.

Alisi, Art. Personal interview. 10 May 2011.

Arar, Yardena. "Allen Ludden Succumbs, Longtime 'Password' Host." *Spokane Daily Chronicle.* 10 Jun. 1981.

"Arlene Francis Biography." *Film Reference.* Web. 31 Jul 2011. <http://www.filmreference.com/film/10/Arlene-Francis.html>

"Art Fleming Hosting College Bowl." *Kingman Daily Miner.* 12 Oct. 1979.

"Art Linkletter gets Odd Assortment of Mail." *St. Joseph News-Press.* 31 May 1958.

"Art Linkletter Lit Sign for Actress." *The Milwaukee Journal.* 16 Jan. 1960.

Ashe, Isobel. "Berle's Jackpot Bowling is a Really Striking TV Series." *Reading Eagle.* Reading, PA. 27 Nov. 1960.

"Ask TV Scout." *The News and Courier.* Charleston, SC. 14 Oct. 1973.

"Astronomical Prizes Doom Quiz Shows." *The Miami News.* 20 Apr. 1957.

"Aughtor Guest on Broadcast." *Pittsburgh Post-Gazette.* 16 Oct. 1943.

Baber, David. *Television Game Show Hosts: Biographies of 32 Stars.* Jefferson, NC: McFarland &, 2008. Print.

Bacon, James. "Bert Convy is Making Third Comeback." *The Sumter Daily Item.* 6 Apr. 1961.

Bailey, Paul, Fred Wostbrock, and Steve Beverly. *Game Show Congress 7 Program* Nov. 2009. Print.

Barry, Les. "Mumps May Give Yankees a Real Pain in the Neck." *The Miami News.* 8 Jun. 1956.

Belcher, Jerry. "Game Show Comic Paul Lynde Dead at 55." *The Montreal Gazette.* Page 22. 12 Jan. 1982.

Berger, Marilyn. "Kitty Carlisle Hart, Actress and Arts Advocate, Dies at 96." *The New York Times.* 18 Apr. 2007.

" Betty White." *Intimate Portrait.* Lifetime Cable Network. 4 Sept. 2000. Television.

Bianculli, David. "Pax Network: 3 Shows, 1 ½ Stars, You Do the Math." *New York Daily News.* 1 Sep. 1998.

"The Big Fix." *Time Magazine.* 19 Oct. 1959. Web. 05 June 2011. <http://www.time.com/time/magazine/article/0,9171,869307-3,00.html>.

"Big Spotlight Turns on Sam, Surprised Organ Grinder." *The Milwaukee Journal.* 27 Apr. 1947.

"Bill Cullen: Emcee of 'Price is Right.'" *Gettysburg Times.* 10 Jun. 1961.

"Bill Cullen's Game is TV Games." *Sarasota Herald-Tribune.* 20 Aug. 1970.

"Bill Cullen: The Talk Show King." *The Times-News.* Hendersonville, NC. 17 May 1975.

"Bill Todman of TV Game Shows Dies at Age 62." *The Montreal Gazette.* 31 Jul. 1979.

"Biography: John Reed King." *The Sherbrooke Telegram.* 18 May 1950.

"Bonanza Winner Taken By Surprise." *Spokane Daily Chronicle.* 5 Mar. 1948.

Bowles, Jerry. *The Gong Show Book.* New York: Tempo Books. 1977.

"Boy Hero Wins $2,500 TV Prize." *Chicago Tribune.* 16 Sep. 1953.

Blair, Tom. "Rolf Benirschke." *San Diego Magazine.* Nov. 2006. Web. 17 May 2011. <http://www.sandiegomagazine.com/media/San-Diego-Magazine/November-2006/Rolf-Benirschke-with-Tom-Blair/>.

Bobbin, Jay. "Jim Perry Juggles Three Game Shows." *The Calgary Herald.* 20 Jul. 1979.

Bombeck, Erma. "To Each His Own Goodbye Style." *Sunday Star-News.* Wilmington, NC. 18 Jan. 1981.

Bowles, Jennifer. "Game Show Caters to Debt-Free Dreams." *Lawrence Journal-World.* 9 Jun. 1997.

"Boy Buys Toys for Needy." *The Deseret News.* 25 Dec. 1949.

Boyle, Hal. "Giveaways are Out of Hand." *Kentucky New Era.* Hopkinsville, KY. 21 Sep. 1949.

Boyle, Hal. "Giving Away Cash on TV Programs Exciting Experience for Emcee, Too." *Spokane Daily Chronicle.* 3 Nov. 1955.

Boyle, Hal. "How to Get on a Quiz Show." *The Evening Independent.* St. Petersburg, FL. 4 Aug. 1949.

Boyle, Hal. "The Man with the $100,000 Answer." *The Evening Independent.* St. Petersburg, FL. 11 Nov. 1948.

"Boy's Idea Snares Gorilla Prize from ABC." *Spokane Chronicle.* 23 Jul. 1987.

"'Break the Bank' Emcee Works Full Schedule." *Oxnard Press-Courier.* 6 Apr. 1953.

"'Break the Bank' Winner has New Problem to Face." *The Victoria Advocate.* 21 Aug. 1949.

"Bridegroom wins $5100, New Job on Radio Program." *The Pittsburgh Press.* 10 Jan. 1948.

"Brooklyn Boy, 5, is Sensation, Especially in Dope on Baseball." *The Sunday News-Press.* St Joseph, MO. 15 Aug. 1954.

Brooks, Tim, and Earl Marsh. *The Complete Directory to Prime Time Network and Cable TV Shows 1946-Present.* Ninth ed. New York: Ballantine, 2007. Print.

Bruno, Michael. Personal interview. 3 Aug. 2011.

Buck, Jerry. "Allen Ludden Turns Game Player." *Schenectady Gazette.* 17 Jul. 1974.

Buck, Jerry. "Tom Skerritt Stars in Political Thriller." *Lawrence Journal-World.* 24 Nov. 1989.

"Busy Bill." *St. Joseph News-Press/Gazette.* St. Joseph, MO. 3 Mar. 1984.

Campbell, Tom. "Packaged in a Blank Shuck. *The Palm Beach Post*. 17 Oct. 1971.

"Can You Top This?" *The Museum of Broadcast Communications.* Web. 17 May 2011. <http://www.museum.tv/rhofsection.php?page=274>.

"Car Crash Injuries Fatal to Larry Blyden." *Sarasota Herald-Tribune.* 7 Jun. 1975.

Caro, Mark. "His Latest Challenge: Dick Clark is Back with a New Game Show and High Hopes." *Chicago Tribune.* 3 Sep. 1990.

http://www.carsonscrafts.com/igas/index.htm

Carter, Bill. "Mark Goodson, Game Show Inventor, Dies at 77." *The New York Times.* 19 Dec. 1992.

Carter, Bill. "TV Notes; TV Game Wins Regis." *The New York Times.* 11 Aug. 1999.

"Change Speed." *The Modesto Bee.* 7 Oct. 1973.

"Chicago Widow 'Walking Man' Contest Winner." *The Florence Times.* 6 Mar. 1948.

"City Code Violated by TV Strike It Rich." *Saskatoon Star-Phoenix.* Saskatoon, Sask. 29 Dec. 1954.

http://www.classicsquares.com

"Clayton 'Bud' Collyer 1908-1969." *Superman Super Site.* Accessed 22 Aug. 2011. < http://www.supermansupersite.com/bud.html>

Cohen, Sandy. "Priceless Bob Barker Ends Record TV Run." *The Washington Post.* 6 Jun. 2007.

"College Bowl is Back, This Time on Radio." *The Miami News.* 27 Nov. 1979.

"College Bowl is Returning." *Youngstown Vindicator.* 24 Apr. 1984.

Collins, Glenn. "Game Show Wins Big—with Kids." *The Palm Beach Post.* 4 Aug. 1987.

"Comic, TV Host Jan Murray Dead at 89." *Fox News.* 3 Jul. 2006. <http://www.foxnews.com/story/0,2933,201978,00.html>

"Contestant Burned When Stunt Backfires on Television Show." *Ocala Star-Banner.* 7 Apr. 1959.

"Country Gal Does a Lot!" *The Robesonian.* Lumberton, NC. 13 Jul. 1980.

"'County Fair' Wins Viewing Honors on TV." *Gettysburg Times.* 13 Nov. 1958.

Crosby, John. "Audience Participation on TV." *Toledo Blade.* 1 Aug. 1957.

Crosby, John. "The Five Faye Emersons." *The Portsmouth Times.* 15 May 1950.

Crosby, John. "Charades Burgeon Into Pantomime on Television." *St. Petersburg Times.* 10 Aug. 1951.

Crosby, John. "Radio and TV: Heartache on Display." *Pittsburgh Post-Gazette.* 4 Jan. 1954.

Crosby, John. "Herb Shriner Doing Well as 'Give Away' Humorist." *Hartford Courant.* 17 Oct. 1952.

Crosby, John. "Radio and Television in Review." *Pittsburgh Post-Gazette.* 13 Aug. 1951.

Crosby, John. "Radio and Television in Review." *Pittsburgh Post-Gazette.* 20 Aug. 1952.

Crosby, John. "Radio in Review: How to Live Like a Millionaire and Like It." *The Portsmouth Times.* Page 16. 5 Jul 1950.

Crosby, John. "TV Writer Doubts Any Wide Yearnings to Lead a Band." *The Modesto Bee.* 27 Aug. 1954.

Crosby, John. "U.S. Custom: Make Loot the Quiz Show Way." *St. Petersburg Times.* 31 Dec. 1956.

Cummings, Judith. "Luck Runs Outfor a Winner as TV Publicity Boomerangs." *The New York Times.* 16 Jan. 1988.

http://www.curtalliaume.com/

"Daly to Leave What's My Line." *The Fort Scott Tribune.* 16 Jan. 1964.

Danzig, Fred. "Channel Chips." *Oxnard Press Courier.* 24 Jul. 1958.

Danzig, Fred. "New Show Comes Up with Innovation to 'Intros'." *The Bend Bulletin* [Bend, OR] 3 Jan. 1962: 8. Print.

Danzig, Fred. "Television in Review." *The Times-News.* Hendersonville, NC. 2 Jan. 1961.

Davis, Alex. "ABC Plans Redo of Dream House." *Buzzerblog.* 04 Apr. 2007. http://buzzerblog.flashgameshows.com/abc-plans-redo-of-dream-house

"Daytime Host of Weakest Link Upbeat." *Daily News.* Bowling Green, KY. 4 Jan. 2002.

"Dennis James, Host of Many Firsts in Television, Dies of Cancer at 79." *The Deseret News.* Salt Lake City, UT. 5 Jun. 1997.

"Dick Clark." *Larry King Live.* CNN. 16 Apr. 2004.

"Dick Clark Denies Ever Taking Payola." *Ocala Star-Banner.* 29 Apr. 1960.

"Dick Clark Returning with New Show 'The Challengers.'" *The Prescott Courier.* 8 Dec. 1989.

Dinan, James. "Chris Jericho Steps into Downfall Ring." *CNN.com.* 3 Jun 2010.

Donlon, Brian. "Game Shows Rebound." *USA Today.* McLean, VA. 12 Jan. 1990.

"Don Pardo." Interview by David Schwartz. Archive of American Television. Web.

Dube, Bernard. "Dial Turns." *The Montreal Gazette.* 13 June 1960.

Du Brew, Rick. "Tennessee Ernie is Back." *The Press Courier.* Oxnard, CA. 3 Apr. 1962.

Duffy, Mike. "TV Geek Paul Goebel Knows His Tube and Loves It." *Detroit Free Press.* 29 Jan. 2002.

"Durham Woman Breaks the Bank." *The Meriden Daily Journal.* 15 May 1951.

"Ed McMahon : Obituary." *This Is Announcements.* Web. 05 June 2011. <http://www.thisisannouncements.co.uk/5883933>.

"Ed McMahon." Interview by Michael Rosen. Archive of American Television. 15 Aug. 2002. Web.

Edwards, Ralph. "Some Things the Quiz Men Learned from Quizzing." *St. Petersburg Times.* 18 Jan. 1943.

Edwardsen, Elizabeth. "Superstars of TV's College Bowl Return to Bates." *Sun-Journal.* Lewiston, ME. 11 Jun. 1993.

Endrst, James. "Messy 'Double Dare' Cleans Up in Ratings." *The Pittsburgh Press.* 17 Apr. 1988.

"Entertainment Legend Merv Griffin Dies at 82." *Billboard.* Accessed 11 Aug. 2011.

ernieford.com

"Ernie Kovacs Now Doing Panel Show on Thursdays." *The Modesto Bee.* 8 Nov. 1959.

Eubanks, Bob, and Matthew Scott Hansen. *It's in the Book, Bob!* Dallas, TX: BenBella, 2004. Print.

Ewald, Willian. "Concentration Found Harmless in TV Opening." *Meriden Journal.* 26 Aug. 1958.

Ewald, William. "Jan Murray Ditches His Program for a New Game." *The News-Dispatch.* Jeanette, PA. 11 Sep. 1956.

Ewald, Williams. "Kudoes to Pat Boone's Substitute." *The Miami News.* 16 Aug. 1958.

"Ex-Game Show Host Ray Combs Dies at 40." *The Lakeland Ledger.* 4 Jun. 1996.

Fanning, Win. "Two Veterans Recall Early Experiences." *Pittsburgh Post-Gazette.* 6 Apr. 1952.

Fates, Gil. *What's My Line?: the inside History of TV's Most Famous Panel Show.* Englewood Cliffs, NJ: Prentice-Hall, 1978. Print.

"Finds Key to Leg Irons 32,744 Keys and Six Days Later."

Fleming, Robert. "Out of the Mouths of Babes Comes Juvenile Jury." *The Milwaukee Journal.* 23 Feb. 1947.

"For Men Who Do the Cooking: TV's Art Fleming is Considered a Master Chef by His Wife and Friends." *The Milwaukee Journal.* 20 Aug. 1967.

Fox, Dan. Personal interview. 10 May 2011.

Gamble, Jack. "Want to Get Rick Quick? Here's How Some People Make Dollars Per Minute." *The Milwaukee Journal.* 19 Sep. 1946.

"Game Show Lets You 'Win Ben Stein's Money." *CNN.com* 4 Aug. 1997. <http://www.cnn.com/SHOWBIZ/9708/04/win.steins.money/index.html?

www.game-show-utopia.net

http://gameshow.ipbhost.com/index.php?showtopic=21339&view=findpost&p=256722

"Games Continue Popular as TV Fare." *Waycross Journal-Herald.* Waycross, GA. 31 May 1972.

"Game Show Resurgence." *The Bryan Times.* Bryan, OH. 2 Nov. 1984.

Gardner, Marilyn and Hy. "Adam Wade Worked in a Lab." *Youngstown Vindicator.* Youngstown, OH. 1 Jul. 1975

Gaver, Jack. "Job of Getting Show Guests Perplexing." *Beaver County Times.* 20 Aug. 1953.

Gaver, Jack. "TV Host Wants a Dream House." *St. Petersburg Times.* 30 Apr. 1969.

"Geoff Edwards: He Knows All the Ropes of Hosting." *Beaver County Times.* Beaver County, PA. 19 Mar. 1977.

www.georgegray.com

Gerhard, Inez. "Stardust." *The Mount Washington News.* 30 Jan. 1948.

Gibson, John. "Talk Show Pioneer Jack Paar Dead at 85 - The Big Story W/ Gibson and Nauert." *FoxNews.com - Breaking News | Latest News | Current News.* 28 Jan. 2004. Web. 17 May 2011. <http://www.foxnews.com/story/0,2933,109763,00.html>.

"Gil Fates, 86, a TV Producer of Shows Like 'What's My Line?'" *The New York Times.* 16 May 2000.

Glazer, Barney. "Televents." *The Press-Courier.* Oxnard, CA. 17 Feb. 1974.

Glover, William. "Jan's Gamble Sends Career on New Slant." *Sarasota Journal.* 5 Sep. 1957.

Glover, William. "Jan Murray is New Video Find for '57." *Ludington Daily News.* 5 Sep. 1957.

"Going…Going…GONG!" Las Vegas Sun. 27 Aug. 1999.

"Goldberg Enjoying Squares Schedule." *Daily News.* Middlesboro, KY. 8 Feb. 1999.

"Goldberg Takes Job on New 'Hollywood Squares.'" *The Tuscaloosa News.* 10 Jul 1998.

Gorron, Barry. "Life's Too Short for Minute to Win It." Reuters. 10 Mar. 2010. <http://www.reuters.com/article/2010/03/11/us-television-minute-idUSTRE62A0EO20100311>

Grace, Art. "He Didn't Quit Quiz; He was Canned." *The Miami News.* 13 Sep. 1958.

Graham, Jefferson. *Come on Down!!!: the TV Game Show Book.* New York: Abbeville, 1988. Print.

"Grandma Hush Solution Brings $30,000." *The Deseret News.* 16 May 1951.

"Grandmother Named As Queen for a Day." *The Tuscaloosa News.* 31 Dec. 1949.

Griffin, Merv, and David Bender. *Merv: Making the Good Life Last.* New York: Simon & Schuster, 2003. Print.

"Griffin Says He Chose Vanna Because of Her 'Big Head.'" *The Milwaukee Sentinel.* 15 Dec. 1987.

"Groucho on New Network with Different Format." *St. Joseph News-Press.* 21 Jan. 1962.

Hagen, Lois. "Quiz Kids Find No Answer to Tax Problems." *St. Petersburg Times.* 13 Mar. 1942.

Hanauer, Joan. "Martindale Invents 'Headline Chasers.'" *Record-Journal.* Meriden, CT. 28 Aug. 1985.

Hanauer, Joan. "People in the News." *The Bryan Times*. Bryan, OH. 31 Mar. 1981.

"The Happy Monarch." *Pittsburgh Post-Gazette*. 25 Oct. 1946.

Hayes, Dixon. *The Classic Hollywood Squares Site*. Web. 18 May 2011. <http://www.classicsquares.com>.

Hazlett, Terry. "Steppin' Out: Daytime Emmy Awards to be Given Tomorrow." *Observer-Reporter*. Washington, PA. 10 May 1976.

Herzog, Buck. "Customer Bought Drinks for the House." *The Milwaukee Sentinel*. 6 Jun. 1956.

"He's Passed Go and Collected Much More Than $200." *Pittsburgh Post-Gazette*. 8 Jul 1990.

Hohl, Verne. "Charity Fete Amused by Jan Murray." *The Milwaukee Sentinel*. 7 Apr. 1957.

Holley, Joe. "Rhyming Funnyman Nipsey Russell Dies." *The Washington Times*. 4 Oct. 2005.

Holston, Noel. "Nickelodeon's Game Show." *Minneapolis Star and Tribune*. 1 Nov. 1986.

Hooper, Carl. "Views on Television." *The Victoria Advocate*. 15 Oct 1960.

Hooper. Joseph. "It's Ben Stein's World; the Rest of Us Just Watch It." *The New York Times*. 20 Feb. 2000.

"Hugh Downs." Interview by Bill Tynan. Archive of American Television. 22 Oct. 1997. Web.

"Hush Family Can't Be Hushed." *The Gettysburg Times.* 26 Feb. 1948.

"Hush Money Nets $18,000 for Housewife." *The Milwaukee Journal.* 16 Mar. 1947.

IMDB.com

Ingram, Billy. "Gleason's Big Bomb!" *TVparty!* Web. 17 May 2011. <http://www.tvparty.com/picture.html>.

Ingram, Billy. "Oddball Game Shows of the '50s." *TVparty!* Web. 26 May 2011. <http://www.tvparty.com/ >.

"It Happened Last Night." *Sarasota Herald-Tribune.* 3 May 1975.

"It Pays to be Ignorant." Old Time Radio Catalog. Web. < http://www.otrcat.com/it-pays-to-be-ignorant-p-1419.html>

"It's Best to be a Mess." *Ellensburg Daily Record.* 24 Aug. 1987.

"Jack Barry Has Been from Top to Bottom and Back to Top." *Herald-Journal.* Spartansburg, SC. 30 Mar. 1980.

James, Caryn. "Critic's Notebook: Game Shows, Greedy and Otherwise." *The New York Times.* 18 Nov. 1999.

"Jan Murray Says Comedians Should be Close to Audience." *Ocala Star-Banner.* 18 Jan. 1955.

www.j-archive.org

"J.D. Roth: Chief Executive Officer." *3 Ball Productions.* http://www.3ballproductions.com/bios.html

"Jeff Foxworthy Interview for Syndicated 'Are You Smarter Than a 5th Grader?' | Radio & TV Talk." *AccessAtlanta.com*. Web. 05 June 2011. <http://blogs.ajc.com/radio-tv-talk/2009/09/23/jeff-foxworthy-interview-for-syndicated-are-you-smarter-than-a-5th-grader/>.

"Jeff Foxworthy Interview, Are You Smarter Than a 5th Grader?" *Www.35pv.com - Online Men's Magazine*. Web. 05 June 2011. <http://www.35pv.com/television/interviews/2007/jeff_foxworthy.php>.

"Joe Garagiola Statistics and History." *Baseball-Reference.com - Major League Baseball Statistics and History*. Web. 05 June 2011. <http://www.baseball-reference.com/players/g/garagjo01.shtml>.

"Jim Peck is Net's Good Boy." *The Milwaukee Journal.* 28 Dec. 1976.

"Johnny Gilbert: Three Talents and Two Voices." *Milwaukee Sentinel.* 17 May 1959.

"John Reed King, Former Radio, TV Personality Here in the 1960s." *Pittsburgh Post-Gazette.* 11 Jul 1979.

Kagan, Ben, and Bob Stahl. "I've Got a Secret's Two Greatest Assets." *TV Guide* 18 Aug. 1962: 18-24. Print.

Kalter, Suzy. "Richard Dawson: The Emcee They Love to Hate." *Daytona Beach Morning Journal.* 18 Aug. 1979.

Kassewitz, Jack. "Trying to Buy Stamps on a Sunday Cancels the Day." *The Miami News.* 14 Nov. 1979.

Kaufman, Joanne. "He Drives This Game Show Vehicle." *The Wall Street Journal.* 26 Jun. 2008.

Kern, Janet. "'Wagon Train' Getting to be 'Topper' on TV." *The Milwaukee Sentinel.* 10 Dec. 1957.

Kisseloff, Jeff. *The Box: an Oral History of Television, 1920-1961.* New York: Viking, 1995. Print.

Kleiner, Dick. "Astronomical Prizes May Spell Doom of Super Television Quiz Programs." *Sarasota Journal.* 15 Apr. 1957.

Kleiner, Dick. "Finding Top-Flight Jokes Tough for Video Crew. *The Victoria Advocate.* 9 Jun 1963.

Kleiner, Dick. "Woody Woodbury: Switch May Lift Him to Stardom." *The Tuscaloosa News.* 18 Nov. 1962.

Kleinfield, N.R. "David Boehm: The Man Behind Guinness Fame." *Times-Union.* Warsaw, IN. 24 Jul. 1980.

Kornheiser, Tony. "A Quiz Show for the Ugly." *Reading Eagle.* 19 Nov. 1999.

Kramer, Chris. "Carmen Sandiego Tests Knowledge." *Beaver County Times.* Beaver County, PA. 14 Nov. 1994

Krause, Marla. "Dealer Hall Trades Tube for Live Stage." *The Milwaukee Sentinal.* 7 Jul. 1978.

Kubicek, John. "Don't Forget the Lyrics, but Please Forget This Show." BuddyTV. 11 Jul 2007. <http://www.buddytv.com/articles/the-singing-bee/dont-forget-the-lyrics-but-ple-8166.aspx>

Kyle, Shirley. "Barbara is a Darling." *The Afro-American.* Baltimore, MD. 3 Mar. 1956.

Lasswell, Mark. *TV Guide: Fifty Years of Television.* New York: Crown, 2002. Print.

Lee, Jennifer. "Jan Murray, 89, Stand-Up Comic Who Became TV Host, Dies." *The New York Times.* 3 Jul. 2006.

Levesque, John. "Martindale Goes into Debt—His 19th Game Show Gig." *The Deseret News.* 10 Jun 1966.

Lewis, Dan. "Daytime Television is Full." *Sarasota Journal.* 15 Mar. 1976.

Lewis, Dan. "Perry Popular Host of Shows." *Waycross Journal-Herald.* 1 Jul. 1983.

Lipton, Lauren. "Reilly's Monopoly on Cockiness." *Los Angeles Times.* 16 Jun. 1990.

"Lisa Jane Persky, Andrew Zax." *The New York Times.* 20 Jan. 2008.

"Love Online." *Lakeland Ledger.* Lakeland, FL. 5 Apr. 1999.

Lowry, Cynthia. "Allen Ludden Gives Up College Bowl for Password." *Ocala Star-Banner.* 9 May 1962.

Lowry, Cynthia. "Cullen Can't Act, but He Can 'Game.'" *The Eugene Register-Guard.* 30 Jun. 1971.

Lowry, Cynthia. "Concentration in 14th Season on TV." *St. Joseph News-Press.* 6 Feb. 1972.

Lowry, Cynthia. "Game's the Thing with Allen, Betty Ludden." *The Victoria Advocate.* 16 May 1965.

Lowry, Cynthia. "New Celebrity Game As Bright as Phone Book." *The Evening News.* Newburgh, NY. 6 Apr. 1964.

Lowry, Cynthia. "Supermarket Sweep Making It Big on TV." *The Florence Times.* Florence, AL. 3 May 1966.

Lowry, Cynthia. "To Tell the Truth, Kitty Carlisle Rates as a Gal with Sleek Class." *Toledo Blade.* 21 Oct. 1962.

Lowry, Cynthia. "What's My Line? Addicts Find Many Similar Shows." *The Florence Times.* 2 Jan 1963.

Lowry, Cynthia. "What's My Line? Starts 15th Year." *The Montreal Gazette.* 1 Feb. 1964.

"Lucky Girls to Present Richards with Whole Rabbit." *St. Joseph News-Press.* 21 Jun. 1951.

MacPherson, Virginia. "24,000 Miles Free Travel Produces Ring in Radio Gag." *Spokane Daily Chronicle.* 29 Nov. 1950.

MacPherson, Virginia. "Hollywood Report." *Oxnard Press-Courier.* 27 Jan. 1949.

"Make Me Laugh Gets No Smile from TV Critic." *The Free-Lance Star.* Fredericksburg, VA. 27 Mar. 1958.

Mann, Arnold. "Acheivers: Preacher's Kid." *Time Magazine.* 11 Nov. 2002.

"Manners & Morals: Americana." *Time Magazine.* 25 Oct. 1948.

"The Many Lives of Monty Hall." *The Press-Courier.* Oxnard, CA. 16 Apr. 1966.

"Many Wish Ralph Could Hush Those Hush Deals." *The Deseret News.* 28 Feb. 1948.

Marshall, Peter, and Adrienne Armstrong. *Backstage with the Original Hollywood Square*. Nashville, TN: Rutledge Hill, 2002. Print.

Marx, Groucho. *The Groucho Letters: Letters from and to Groucho Marx.* New York: Simon & Schuster Papberbacks, 2007. Print.

McDermott, Marc. "Goodson, Mark and Bill Todman." *The Museum of Broadcast Communications*. Web. 19 May 2011. <http://www.museum.tv/eotvsection.php?entrycode=goodsonmark>.

McDonough, Kevin. "Greed May be a Result of Envy." *Record-Journal.* Meriden, CT. 4 Nov. 1999.

McGeehan, Patrick. "Charles Nelson Reilly, Tony-Winning Comic Actor, Dies at 76." *The New York Times*. Web. 05 June 2011. <http://www.nytimes.com/2007/05/28/theater/28reilly.html>.

McMahon, Tom. "Television Just a Game for Chuck Woolery." *The Windsor Star.* Windsor, Ont. 20 Jul 1984.

"Meet Geoff Edwards." *The Dispatch.* Lexington, NC. 21 Mar. 1975.

http://members.multimania.co.uk/gameshowpage/MG/Conv.html

Mendoza, N.F. "Shows for Youngsters and Their Parents Too." *The Los Angeles Times.* 28 Aug. 1994.

Mercer, Charles. "Half-Hour Drama Show Makes Hit on Goodyear's Theater." *Ocala Star-Banner.* Ocala, FL. 25 Nov. 1958.

Mercer, Charles. "New Give-Away Boom in Television." *The Michigan Daily.* Ann Arbor, MI. 19 Oct. 1955.

Mercer, Charles. "TV Report." *The Dispatch.* Lexington, NC. 22 Jan. 1959.

"Merv Griffin." NNDB. Accessed 20 Aug. 2011. <http://www.nndb.com/people/418/000022352/>

"Merv Griffin Hopes Game Show will 'Click' with Teens." *The Vindicator.* Youngstown, OH. 25 Oct. 1997.

Michals, Bob. "Test Trivia Mettle on College Bowl." *Palm Beach Post.* 22 May 1984.

"Million Dollar Password: Password Gets a 21st Century Makeover." Vindy.com. 1 Jun. 2008. <http://www.vindy.com/news/2008/jun/01/8220million-dollar-password8221-8-pm/>

"Milton Bradley Company." Funding Universe. Accessed 21 Aug. 2011. <http://www.fundinguniverse.com/company-histories/Milton-Bradley-Company-Company-History.html>

Mink, Eric. "Six Ideas for an Even More Winning Game." *New York Daily News*. 1 Sep. 1999.

"Minnesota Fats Will Hustle Hackett When 'Celebrity Billiards' Debuts." *Schenectady Gazette*. 13 Jan. 1968.

"Miss California Wins Runner-Up in Miss USA Pageant." *Lodi News-Sentinel*. 2 Mar. 1988.

"Mister Wickel Finds Himself in Very Much of a Pickle." *St. Petersburg Times*. 2 Dec. 1944.

Mooney, George A. "Radio Notes and Comment: A Radio Quiz is Quizzed and a Plot is Suspected." *The New York Times*. 18 May 1941.

Moorhead, Jim. "Gong Show Movie Complete with Plot, Storyline and Cast." *The Evening Independent*. St. Petersburg, FL. 28 May 1980.

"Mother Finds Child Alive; Plans Trip." *Star-News*. Wilmington, NC. 16 Apr. 1956.

"Monty Hall Answers Charges Against 'Let's Make a Deal.'" *Sarasota Herald-Tribune*. 15 Dec. 1975.

"Monty Hall Tapes Final 'Let's Make a Deal' Show." *The Press-Courier.* Oxnard, CA. 23 Dec. 1976.

Moore, Frazier. "New Hollywood Squares Lacks Charm of First Show." *The Albany Herald.* 3 Feb. 1999.

Moore, Garry. "They'll Do Anything to Get on TV." *The Spokesman-Review.* Spokane, WA. 31 Oct. 1954.

Moore, Scott. "Getting There From Here; Lynn Thigpen First Said No." *The Washington Post.* Washington, DC. 3 Oct. 1993.

"More 'Information Please' Information." *The Milwaukee Journal.* 16 Feb. 1943.

Murphy, Mary. "The Prizes…The Applause…The Pain." *TV Guide* 21 Jan. 1984: 35-42. Print.

http://www.museum.tv/eotvsection.php?entrycode=downshugh

"N.C. State Wins College Bowl Title." *Milwaukee Journal.* 30 May 1988.

Nest, Eugene. "Wheeler-Dealer." *The Pittsburgh Press.* 25 Jul. 1964.

"New Game Show '1 vs. 100' Unlikely to Drain Brain Cells." *Philadelphia Inquirer.* 13 Oct. 2006.

"New Game Show Debuts Dec. 30." *St. Joseph News-Press.* 16 Nov. 1963.

"New Jersey Couple Break 'Radio Bank,' Win $7,440." *St. Petersburg Times.* 2 Aug. 1947.

Newman, Kathy M. "Beat the Geek." *The Pacific Northwest Inlander.* Spokane, WA. 19 Dec. 2001.

"New Quiz Kids to be Based on Radio Show." *The Rock Hill Herald.* 22 Feb. 1978.

"New Quiz Show Brings Some Levity to All-News Channel." *The New York Times.* 18 Feb. 1997.

"New York Cracks Down on Strike It Rich Show." *Pittsburgh Post-Gazette.* 4 Feb. 1954.

nfl.com

Nguyen, Daisy. "Former Game Show Host Peter Tomarken Killed in Santa Monica Plane Crash." *North County Times.* San Diego, CA. 14 Mar. 2006.

O'Brian, Jack. "It's Not the Game, but the Players." *St. Petersburg Times.* 8 Jul. 1957.

Ochiltree, Tom. "Gets Thousands of Gifts as Penalty." *The Lewiston Daily Sun.* 28 Jan. 1943.

O'Connor, John J. "TV Weekend: 'The Rousters' To Begin.'" *The New York Times.* 30 Sep. 1983.

Oliver, Wayne. "Bill Cullen Has Seven TV, Radio Shows on 5 Networks." *Ocala Star-Banner.* 15 Dec. 1954.

Oliver, Wayne. "Billion-Dollar Give-It-Back TV Show Planned by Framer." *Reading Eagle.* 30 Mar. 1955.

Oliver, Wayne. "Masked Celebrities Called Good Sports." *The Miami News.* 11 Jan. 1955.

Othman, Frederick C. "Quiz Kids Go to Hollywood, Have Run-In with Fields." *St. Petersburg Times.* 23 Apr. 1941.

Ottinger, Matt. *The Bill Cullen Homepage*. Web. 19 May 2011. <http://www.billcullen.net>.

Oviatt, Ray. "Boy! How Exciting Can It Get?" *Toledo Blade.* 3 Jun 1958.

Oviatt, Ray. "TV-Motion Picture Wedding Flops as Sullivan Cancels Film Trailers." *Toledo Blade.* 12 Jul. 1953.

"Game Shows." *Pioneers of Television*. 2009. Television.

Pack, Harvey. "Charles Nelson Reilly is All Over the Tube." *The Miami News.* 9 Dec. 1971.

Pack, Harvey. "Dennis Wholey to Host The Generation Gap." *The Morning Record.* Wallingford, CT. 15 Feb. 1969.

Pack, Harvey. "Why Art James Looks Quizzical." *The Miami News.* 1 Jul 1971.

"Page 13 Still Important After Books Reach Camp." *Youngstown Vindicator.* 14 Dec. 1944.

Paul, Péralte C. "Protest Set Today over Cox's Winnings." *AJC.com*. Aug. 2009. Web. 05 June 2011. <http://www.ajc.com/news/fayette/protest-set-today-over-118789.html>.

Pearson, Drew. "Big Money in Plugging Products on TV." *The Press-Courier.* Oxnard, CA. 24 Nov. 1959.

"Peck Leaves for NY to Fill In on Show." *The Milwaukee Journal.* 27 Dec. 1976.

"Peggy Cass: Truth Teller." *People.* 29 March 1999. Web. Accessed 3 Aug. 2011.

<http://www.people.com/people/article/0,,20127810,00.html>

"Pennies Flow to Marine." *The News and Courier.* Charleston, South Carolina. 31 Jan 1943.

"Penn Jillette Finds New Identity As Game Show Host." Artisan News Service. 3 May 2007. <http://youtu.be/UkiGSG3TQHE>

"People." *Sports Illustrated.* 08 June 1970. Web. 05 June 2011. <http://sportsillustrated.cnn.com/vault/article/magazine/MAG1083693/index.htm>.

"People are Funny." *Old Time Radio Catalog.* Web. 9 Sep. 2011. <http://www.otrcat.com/people-are-funny-p-1717.html>

"People in the News." *Eugene Register-Guard.* 16 Mar. 1982.

"People in Sports." *Houston Chronicle.* Sports, Pg. 3. 9 Feb. 1989

Perotin, Maria M. "Luck Runs Out for Trivia Champ." *Orlando Sentinel.* 10 Dec. 1998.

Petrazello, Donna. “Fox Eying Ace Host for ‘Greed’ Net’s New $2M Game Show Aims to Give ‘Millionaire Run for Money in November.” *New York Daily News.* 14 Oct. 1999.

“Pike Woman Named Queen on Radio Show.” *Williamson Daily News.* Williamson, WV. 7 Jan. 1950.

Poniewozik, James. “Art Linkletter, 1912-2010. *Time.com.* 26 May 2010. <http://tunedin.blogs.time.com/2010/05/26/art-linkletter-1912-2010/>

“Posters Accelerate Ticket Sales for Queen for a Day.” *The Evening Independent.* St. Petersburg, FL. 3 Apr. 1948.

“‘Price is Right’ Host Bob Barker to Retire from TV After 50 Years.” *Fox News.* 31 Oct. 2006. <http://www.foxnews.com/story/0,2933,226520,00.html>

“Queen for a Day Host Jack Bailey Dies at 72.” *The Albany Herald.* 3 Feb. 1980.

Quigley, Bob. “His ‘System’ Working.” *Daytona Beach Morning Journal.* 24 Jul. 1961.

“Quiz Bans Draw Ire.” *Spokane Daily Chronicle.* 17 Oct. 1959.

“Quiz Kids Celebrate.” *The Pittsburgh Press.* 1 Jul. 1945.

“Radio: Fun in the Living Room.” *Time Magazine.* 20 Oct. 1952.

“Radio: Hot Out of Vassar.” *Time Magazine.* 1 May 1950.

“Radio: The Idea Business.” *Time Magazine.* 31 May 1954.

"Radio Jackpot Hit By Woman." *St. Petersburg Times.* 7 Mar. 1948.

"Radio: Juvenile Jury." *Time Magazine.* 17 Jun. 1946.

"Radio: Moore for Housewives." *Time Magazine* 2 Feb. 1953. Web. 18 May 2011. <http://www.time.com/time/magazine/article/0,9171,817877,00.html#ixzz1MjQlotD9>.

"Radio: No Chance." *Time Magazine.* 29 Aug. 1949.

"Radio: Not Caviar." *Time Magazine.* 29 Dec. 1952.

"Radio: Program Preview." *Time Magazine.* 30 Dec. 1946.

"Radio: Shindig." *Time Magazine.* 27 Nov. 1939.

"Radio Star Here to Entertain Troops." *Spokane Daily Chronicle.* 28 Apr. 1943.

"Radio: The Experts." *Time Magazine.* 14 Jul. 1952.

"Radio: The Search for the Gimmick." *Time Magazine.* 17 Dec. 1951.

"Radio: The Troubled Air." *Time Magazine* 12 Jan. 1953. Web. 18 May 2011. <http://www.time.com/time/magazine/article/0,9171,817722,00.html#ixzz1MjWC0REd>

"Radio: Wow!" *Time Magazine.* 4 Aug. 1947.

"Radio: You Bet Your Shakespeare." *Time Magazine.* 17 Nov. 1952.

"Radio & TV: The $35,250 Answer." *Time Magazine.* 21 Mar. 1949.

"Ralph Edwards." *Radio Hall of Fame.* Accessed 22 Aug. 2011. <http://www.radiohof.org/musicvariety/ralphedwards.html>

The Real Match Game Story: Behind the Blank. GSN. 26 Nov. 2006. Television.

Rayburn, Gene. Interview. Game Show Network. 1999. Television.

"Ray Combs." *The E! True Hollywood Story.* E! 1997.

"Reagan's Son Quits TV Job, Sues Producer." *San Jose Mercury News.* 23 Nov. 1988.

Reedy, Tom. "Four Senators Bow to Quiz Kids in Red Cross Radio Show." *Reading Eagle.* 19 Mar. 1945.

Reid, Don. "Quiz Show Security Rigorous." *Daily News.* Bowling Green, KY. 25 Jul. 1968.

Remenih, Anton. "Queen for a Day Finds Crown is Target for All." *Chicago Tribune.* 6 May 1950.

Roosevelt, Eleanor. "My Day." *St. Petersburg Times.* 14 Jan. 1941.

Rosenberg, Howard. "Puh-leeze! Pull the Sheet Over 'Buddies.'" *Los Angeles Times.* 12 Aug. 1992.

Rosenburg, John. "Radio Answer Man Kept Busy." *Warsaw Daily Times.* Warsaw, IN. 21 Apr. 1949.

Rowan, Robert. "Play Your Hunch Tops Day Shows." *The Southeast Missourian.* Cape Girardeau, MI. 24 Jun. 1960.

Ryan, Steve, and Fred Wostbrock. *The Ultimate TV Game Show Book: with a Tribute to Bill Cullen.* Los Angeles, CA: Volt, 2005. Print.

Sagi, Douglas. "You May Get a Prize—Or It Might be a Zonk." *Ottawa Citizen.* 24 Dec. 1971.

"Sale of the Century Features Couples as Contestants." *The Rock Hill Herald.* Rock Hill, SC. 2 Apr. 1973.

Schwartz, David, Steve Ryan, and Fred Wostbrock. *The Encyclopedia of TV Game Shows 3rd Edition.* New York, NY: Facts On File, 1999. Print.

Schwed, Mark. "New 'Bargain Hunters' Combines Home Shopping with Game Show." *Schenectady Gazette.* 3 Jul. 1987.

Scott, Jeffry. "Kathy Cox Outsmarts 5th Graders, Wins a Million." *Atlanta News, Sports, Atlanta Weather, Business News | Ajc.com.* 8 Sept. 2008. Web. 05 June 2011. <http://www.ajc.com/metro/content/metro/stories/2008/09/05/cox_fifth_grader.html>.

Scott, Vernon. "Betty White Right for TV's 'Just Men'" *Florence Times-Tri-Cities Daily* 18 Mar. 1983: 28. Print.

Scott, Vernan. "Cullen's Quiet Popularity Survives Fifteen Years." *Bangor Daily News.* 6 Aug. 1971.

Scott, Vernon. "Generation Gap Clearly Etched." *Beaver County Times.* Beaver County, PA. 22 Feb. 1969.

Scott, Vernon. "Initial Reaction is Astonishment for Winners on Dream House." *Sarasota Herald-Tribune.* 29 Sep. 1983.

Sedore, David. "Reel Producer's Disappearance Leaves Everybody Reeling." *The Palm Beach Post.* 9 Dec. 1998.

Shales, Tom. "Worth a Closer Look." *The Washington Post.* 31 May 2008.

Shapiro, Charles. "John Reed King Left Wilmington to Become a Junk Collector for a Television Network." *Wilmington Sunday Star.* 24 May 1953.

"Sh-h-h! Don't Tell a Soul...Except 25,000,000 Viewers: Some of the More Wacky Moments on 'I've Got a Secret.'" *TV Guide* 22 Aug. 1959: 17-21. Print.

Shister, Gail. "Glenn Frey Returns to Miami Vice." *Beaver County Times.* 6 Mar. 1986.

Shister, Gail. "Nicelodeon Finds Home in Philadelphia." *Ocala Star-Banner.* 13 Oct. 1987,

Shister, Gail. "Tubenotes." *The Lewiston Journal.* 28 Sep. 1988.

"Show Allows Kids to Have Messy Fun." *The Palm Beach Post.* 18 Apr. 1988.

"Showoffs Premieres This Summer on TV." *The Dispatch.* Lexington, NC. 22 May 1975.

Shull, Richard. "The Rigors of Being a Contestant." *Lakeland Ledger.* 21 Jul. 1974.

"Side Splitter." *Gettysburg Times.* 28 Dec. 1948.

"Silver Spoon is Offered Every New Year's Day Baby." *St. Petersburg Times.* 28 Dec. 1950.

Smith, Ben. "School Chief's Bankruptcy Has $1M Prize in Limbo." *AJC.com.* 28 Jan. 2009. Web. 05 June 2011. <http://www.ajc.com/metro/content/metro/stories/2009/01/28/cox_prize_bankruptcy.html?cxntlid=homepage_tab_newstab>.

Smith, Christian. "NBC: You are the Weakest Link, Goodbye." *The Michigan Daily.* University of Michigan. 16 Apr. 2001.

Smith, Patricia. "Rafferty Roves for 'Real People.'" *The Spokane Chronicle.* 15 Feb. 1982.

"Stars Assume Guises." *Lakeland Ledger.* Lakeland, FL. 29 Aug. 1976.

"Stefan Hatos." *The Official Let's Make a Deal Website.* Accessed 1 Sep. 2011. <http://www.letsmakeadeal.com/stefan.htm>

"Stefan Hatos." *Toledo Blade.* 12 Mar. 1999.

Steinhauser, Si. "'Certain Failure' Succeeds." *The Pittsburgh Press.* 17 Apr. 1952.

Steinhauser, Si. "Quiz Kids' Dads to Broadcast Father's Day." *The Pittsburgh Press.* 18 Jun. 1943.

Stiff, Robert. "Quiz Show Utterly Tasteless. *The Evening Independent.* St. Petersburg, FL. 10 Nov. 1979.

"Strange People Visit TV Show: Panelist." *The Montreal Gazette.* 24 Jan. 1979.

Strauss, Gary. "Lots of Entertainment Under Al Roker's Umbrella." *USA Today.* McLean, VA. 8 Apr. 2008.

"Strike It Rich Ordered to Get Solicitor Tag." *The Miami News.* 3 Feb. 1954.

"Strikes Net 75 Grand." *The Bend Bulletin.* Bend, OR. 3 Jan. 1961.

Susman, Gary. "Goodbye: Tonight Show Icon Jack Paar Dies | EW.com." *Entertainment Weekly's EW.com | Entertainment News | TV News | TV Shows | Movie, Music and DVD Reviews.* 27 Jan. 2004. Web. 17 May 2011. <http://www.ew.com/ew/article/0,,583933,00.html>.

Taylor, Chuck. "'Fortune' Visits Its Friendly Fans—Devoted Audience Loves Pat, Vanna, and Money." *The Seattle Times.* 21 Sep. 1995.

"Telecastings." *Broadcasting* 28 January 1985: 99. Print.

"Television Notebook." *Sarasota Journal.* 11 Feb. 1969.

"Television: Off the Map." *Time Magazine.* 28 Mar. 1960.

"Tell It to Groucho Has a Game, but People Are Chief Ingredient." *St. Petersburg Times.* St. Petersburg, FL. 11 Jan. 1962.

"Texas Woman Hits Jackpot in Naming Radio's Miss Hush." *The Miami News.* 7 Dec. 1947.

Thomas, Bob. "Art Says Our Show is Good as Russia's." *Lewiston Morning Tribune.* 21 May 1958.

Thomas, Jr., Robert McG. "Dennis James, 79, TV Game Show Host and Announcer." *The New York Times.* 6 Jun. 1997.

Thomas, Jr., Roger McG. "Art Fleming, 70, Television Host Who Gave Polish to Jeopardy!" *The New York Times.* 27 Apr. 1995.

Thompson, Ruth. "Bob Eubanks' Dreams Go to Commentating. *The Free-Lance Star.* Fredericksburg, VA. 10 Dec. 1983.

Thompson, Ruth. "Rafferty's Success is the 'Real' Thing." *Sarasota Journal.* 29 Jul 1981.

Those Wonderful TV Game Shows. NBC. Los Angeles, CA, 1984. Television.

"Tic Tac Dough TV Quiz Show Chief is Fired." *St. Petersburg Times.* 8 Oct. 1959.

"Tic Tac Dough Winner Sets Record." *Reading Eagle.* 26 Jun. 1980.

"Top Stars Battle it Out on TV Sports Quiz Show." *Kingsport Post.* 20 Apr. 1972.

Trebek, Alex, and Merv Griffin. *The Jeopardy! Challenge: the Toughest Games from America's Greatest Quiz Show! ; Featuring the Teen Tournament, the College Tournament, the Seniors Tournament, the Tournament of Champions.* New York, NY: HarperPerennial, 1992. Print.

Trebek, Alex, and Peter Barsocchini. *The Jeopardy! Book: the Answers, the Questions, the Facts, and the Stories of the Greatest Game Show in History*. New York, NY: HarperPerennial, 1990. Print.

Tucker, Ken. "Who is the Weakest Link?" *Entertainment Weekly.* 20 Apr. 2001.

Tucker, Ken. "Win Ben Stein's Money." *Entertainment Weekly.* 19 Jun. 1998.

"TV Contestant Gets Trapped in Quiz Booth." *The Modesto Bee.* 10 Sep. 1958.

"TV Contestants Sweep Supermarket." *St. Petersburg Times.* 14 Feb. 1967.

"TV Man Denies 'It Could Be You' Was Rigged." *Meriden Record.* 29 Dec. 1960.

"TV Producer Stefan Hatos Dies." *Record-Journal.* Meriden, CT. 11 Mar. 1999.

"TV's 'Laugh-in' Comic Dick Martin Dies." *TODAY.com.* MSNBC/Associated Press, 25 May 2008. Web. 18 May 2011. <http://today.msnbc.msn.com/id/24810404/ns/today-entertainment/t/tvs-laugh-in-comic-dick-martin-dies-calif/>.

"United Fund in Good Start." *Beaver County Times.* 5 Oct. 1963.

www.usgameshows.net

"The Warm-Upmanship of Don Pardo." *The Rock Hill Herald.* 25 Nov. 1971.

Watkins, Mel. "Nipsey Russell, a Comic with a Gift for Verse, Dies at 80." *The New York Times.* 4 Oct. 2005.

Wedge, Pep. "Beat the Clock." *Canadian Communications Foundation.* Aug. 2002. http://www.broadcasting-history.ca/programming/television/programming_popup.php?id=108

Wedman, Les. No title. *The Sunday Sun.* Vancouver, B.C. 20 Oct. 1965.

West, Randy. *Johnny Olson: A Voice in Time*. Albany, GA: BearManor Media, 2009. Print.

West, Randy. Personal interview. 2 Aug. 2011.

"Westinghouse Presents—" *Meriden Record-Journal.* Wallingford, CT. 16 Jun. 1962.

"Wheel of Fortune." *True Hollywood Story*. E! Entertainment Television. 23 Jan. 2005. Television.

"When in Doubt, Punt!" *Lakeland Ledger.* 15 May 1960.

White, Betty. "Panelist Likes Work." *The Montreal Gazette.* 31 Jul. 1964.

"Why Our Marriage Works." *The Spartansburg Herald-Journal.* 23 May 1976.

"Will Serve as Host, Hostess, and Emcee on Miss Universe Pageant." *The Southeast Missourian.* Cape Girardeau, Missouri. 12 Jul 1963.

Wilson, Earl. "Country Star Goes by Day." *Sarasota Herald-Tribune.* 23 Apr. 1971.

Wilson, Ernie. "Ernie Kovacs is Happy (Guest) Without a Steady Job." *The Milwaukee Sentinel.* 31 Oct. 1957.

Wilson, Earl. "Fred Allen Rings Bell in 'Judge for Yourself.'" *The Milwaukee Sentinel.* 23 Aug. 1953.

Wilson, Earl. "New Stage Name Got Van Rolling." *The Milwaukee Sentinel.* 24 May 1976.

Wilson, Earl. "War Rages Among TV Quiz Shows." *St. Petersburg Times.* 20 Jun. 1957.

Wilson, Earl. "The Weekend Windup." *Daytona Beach Morning Journal.* 25 Nov. 1961.

Wilson, Earl. "Wife Finds Office for Busy TV Packager Merv Griffin." *St. Petersburg Times.* 15 Apr. 1964.

Wilson, Jean Sprain. "'I Met Toni and was Reborn' is Love Story of Jan Murray." *The Miami News.* 27 Jan. 1959.

Winchell, Walter. "Broadway Chisler Definition has Revolving Door." *Spartansburg Herald-Journal.* 15 Feb. 1948.

Witbeck, Charles. "A Chance to Win a Dream House." *The Times-News.* Hendersonville, NC. 31 May 1983.

Witbeck, Charles. "TV Keynotes." *Meriden Journal.* Southington, CT. 10 Feb. 1964.

"The Wizard of Quiz." *Time.* 11 Feb. 1957. Web. 24 May 2011. <http://www.

Index

Numbers in **bold** indicate photographs

CPSIA information can be obtained
at www.ICGtesting.com
Printed in the USA
BVHW050945010720
582654BV00004B/124